THE JOURNEY

OTHER FAMILY HERITAGE BOOKS:

Broadway Generations

Butterfly Press Online Book Store
Visit http://butterflypress.net/store/

THE JOURNEY

Celebrating Family Heroes, Stories
and Legends of Broadway Generations

Eugene Broadway

EBuy

*Rudy you are always
Family*

Butterfly Press
Dallas, Texas

THE JOURNEY
Copyright © 2012 by Eugene Broadway

Requests for information should be addressed to:

Butterfly Press
P.O. Box 944
Little Elm, Texas 75068
http://butterflypress.net

ISBN 978-0-9830822-5-5

Published in the United States of America.

DEDICATION

This book is dedicated to

My late Father, Daniel Lee Broadway, Sr. (1920-1999)
and
In memory of my Brother, Daniel Lee Broadway, Jr. (1950-1972)

ACKNOWLEDGMENTS

I am excited to present to you a continuation of our *Broadway Family History* with this book. I acknowledge my wife *Shianne*, my cousin *Marie Broadway Toms*, many family members, and friends who are responsible for preserving pictures, memories, writing stories, poems, interviews and prayers to see this project to fruition.

I acknowledge the *1983 Broadway-Clark-Beasley* committee members and other relatives who began the research of our ancestors back to Marshall Broadway and Silvia Clark. Their work encouraged me to continue the backward journey to find out more about the Broadway dynasty's contribution to this world.

Last, but not least, I acknowledge the official *2009-2010 Broadway Family Reunion Committee Members*. The committee produced a reunion beyond measure setting the standard and foundation for future *Broadway Family Reunion Committees* to come.

INTRODUCTION

The researchers for this book and I have gathered information on over 6,000 Broadway family members. The intent of this book is to share our ancestral history and to bring descendants even closer. The 1983, 1993 and 2010 family research committees gave us some fantastic history. The research group for this book discovered a tremendous amount of information about the Broadway family that is interesting, surprising, detailed, and factual.

I have always wanted to know more about my family. I started research several years ago. A special thing happened; I joined the 2010 Broadway research team and fell in love with my new found Broadway family members and all aspects of ancestry research. After the 2010 reunion, I was so proud of the accomplishment of the event; I could not stop researching about my Broadway ancestry. This paved the way to a sequel to the *Broadway Generations* book, by Marie Toms.

The major responsibility for researching and financing this book project was taken on by me. Of course, Marie Toms graciously contributed a lot of time and work into the project. Even though I did a lot of research on my immediate family; I left no stone unturned with other family members. My research led every which way, thus is spanning the entire Broadway family. This book is to be treasured and every Broadway descendent will benefit from the history unfolded.

My heart's desire is to encourage unity in our vast family. It is my wish that this book will be an inspiration to you to dig deeper and go even further in our ancestral history. After reading this book, created out of love for you all, I charge you to bring even more ancestors to the forefront for us to meet.

Lastly, please know this book is not all-inclusive. It is just another piece of the Broadway history unfolded. I cannot begin to say every family member was noted or even accurately portrayed. This book reflects submissions from various contributors. Notably, family names were gathered from many sources, sometimes they were spelled differently; it all depended on the source and who was spelling or writing.

For example, James Broadway was spelled "Broadaway" and Sylvia was spelled "Silvia". Please know we did our best to prepare an excellent work and contacted everyone we knew who would want to be a part of this project. With loving hands and hearts, we present to you "The Journey." May God add a blessing to you as you read and view the many pictures in this book!

Eugene Broadway

EPIGRAPH

When times get tough, rejoice in the knowledge that you are one in a long line of proud, courageous people who have a history of surviving.

Denise L. Stinson

Contents

Introduction - Eugene Broadway   09

A Letter to Eugene by Shianne C. Broadway   15

SECTION ONE: The Broadway's Journey   17

SECTION TWO: Slave Owners   39

SECTION THREE: Slave Ancestors from North Carolina   53

SECTION FOUR: Broadway Slave Community   65

SECTION FIVE: Freed Broadways   73

SECTION SIX: Living Free In Arkansas   81

SECTION SEVEN: Memoirs of Eugene Broadway   97

SECTION EIGHT: Life Journey Stories – Other Broadways   111

SECTION NINE: Featured People and Events   191

SECTION TEN: Broadway Family Tree   199

SECTION ELEVEN: Family Photo Album   205

NOTES   241

BIBLIOGRAPHY   245

STORY INDEX   253

ABOUT AUTHOR   257

A LETTER TO EUGENE:

My Dearest Eugene,

I remember several years ago, early in our relationship, the conversations we had about one of your goals in life to write a book. The dedication and commitment you have shown has been remarkable. I watched you work for the last couple of years so diligently researching and gathering information about your family genealogy.

I love listening to you talk and seeing how excited you get when you discover new and valuable information about the Broadway family. I watched the many hours you spent in conversations you had with family members. I noticed the early mornings and the late nights you would spend at the computer.

I remember the trips we took to North Carolina and Arkansas to visit some of the sites of your ancestors and the conference calls you and Cousin Marie Broadway-Toms had. She was and still is one of your biggest supporters in helping make this dream of yours come true.

Eugene, I want you to know how proud I am of you. The love and respect I have for you is immeasurable. It gives me such joy to see how strong, focused and dedicated you are. This book is something that will live on for generations to come in the Broadway family.

As your wife, I thank you for allowing me to have the pleasure of experiencing this great milestone in your life with you. It has been an amazing journey which you have brought to life. "I love you" with all my heart and soul.

Your wife,
Shianne C. Broadway

SECTION 1

THE BROADWAY'S JOURNEY
LIFE FOR OUR ANCESTORS AND
COLORED PEOPLE IN GENERAL

AS SLAVES

A WEEK IN THE LIFE OF JAMES BROADWAY, A SLAVE BY OUR ANCESTOR

The journey of colored people in general started a long time before the mass slavery of our people in the sixteenth through nineteenth centuries. However, the slavery of my Great[3] Grandfather James Broadway is where I will start the journey of our colored people.

Imagine the week, Monday through Saturday, James started at daybreak. He was most likely a leader, since history records that James' son, Marshall, was a recognized leader. James started Monday mornings getting all the slaves motivated to get through the work week. He was a good horse trainer and a good farmer.

The family probably grew lots of corn, wheat, cotton, soybeans and cane in North Carolina. In addition, they probably had access to dairy farms, orchards, vegetable gardens, preserved food for the winter by canning, poultry farms, hunting and/or fishing.

Knowing that Frederick Staton was the father of John Broadaway's (slave owner) wife, Harriett, the assumption is that Frederick could have been the previous slave owner of James Broadway. Some of the slaves were trained by Frederick Staton who knew how to rotate and fertilize the soil to make good crops.

Grains were grown and harvested for flour and meal. Off seasons, when they weren't planting or harvesting, the slaves would clear the land of trees to prepare the lands for additional farmlands. All of the work was really manual labor. The work week was really hard work, but it was reported by "Staton History" that Frederick Staton treated his slaves' well. (Staton, 1960)

Then came Sunday, which was the best day of the week for the slaves. According to the "Staton History" book, the slaves were known to be treated better than other slaves. What a blessing. The slaves looked forward to Sunday. They were sometimes invited up to the slave master's house for Bible stories, song, prayer and dance.

The slaves were told about life in other places up north. They were treated decently by the Statons. A few of them were invited to attend church and a select few were selected to join the White church at Rocky River Baptist Church.

Frederick was raised on a large plantation where he received a good education, presumably from the circuit instructors who were hired to travel from farm to farm.

He knew the importance of education; James Broadway and other slaves may have been allowed a moment during the week to be taught how to read. (Stoddard, Brooke C. and Daniel P. Murphy, Ph.D.)

GENERAL TREATMENT OF SLAVES

Some slaves were treated poorly and others treated badly. For the most part, the treatment of slaves was extremely

- exhausting
- violent
- degrading
- unacceptable

Exhausting: Those employed as farmhands faced back-breaking labor and demanding hours. Slaves seldom benefited from their labor. They had nothing to look forward to except hard labor until the day they died.

Degrading: Merely, being a slave was degrading enough. Slaves were expected to obey their masters without question and to always show great humility by lowering their gaze and speaking softly whenever they were in the company of Whites. Dead slaves were often buried at night because their families and friends had to work all day. In the eyes of many slave owners, a slave's death wasn't sufficient cause to lose even an hour of work time. Plantation and farm owners worked hard to keep their slaves submissive. This mentally was evident throughout the 1960's in Arkansas; it was depicted in riots, massacres, hangings, peonage systems, Elaine 12, Little Rock Central, and more.

Violently: Slaves who tried to escape were sometimes hobbled with a spike through the ankle or placed in iron fetters. Some slaves were forced to wear slave collars that had bells on them; a more punishing version had lengthy prongs sticking out on four sides that prevented its wearer from lying down. Dissent was met with harsh punishment, including vicious beatings with whips. Minor offenses such as drunkenness or simple disobedience were often punished by a day in wooden stocks, which clamped tightly around the slave's neck and wrists.

Insupportable: Slaves were not allowed to do many things, such as own property, gather for meetings, marry whom they chose, learn to read and write, speak their native African languages, practice their native religions, escape or fight back, nor question their master. The Arkansas Elaine 12 Massacre is an example of the mentality of not questioning the Whites. Farmers were planning to question a group of Whites about buying their cotton at the same price that they were buying the other White farmers. For that effort, the Blacks were brutally and fatally beaten or they were massively shot and buried in the same grave just for questioning Whites.

So to say that one had a good Master says to me that the Master knew it was wrong to enslave another human being but society allowed him a way out. They justified it as the way it was supposed to be; so they could get free labor. Slaves were worked like horses; they cleared the land, chopped and picked the cotton, raised the food and cooked it too but still received rations.

CAUSES OF DEATH DURING MID 1800S

Records state that many slaves died a premature death from the abuses of slavery. But generally, many of the young were the ones who were often plagued with illnesses. There were many illnesses that caused death during slavery times, such as dropsy, typhoid, scarlet fever and cholera.

However, the majority of the deaths were related to pneumonia, scarlet fever, cholera and croup. A point to note, a few of the causes of death were not related to illnesses. Slaves were being shot, hung, drowned, suicide related, and occasionally died of old age.

It is noted that Marshall and Silvia had six children to die young and ten lived and achieved adulthood. Additionally, many other relatives had approximately one-third of their children to die from various illnesses.

IN COMMUNITY

To get a sense of what the North Carolina community was like during our Great Grandparents' lifetime, the Plantation was looked at as a mini community. The county was Anson, North Carolina. There were several townships or settlements in Anson County (Burnsville, Lanesboro, Ansonville,) where the Broadway ancestors were from. The Broadway ancestors were from Anson County, North Carolina and mainly, they lived on two plantations (Statons and Broadaways).

Later, during the late 1800's, the Broadways moved to Lee County, Arkansas, multiplying and populating several townships (Hampton, Moro, Marianna, Oak Forest, and Fleener).Two closely related families (Broadway and Clarks) lived near each other.

It seemed they connected through Silvia's family and Marshall. Through certain indicators the families may have been friends even before Silvia's and Marshall's union. History indicates Marshall may have been friends with Silvia's brother before they met.

Back then, chopping cotton was looked at as the main crop for their livelihood.

PLANTATIONS

To some people, plantations were associated with slavery and the "Big House". But according to Microsoft's reference books, a plantation is a large estate or farm, especially in a hot climate, where crops such as cotton, coffee, tea, or rubber trees are grown and usually worked by resident laborers. (Morgan)

Plantations were plentiful back during slavery and they still existed through the sharecropping era during the 1940s. Of course after slavery, the labor intensive system of sharecropping was used. However between 1940 and 1970, much of the agricultural labor force in the southern states, primarily African Americans, left the area to take better-paying, less demanding industrial jobs elsewhere. As a result, agriculture on the plantations became more mechanized.

The African American Broadways started life in slavery in North Carolina, but during the 1880s, they moved to Arkansas and became land owners and some family members were farm laborers. For those who were sharecroppers, life revolved around each year's cotton crop. In early spring, mule-drawn plows broke the ground for planting, and then followed repeated de-weeding with hoes (known as chopping cotton). Usually, by late September, the first cotton bolls were ready to be picked by hand. To supplement their income, after the Harvest ended around December 1st, many tenants cut wood to sell to the plantation.

If a family was sharecropping, each family set its own routine. Most began work by 7 a.m., took a break, and then worked until sundown. Young children worked alongside their parents, who toiled Monday through Saturday.

Plantation supervisors would travel around the area checking on each cropper's progress, but generally allowed each tenant to tend the crop as he or she saw fit. Soon after Harvest and cotton ginning ended, tenants met individually with plantation owner to settle accounts.

Generally, sharecroppers received a one-third share and the planter took two-thirds. From the farmer's share, charges at the plantation store during the year were subtracted. Any cash advances made during the year were also tallied. The tenant then received, in cash, the amount left after the deductions, leaving those who finished the year with little or no money.

Many landlords who kept the books, frequently abused the furnish system by using fraudulent charges to keep Black laborers in peonage (deliberately indebted). Those tactics not only happened during slavery but they were happening during the mid 1900's.

Judd Hill's plantation in Arkansas shows a good example of what plantation life was like. Back in 1925, a purchase of a 5,800-acre tract was added to his plantation. It was a heavily-forested land that was cleared. The lumber sold made him wealthy and the land was later used to farm. The work force on Judd Hill's land consisted of three groups: sharecroppers, renters, and day (i.e., wage) laborers.

Sharecroppers grew most of the cotton in exchange for a house and a share of the proceeds from their crop. In 1934, sixty-eight families, all African Americans, tended plots of ground ranging from 5 to 40 acres. (Vernon)

Plantation-like situations happened with many Arkansans. However, one situation wasn't so bad. During the late 1930's in this example, the African American owner found the family of good workers and asked if they would sharecrop his land. The family agreed. Two-thirds went to the family and one-third went to the owner. The house, 40 acres, and supplies were provided by the owner.

The family farmed and harvested the land. They would then divide the profits. Plus for additional income, the family would work as day laborers on another's farm.

This was profitable for them because the family had eleven children. When they were all old enough to be hired out, they would gather in a field and get the job done. Ocie Broadway loved to hire this family to work on his farm. Ocie and other farmers would race to hire the family.

AFTER SLAVERY

Directly after slavery was abolished, did our ancestors stay on the plantation with their slave masters John and Harriett Broadaway? Did James Broadway and family sharecrop? Did they move to another town? Could our ancestors read and write? Or just what did our ancestors do after slavery?

HOW LONG DID THE BROADWAYS STAY ON THE PLANTATION AFTER SLAVERY WAS ABOLISHED?

It is believed that James (Great[3] Grandfather) and Marshall Broadway (Great[2] Grandfather) remained on the Broadaway Plantation for approximately five years. Number one, the former slave master, John Broadaway died in 1870.

It is suspected that James stayed around to help the slave master's wife, Harriett Staton Broadaway and William Cannie Staton with the farm. James and his family worked and saved enough money in five-to-ten years for Marshall and his wife Silvia to buy 133 acres of land in 1875.

SHARECROPPING IN 1865

Sharecropping was not much different from the slavery system, but that was one of their options. They could leave and starve to death or sharecrop. It is believed that they sharecropped for a living in order to get paid. James had done hard slave work all his life; he wanted to help his family do a great job after acquiring their freedom.

Brothers Harry and Robert left the plantation on their own in search for a better life. James kept his young son Marshall to continue to build his self esteem and work ethics. James' daughter who was married, Jane Watson and her two children were living with him in 1880. Actually, Marshall was head of household in 1880 according to the 1880 U. S. Federal Census.8

PLANTATION GOOD BYES

As slaves, James and his family lived in Burnsville, Anson County, North Carolina (NC). According to the 1870 United States Federal Census, James was living at household number seventy-two and the former slave master, John Broadaway, was living at number seventy-one as recorded by the Census takers.

Living in James Broadway's household was Marshall Broadway at age seventeen (1853), Margaret Broadway at age thirty (1840), Jane Broadway at age fourteen (1856) and Mack Broadway at age ten (1860). (Ancestry.com, 2009)Marshall and his family moved to Lanesboro, Anson County, NC after he purchased land in 1875. Additionally, they were seen in Lanesboro during the 1880 U.S. Federal Census.

COULD OUR ANCESTORS READ AND WRITE?

No one in the household in 1870 could read or write. Marshall, Margaret, Jane and Mack Broadway were staying with James Broadway. According to the 1880 United States Federal Census report, James Broadway, our great[3] grandfather, was living with his son and daughter-in law, Marshall and Silvia Broadway. No indication was made to whether they could read or write in 1880.

When the land deed was found where Marshall and Silvia Broadway purchased their land from Charles W. Beverly in 1875 and sold their land to William Canny (W.C.) Staton in 1885 it seemed that Silvia used an "X" and Marshall signed his own signature which indicates that he could read and write. Their mark and signature are shown next:

(Deeds, 1875)

The "X" that Silvia made is a depiction of her name as proof of her identity and intent to buy and later sell the land. An "X" was made by Silvia in lieu of her signature. The traditional function of a signature is evidential: it is to give evidence of deliberation and informed consent. This is why the signature often appears at the bottom or end of a document.

Additionally, signatures may be witnessed and recorded in the presence of a Notary Public to carry additional legal force. On legal documents, an illiterate, incompetent, or disabled person can make a "mark" (often an "X"), so long as the document is countersigned by a literate witness. The person who witnessed and countersigned was R. B. Gaddy.

In North Carolina, where our ancestors were from, land was a commodity to many, especially to two families, the Statons and the Broadaways, who had connections to our ancestors. John Broadaway was slave owner to James Broadway. Frederick Staton was a parent of John Broadaway's wife, Harriet Staton Broadaway. Frederick Staton owned so much land that one could not ride across it in a day's time; in addition, John owned over 9,000 acres of land.

So, they developed patterns and procedures to purchase, sell, and gift land. They knew exactly what to say, what to do, how to do it, and when to do it. They knew how to buy and sell land. Matter of fact, Frederick Staton's son, Uriah was taken to court and even the Supreme Court at least four times from people who were trying to get their land back because they felt the family had defrauded them out of the land, but the Staton family won each time. Consequently, they developed a procedure when people were literate and illiterate, evidently; it was a good one. (Staton, 1960)

Was the "X" used in Arkansas by our ancestors?

Once Marshall and Silvia moved to Arkansas from North Carolina, Marshall and Silvia purchased land. An "X" is indicated for Silvia's signature and whoever signed the names, the last names were misspelled. (Lee County, 1885)

Yet, another record that showed a family member's signature and whether he made a mark of "X" on his Draft Card. Our great grandparents were not formally educated, but they learned fast. According to the draft card of Oliver (James) Broadway, he signed his own signature. (Ancestry.com, Draft Registration of James (Oliver) Broadway, 1942) What Did Our Ancestors Do After Slavery?

REGISTRATION CARD—(Men born on or after April 28, 1877 and on or before February 16, 1897)

SERIAL NUMBER — U - 1879   1. NAME (Print)   JAMES   BROADWAY   ORDER NUMBER

2. PLACE OF RESIDENCE (Print) RFD No 7 Box 54 MORO LEE ARKANSAS
(Number and street) (Town, township, village, or city) (County) (State)
[THE PLACE OF RESIDENCE GIVEN ON THE LINE ABOVE WILL DETERMINE LOCAL BOARD JURISDICTION; LINE 2 OF REGISTRATION CERTIFICATE WILL BE IDENTICAL]

3. MAILING ADDRESS SAME
[Mailing address if other than place indicated on line 2. If same insert word same]

4. TELEPHONE None   5. AGE IN YEARS 63   6. PLACE OF BIRTH CHARLOTTE (Town or county)

DATE OF BIRTH November 19 1878   NORTH CAROLINA
(Exchange) (Number)   (Mo.) (Day) (Yr.)   (State or country)

7. NAME AND ADDRESS OF PERSON WHO WILL ALWAYS KNOW YOUR ADDRESS WILL CLARK RFD No 7 MORO, ARK

8. EMPLOYER'S NAME AND ADDRESS SELF EMPLOYED

9. PLACE OF EMPLOYMENT OR BUSINESS RFD No. 7 MORO LEE ARK.
(Number and street or R. F. D. number) (Town) (County) (State)

I AFFIRM THAT I HAVE VERIFIED ABOVE ANSWERS AND THAT THEY ARE TRUE.

D. S. S. Form 1 (Revised 4-1-42)   (over)   16-21630-2   James Broadway (Registrant's signature)

So, the Broadways were somewhat literate. Even though, they were not excellent readers and writers, they learned how to read people. They found other ways to succeed. They became Broadway entrepreneurs.

STARTING A NEW LIFE

Satisfied in Full

The first known African American Broadways in Lee County were Marshall and Silvia Broadway's family, who migrated to Arkansas from North Carolina in 1885. Marshall purchased land and he and his family mainly farmed cotton. When their children got old enough to be on their own, some of them purchased land and others worked as hired hands and/or sharecroppers. Marshall, as well as many Whites, felt the gateway to wealth and making a living was through owning and farming land, plus working hard to receive the stamp on the deed "Satisfied in Full".

Dream Come True

White neighbors Charles and Charlotte Beverly sold Marshall and Silvia 133 acres of land in North Carolina in 1875. The land was purchased ten years after slavery was abolished. Their first son, Oliver, was just a baby in North Carolina. Oliver was born in 1874. Marshall was twenty-one years old and Silvia was eighteen years old when they purchased land for the first time. I am sure; it was a "dream come true".

Marshall owned the land for ten years until he moved to Arkansas in 1885. When Marshall and his family arrived in Arkansas, he knew just what to do to continue his dream. He immediately purchased eighty acres of land in Lee County, Arkansas. The process of owning the land: acquiring it in 1885; approved 1887, certificated 1888 and owning it in 1891/1892. It got harder and harder for Marshall to make ends meet. Marshall began to borrow against his land.

In 1898, not only his land was used as collateral on a loan, but all of his farming assets were required as collateral: the West half of South West quarter of section twenty-seven in township two north and range one east containing eighty acres more or less [W1/2 S.W.1/4, Sec. 27, T2 N R 1 E 80], plus one black horse; mule one year old; one bay mare sixteen years old; one bay mare six years old; one black and white cow; one red yearling; one two-horse wagon. The note was for $281.28 including interest to October 15th, 1898, plus $110.00 was for supplies to be advanced that year.

Economic and Political Climates

During the 1890 – 1920, the economic and political climates were not far removed from slavery. "The powers that be" thought African Americans should not own land anyway, so whatever it took to cause them to lose their land and make African Americans dependent totally on the Whites, it was tried. Basically, they were looking for free labor.

African-American sharecroppers' Cotton Pickers Strike of 1891 in Lee County was a failed, but legal attempt to fight back because of the White owners' disturbingly wronged the African Americans in that they were paying wages 100% less than the going rate. According to the Encyclopedia of Arkansas History & Culture, Cotton Pickers Strike of 1891, many White owners were paying 50 cents per 100 pounds and the going rate was $1 per 100 pounds. This strike ignited a White mob to kill fifteen African Americans and imprison another six. (Lancaster, 2010)

Some thirty years later, the Elaine Massacre proved that White landowners and authorities were just as interested in making African Americans a subhuman race as they were in 1891. The Elaine Massacre of 1919 hit a home run in subservience and poverty in protecting their almighty dollar. Conflict began when 100 African Americans, mostly sharecroppers on the plantations of White landowners, attended a meeting of the Progressive Farmers and Household Union of American at a church in Hoop Spur (Phillips County), three miles north of Elaine, Arkansas to strategize for higher wages. Governmental authorities were responsible for over 100 deaths and over 500 imprisonments. But according to many sources, many more deaths and injuries were recorded. (Stockley, 2001)

Dream Still Alive

Then in 1902, Oliver was old enough, experienced enough and had saved enough money to purchase eighty acres of land in Section 28. By 1903, Oliver purchased an additional forty acres in Section 34. Both plots of land were paid in full during 1903. Trust Deeds were placed on both plots of land to EJ Beazley during the years 1904 through 1921. It was found that the deeds were "Satisfied in Full" in 1906, 1907, and 1908. By 1918 and 1921, there was no mention of the forty acres of land; however, the eighty acres were mentioned through 1921.

Oliver's wife, Dora, died in 1921. I am sure that was a difficult time for Oliver. He was raising five sons and one daughter. Sam Broadway was the oldest who was twenty years old at the time of his mother's death. Sam and Cynthia were the only kids of Oliver and Dora who stayed in Arkansas and stuck with owning and farming land.

According to Dora Miller-Word, Oliver owned land during the early 1930's until someone came by and told him that he was living on "Heir land" and that he had to move. During the early 1940's, Frank Miller said he used to stay with Oliver and Mary Broadway during the summers for a while and Oliver did not own any land at that time. Dora and Frank are sister and brother; additionally, Oliver Broadway was their step-grandpa. However, I do wonder if Oliver was lax on checking the deed to see if it was "Satisfied in Full".

Marshall and Silvia had other children who were bitten by the land ownership bug. Morris and Josie Broadway purchased forty acres of land in 1919 and sold it in 1924 (Satisfied in Full). The children of Marshall and Silvia who were born in Arkansas acquired the business ownership trait and purchased land; William Cannie and all of his sons (Ocie, LC, MC, Julius, Earnest, Clayborne); Julius and his sons

(L.A. and Julius); Lessie Broadway and husband, Adolopher Beasley purchased 120 acres. (Broadway Deeds 1885-1920, 2010)

Who among the Broadways who were mentioned in this document were able to acquire "Satisfied in Full" on a consistent basis? Some lost land because of debt, sold to acquire a better life, left as an inheritance, and usually sold by non-farming family members. This caused the average farm land ownership to be 1,000 acres with White owners. Many African American kept their farms in the family, but most are small farms with forty acres or less.

Black Farmers loans were discriminately denied by FHA. A lawsuit was filed. The lawsuit was won. The government paid a few and didn't pay many who rightfully were qualified. Eight years with a Republican president and not a single dime paid out nor a single effort to initiate a payout. The suit was won; the payout is due. Call it how you see it. This lawsuit is not "Satisfied in Full."

The plan was to keep African American in poverty, sharecropping, mortgages indebted, poorly educated and to enforce Jim Crow laws so African Americans could work for them in their cotton fields like in slavery and the Whites could get all the profits.

RAILROAD JOBS

The first job or career that the Broadway ancestors had other than being a farmer or a farm laborer was as a railroad worker in the Lilesville Township of Anson County, North Carolina in 1870. I saw Robert Broadway who was fifty-seven years old working on the railroad. His wife, Harriett, was sixty and keeping house. At home with Robert and Harriett were Lydia (21), Ellen (4), and Harriett (5). They were all listed as Black.

A close neighbor of the Broadways was Sandy Clark, and his sister, Silvia who later married Marshall Broadway. Sandy was listed as head of the household and working on the railroad at age twenty-one. Listed in his household was his mother, Hanah, who was forty-nine years old and kept house. Additionally, his sister, Silvia,

was listed as a farm worker at age thirteen. They were all listed as Black on the 1870 Federal Census.

Jerome Turner and Eugene Broadway, great[2] grandchildren of Silvia Clark Broadway, visited the railroad tracks where Great Uncle Sandy Clark worked in Lilesville. The old tracks of the 1870s had not been dug up, but the new tracks were laid next to the old tracks. They were still there in the year 2011.

A Divorce in 1914

According to the Lee Chancery Court on March 18, 1914, the plaintiff's Attorney W. L. Ward, Esquire and the defendant summoned and heard the complaint and depositions of J.M. Broadway, Sam Carter, and Cannie Broadway. The plaintiff, J.M. Broadway, was alleging desertion as well as all other material allegations was true and fully proven.

It is therefore by the court considered, ordered and decreed that the bonds of matrimony heretofore existing between the plaintiff, J.M. Broadway and defendant, Lella Broadway be dissolved and set aside, and that each party be restored to the possession of all property not disposed of at the commencement of this action, which either party obtained from or through the other during said marriage and in consideration or by reason thereof, and that the plaintiff pay all costs of this action.

A summons was served to Lella Broadway in the State of Arkansas, County of Lee on February 16, 1914. Interestingly enough, the fees were: Service $.50, Mileage $1.50, and Ferriage $.40 for a total of $2.40 and signed by Sheriff A. Cotten. Lella had twenty days to answer the summons. If not, the complaint would be taken as confessed.

In Lee Chancery Court, the depositions of J.M. Broadway, Sam Carter and Cannie Broadway were taken on March 9, 1914, between the hours of 8 a.m. and 6 p.m. at the office of W. L. Ward, Marianna, Arkansas, to be read wherein J.M. Broadway is plaintiff and Lella Broadway is defendant. J.M. Broadway, being first duly sworn deposes and says:

My name is J. M. Broadway, I am the plaintiff in this suit and have lived here all of my life. I was married to my wife in December 1912. She left me in December 1913. Prior before she left me, my wife treated me in every mean way possible; she would curse me and would use violent and abusive language toward me. Along about the first of the fall she began to take up with a man by the name of Albert Beazwell and was often seen with him, especially in my absence or when I would come to town. My brother Cannie and a man by the name of Sam Carter told me they caught my wife in the act committing adultery with this man on or about the 6th of December. I got after her about it and she never denied it. The next day or two after that she and Albert Beazwell left here and went to Little Rock together. She has never been back to my house since that time. I gave her no cause to treat me this way for I was always good to her. I am a resident of this County and have been living here all of my life. Signed: J.M. Broadway

SAM CARTER, being first duly sworn deposes and says: My name is Sam Carter. I am of lawful age and reside in the neighborhood where the plaintiff and defendant live. I have known both of them all of their lives. They were married in the fall of 1912. Lella left her husband sometime about the first of December 1913. She was a woman of very violent temper. I have heard her use abusive language toward her husband. All last fall she took up and was often seen with one Albert Beazwell. Cannie Broadway and I caught Lella and Albert in a very compromising position at the home of J.M. Broadway about the first week in December last year. I told Broadway about it. I know a few days afterwards Lella left here with Albert Beazwell and went to Little Rock. They stayed over there about six weeks. Since she came back here, she has never lived with J.M. Broadway. She is a woman of bad character and it is generally talked about in our community and lodge. J.M. Broadway is a good man and bares a good reputation. I have no interest in this suit and am not related to wither party. Signed: Sam Carter

CANNIE BROADWAY, being first sworn deposes and says: My name is Cannie Broadway and I live here in Lee County. I am of lawful age and a brother of the plaintiff. He was married to Lella sometime in December 1912 and they lived together until she left him last December and went to Little Rock. Lella is a woman of bad character and was all the time cursing and abusing my brother. I know my brother was good to her and gave her no cause to treat him as bad as she did. Last December, I caught her with a man by the name of Albert Beazwell lying on the bed together in my brother's house. I told him about it. The next day, I believe it was; she left here with Albert and went to Little Rock. They were over there for about two months. She has not lived with my brother since she came back. I am a married man and live with my family. Signed: Cannie Broadway

The plaintiff was present with his attorney and the depositions were notarized at that time.

J.M. BROADWAY and defendant Lella were intermarried in Lee County, Arkansas on December 11, 1912 and the defendant without cause on part of the plaintiff left and willfully deserted him more than two months ago, sometime in December 1913.

The plaintiff further alleges that the defendant for some time prior to her leaving him, that she habitually, and systematically pursued a course of personal indignities towards him, consisting of rudeness, abuse in the most violent language and open insult, that said conduct persisted in her until J.M. Broadway's condition was rendered intolerable.

Plaintiff further alleges that the defendant on December 6, 1913 and several other times had committed adultery with one John Broadway and Albert Beazwell and that she was caught in the very act committing adultery with these parties.

Plaintiff states that he is a resident of Lee County Arkansas and has been for more than one year before the filing of this action and that the cause of divorce alleged herein occurred or existed in this State within five years before institution of this proceedings.

Plaintiff prays that the bonds of matrimony now existing between him and the defendant be cancelled, set aside and held for naught and that he be granted an absolute and free divorce and for all other just and proper relief which was signed by W. L. Ward, Sol. or Plaintiff. (Broadway, 1914)

It has been approximately 100 years since this divorce. We still believe that a divorce is sometimes justified.

JOHN BROADWAY USING THE COURTS TO BIND A LAND CONTRACT

The disputed land was owned by Wade Norment. Wade and his wife had no children. The land was earlier leased and rented for five years in 1908 by Cannie Broadway. The price was $450 with 8% interest. Later, that same land was rented with option to buy by John Broadway. The forty acres were located on the SE 1/4 of the NW 1/4 of Sec. 34, 2N, Range 1E in Lee County. A contract and an option to purchase the land was signed by Wade Norment (x mark), Cannie Broadway, and Ella Norment (x mark) on December 14, 1908 and witnessed by C.E. and J.B. Daggett.

Several court documents were located in the Chancery Records, Marianna, Arkansas stating the process that John had to go through to finalize his purchase of land from the deceased Wade and Ella Norment. The Plaintiff acquired an attorney. John Broadway testified in court that he was thirty-six years old, that he purchased the contract between Wade Norment and Cannie Broadway in 1912, that Cannie was in possession of the land, and that Wade Norment died in 1912. John said that he was in possession of the property when Wade Norment died.

Furthermore, witnesses were located and statements were taken. Family history was gathered. Norment heirs were asked to appear in court within thirty days and answer the complaint filed against them. The land and heir information was posted in the newspaper during four consecutive weeks. All heirs were notified or at least an attempt was made. The heirs answered the ad and allowed John Broadway to purchase the land that the heirs of Wade and Ella Norment claimed no interest.

John Broadway further stated that in compliance with the terms and conditions of said contract, he entered into the possession of said lands in Lee County, Arkansas and on October 15, 1909, 1910, and 1911, he paid the sum of $75, $100, and $100 respectively, the same being the rent due under said contract for said years; that he is now desirous of exercising his option to purchase said lands and herewith tenders into Court the sum of $287.43, being the balance due thereon under the exercise of said option.

Everything was final with D.S. Clark serving as administrator of the estate of Wade Norment. Court cost of $40.25 was paid. Additionally noted was that D.S. Clark was a Special Commissioner appointed by the Court because Wade was deceased. (Broadway C., 1908) This is one example of how it happened back in the day.

DURING JIM CROW
Their Rights Halted

Within ten years after the Civil War, Blacks were learning how to "govern by governing"; they were exercising their rights: reading, writing, calculating, running and acquiring political office, managing and buying land, and more. Most of them were farmers. But be reminded that farming wasn't just rote labor. One needed to use all of those educated skills they had begun to acquire from 1865 to 1875. Blacks were tolerated as citizens. The White South saw that in ten years they weren't prospering as in slavery times when they had free labor. The Blacks were advancing too quickly. A plan was implemented to slow and shut Blacks down.

The South was the first to pass laws to disenfranchise Black voters (halt Blacks from exercising their rights). For example in Louisiana in 1896, there were over 130,000 Black voters but by 1900, there were about 5,000. (Eye Witness to History, 2005) This was accomplished with ordinances (legislated laws) in the southern states. Laws were rigged to disqualify Black voters.

1. Poll Tax laws required Blacks to pay to vote. Additionally, Ku Klux Klan was used to terrorize Blacks to prevent them from voting. Blacks were murdered and tortured; the acts were justified because the Whites believed that the Blacks were inferior to Whites. Blacks had been treated inferior for so long and during their life time, they had always been taught that Blacks were inferior. By 1910, Blacks were effectively disenfranchised in eight southern states thus causing the political and economic flight of the Blacks to northern cities.

2. Grandfather laws exempted Whites from either test by a "grandfather clause" that said if your grandfather voted, you could too. Of course, most grandparents were slaves who were not given the right to vote.

3. Good Character law sent Blacks back to physical and mental slavery. The Plessy vs. Ferguson Supreme Court decision of 1896 legalized rigid segregation. This law gave Whites infinite opportunities to physically and mentally display the attitude that Blacks were inferior to Whites. The 1896 decision enabled Whites to treat Blacks inferior and differently from the Whites in the school system, the political arena, and the way business was handled.

4. Understanding Clauses laws required Blacks to take a literacy test in order to vote. Blacks had to show that they could read.

These were some of the things that pushed Blacks from the South and other things that pulled migrants to the North.

HANGINGS

Vigilantes Lynchings to Intimidate and Oppress African Americans as a Race

1865-1870s

One of the strongest messages ever sent was lynching by Ku Klux Klan (KKK). KKK is best known for advocating White supremacy and acting as vigilantes while hidden behind masks and white robes. The first KKK arose in the turmoil after the Civil War which begun in 1865. It used terrorism, violence, and lynching to intimidate and oppress African Americans.

The first Klan was founded in 1866 by veterans of the Confederate Army. The Klan raided and intimidated Black members. Additionally, when they killed Black political leaders, they also took heads of families, and leaders in churches and community groups. Assaults and murders of Blacks and political riots were staged and many more Blacks were killed than Whites. These incidents were consistently reported by agents of Freedmen's bureau; In addition, Black farmers were driven off their land.

1915-1944

In 1915, the second Klan was founded. This was a time of postwar social tensions which included the Great Migration of Southern Blacks. Some local Klan groups took part in lynching, attacks on private houses and public property, and other violent activities. KKK used ceremonial cross burnings to intimidate victims and demonstrate its power. Murders and violence by the Klan were numerous in the South which had a tradition of lawlessness. The second Klan was a formal fraternal organization, with a national and state structure.

The Klan also defended the interest to curb Black education, economic advancement, voting rights, and right to keep and bear arms. As the Wikipedia encyclopedia states, there was a multitude of anti-Black vigilante groups, disgruntled poor White farmers, White workmen fearful of Black competition, employers trying to enforce labor discipline, common thieves, and neighbors with decades-old grudges.

Lynchings escalated from 1918 to 1927, mostly in the South and Klan activities peaked in the mid-1920s. Masks and robes were adopted in the 1920s to hide their identities which added to the drama of their night rides. However, membership fell during World War II beginning 1939 and ending 1945.

Wikipedia statistics show the change in the Klan's estimated membership over time. The first number represents the approximate time period and the second represents the total membership for the year: 1920 – 4,000,000; 1924 – 6,000,000; 1930 – 30,000; 1980 – 5,000; and 2006 – 3,000.

Even during this era, the Klan continued to maintain its dual heritage of hate and violence. As stated in the Encyclopedia of Arkansas History and Culture, the Elaine Massacre was by far the deadliest racial confrontation in Arkansas history and possibly the bloodiest racial conflict in the history of the United States. While its deepest roots lay in the state's commitment to White supremacy, the events in

Elaine stemmed from tense race relations and growing concerns about labor unions. A shooting incident that occurred at a meeting of the Progressive Farmers and Household Union escalated into mob violence on the part of the White people in Elaine (Phillips County) and surrounding areas. Although the exact number is unknown, estimates of the number of African Americans killed by Whites range into the hundreds; five White people lost their lives.

The Elaine Massacre in Arkansas was a heartrending example of hate and violence. All of the Blacks who were murdered may not have been hung but to read about the various ways violence was placed upon man and family, one after another, was a disgrace to mankind and Arkansas history. Even worst, not one person was found guilty of doing anything wrong against a Black, not one.

That is amazing in itself. According to authorities, during one short time period, there were 100-550 Blacks who broke the law and not one White broke the law. Incredible! No jail in Helena and the surrounding area could hold that many prisoners, but maybe with 1,000 White vigilantes, a few of them could think of ways to kill and get rid of the bodies. Oh yeah, they got away with it.

Many of our Broadway ancestors lived in the neighboring Lee County and maybe a few of them lived in Phillips County. Nothing is known of any hangings of Broadways during that time. However, there are a few of our relatives who went missing during that time period. Most of the time when violence was committed against Blacks, they would be taken to another county and stripped of their identity. Then, how could a person be found or recognized by others? They would unwillingly join the Unknown.

Once African Americans secured Federal legislation to protect civil and voting rights, the Klans shifted focus to opposing court-ordered busing to desegregate schools, affirmative action, and more open immigration.

According to Harper's Weekly in 1862 NATHANIEL GORDON was hung for being engaged in the slave-trade on February 21, 1862 in New York. He was probably the most successful and one of the worst of the individuals engaged in the trade.

1945-Present

A third incarnation of the Klan happened in 1945 and they have not gone away. Michael Donald, a Black man, was lynched in 1981 in Alabama; the FBI was involved in investigating his death. Two local Klansmen were convicted of having a role. One was sentenced to death and executed in 1987. It was the first time a White man had been executed for a crime against an African American since 1913. Additionally, it was an all-White jury that found the Klan responsible for the lynching of Michael Donald and ordered it to pay $7 million USD.

Today, the U.S. government classifies KKK as hate groups with the political ideology of White supremacy. KKK members are decentralized and have increased somewhat in recent years, but membership is estimated at 5,000 to 8,000 among an estimated 179 chapters. The latest recruitment drives have used issues such as people's anxieties about illegal immigration, urban crime and same-sex marriage. At first, the Ku Klux Klan focused its anger and violence on African-Americans, on White Americans who stood up for them, and against the federal government which supported their rights. Subsequent incarnations of the Klan typically emerged in times of rapid social change.

WHY NORTH MIGRATION
Migration of African Americans

The great migration of Blacks from the rural South to northern industrial cities is the largest mass population movement in America's history, and, secondly, it resulted in a dramatic environmental change for Black and White Americans.

It was approximately one million Blacks who moved from the southern United States to the Midwest, Northeast and West from 1910 to 1930. (Early) African Americans migrated to escape racism and prejudice in the South, as well as to seek jobs in industrial cities. The Broadway family began moving north around 1920 until the 1970s when they started moving to Atlanta and Dallas.

There were two other movements from 1910-40 and 1940-1970 in which five million or more people moved and to a wider variety of destinations.

According to Nebraska Studies.org "Racial Tensions in Omaha", there were a number of reasons for the exodus.

- From 1913 to 1915, falling cotton prices brought on an economic depression across the South.
- After prices dropped, boll weevil insects destroyed much of the cotton crop.
- In 1915, severe floods destroyed the houses and crops of farmers along the Mississippi River, most of who were Black.
- African Americans suffered under "Jim Crow" laws in the South that segregated schools, restaurants, hotels, railroad cars, and even hospitals. Blacks were effectively kept from voting by laws requiring a literacy test (if you wanted to vote, you had to show you could read) and a poll tax (you had to pay to vote). Whites were exempted from either test by a "grandfather clause" — if your grandfather voted, you could, too.

Furthermore, there were other factors that pulled migrants to the North.

- Northern industries were going through an economic boom, especially as the war in Europe began creating a demand for war goods.
- Those industries could no longer rely on new immigrants from Europe to fill the jobs. The war had limited immigration from Europe.
- When America got into the war, many young White men (and some young Black men) were recruited into the military, leaving their old jobs open.
- Salaries were higher in the North. Wages in the South ranged from 50 cents to $2 a day. In the North, workers could make between $2 and $5 a day.

During these years, there were a number of strikes as unions began to organize and demand decent wages. In general, Blacks were willing to become "replacement workers," as the companies called them, or "scabs," as the unions called them. (Racial Tensions in Omaha - African American Migration, 1921)

During the late 1960's cousins would leave Moro, Marianna, and Brinkley, Arkansas to travel to Chicago to find summer jobs. Marie Broadway went to Chicago during early May on five different occasions to find jobs because she couldn't get a job down South.

BLACK MIGRATION

Black migration happened during 1865-1920 between southern states because Blacks heard land was more fertile elsewhere and they could buy their own farms and earn a living. Or just maybe, they wanted to get as far away from previous slave situations as possible. Others migrated to northern states for better economic conditions.

Most were looking for higher wages. Some moved to Kansas for railroad work and the promised free railroad transportation for employees. Blacks seized the opportunities in large numbers. The Whites resented the lost of cheap labor and begin passing ordinances to stop the exodus of Blacks. Some cities charged recruiters for a license and made it against the law for Blacks to leave with those recruiters. However, if there was a railroad line, wherever it led is where the Blacks went, as long as it was north.

Once Blacks started crowding into the large northern cities, Whites started passing Jim Crow laws barring Blacks from restaurants, theaters, hotels, and stores. Blacks were surrounded by prejudice, discrimination and segregation and were forced to reside in the run-down areas of the city.

Migrants demanded their rights, became aware of their ancestry and identified with Africa; at the same time, they regarded Blacks as a part of America. Today, 97% of the Blacks in America reside in urban areas. However, a new trend has developed in some northern cities; some Blacks are returning to the South, however, not as fast as they left. (Lapucia, 2011)

IN CIVIL RIGHTS
Civil and Political Rights

For so long, African Americans had no rights during slavery. They were taught to be subservient and nonassertive. If the natural instinct of asking why, defending themselves, or of boasting of a discovery or inventions were subdued.

Civil and political rights are a class of rights that protect individuals' freedom from unwarranted infringement by governments and private organizations, and ensure one's ability to participate in the civil and political life of the state without discrimination or repression. That wasn't happening. I thought my grandfather was lazy. My aunt told me he wasn't a lazy man. He used to work hard. He bought a tractor to work more efficiently. What happened is the government told him he was not a successful farmer. So they would not lend him any money; he received a double whammy. He had to go out of business. He had to rent his land out or sell it.

The government ensures compliance with applicable laws, regulations and policies for USDA customers and employees regardless of race, color, national origin, sex (including gender identity and expression), religion, age, disability, sexual orientation, marital or familial status, political beliefs, parental status, protected genetic information or because all or part of an individual's income is derived from any public assistance program.

On December 8, 2010, President Obama signed into law the Claims Resolution Act of 2010, which provided an additional $1.15 billion to fund a Settlement Agreement reached by counsel for the Black farmers. The Claims Settlement Act will allow those that have been waiting to get the relief they deserve and have long been promised. (Claims Resolution Act of 2010, 2011)

SECTION 2

SLAVE OWNERS

SLAVE OWNERS

SLAVE MASTER, CAPTAIN FREDERICK STATON

Researching slavery has always been hindered by the lack of records on slaves. Since slaves were mere property, only the race, sex, age, and owner's name and location were given. But because of a tremendous amount of research by Broadway family members, the Broadway lineage was ascertained by seeing family members on Census reports immediately after slavery was abolished and tracing them back into slave houses. Additionally, slave masters records were analyzed. That is why Captain Frederick Staton and John Broadaway were found to be Broadway slave masters.

According to Staton History, he was born in 1772 near the Tar River in Edgecombe County, North Carolina. He came to Anson in 1796 and died in Anson County in 1864. Frederick's lineage: son of Jesse (1740), son of Thomas (1722), son of James (1689), son of Joseph Sr. (1666), son of John (1644), who emigrated in 1666 to Pennsylvania (now Delaware) from Stratford-on-Avon, England with his wife Anne Matthews.

Fredrick grew up and was educated on a large plantation. He loved horses. He owned a beautiful white Spanish horse. He and his slaves would go back to Edgecombe county and roundup horses, then take them back to Anson County and sell them in exchange for land from people who thought their land was no good. Frederick became wealthy buying land. It was said one could not cross his land if one rode all day.

Frederick became a captain in the War of 1812 after answering the call of military duty. The title of Captain remained with him the rest of his life.

Captain Frederick was married three times; first to Priscilla Coburn, born 1776 and died 1854. They had their first of five children, Ennis Staton, in 1798. Frederick was twenty-six years old when he had his first child. Second child was Uriah Staton (1807), third was Maniza Staton (1812), fourth was Harriet Staton (1815) who married Rev. John Broadway, and fifth was Reddin Staton (1820). After Priscilla died, Frederick married Sally Tomlinson, and after her death, he married Roda Ann Shannon. Frederick did not have children with either of the last two wives. Frederick outlived all three of his wives.

He died at the age of ninety-two and was buried at the Staton cemetery five miles west of Ansonville and two miles southeast of Rock River Church according to Staton History edited by Rev. John Staton.

FROM HORSES TO LAND

Frederick Staton was a horseman. He would take a group of slaves and round up wild horses. Frederick brought horses to farming in North Carolina. He sold horses to the

people who had given up on their land being fertile. Frederick's son, Uriah purchased a lot of land from people who was tired of working with the land and had decided to move on to better land. Once Uriah fertilized the land and began farming it successfully, many people sued for their land back. Uriah's cases were sent to the Supreme Court and he won about four times.

Broadway Slave Masters

To get an understanding of the family, the Broadway forefathers belong to, in this section we'll talk about the Broadaways, Statons and Broadways.

Uriah Staton (1807-1888) willed land to his son, W.C. Staton (1837-1906). W.C. was also the adopted son of John and Harriett Broadaway. In Uriah's will, he stated "I give to my son, W. C. Staton, one lot of land at Ansonville known as the Parker lot lying near the Mineral Spring containing three acres and a fraction." Uriah died in 1888. Uriah had several children and had been married four times to women with the maiden names: Lee, Benton, Crump, and Ingram.

According to the Staton History book, he was a very religious man and served most of his life as Deacon of Rocky River Baptist Church. He also helped organize and develop Red Hill Baptist Church. He was buried with his father, Frederick Staton at the Old Frederick Staton Cemetery, just west of Lanes Creek between Ansonville and Burnsville in Anson County.

Frederick Staton (1772-1864) willed land to his daughter, Harriett Staton Broadaway (1815-1887). In Frederick's will, he stated "I give and bequeath to my daughter, Harriet Broadaway and the heirs of her body, a tract of land, adjoining John Broadaway, containing Two Hundred and Fifty acres more or less.

Also one negro boy named George, if the said Harriet Broadaway should decease without a lawful heir of her body, and then they said property is to return to my surviving heirs." His will was signed in the presence of H.M. Broadaway, D. Hyatt, J.W. Bennett, and R. H. Allen during 1859. Interestingly, James Staton moved with his Uncle Frederick and became foreman on his plantation, thereafter, married Frederick's daughter, Maniza.

The land Frederick Staton willed to Ennis Staton was on Niggerhead Creek. The tract contained 700 acres. What an interesting name for a body of water. Legislation was introduced in North Carolina in 2003 to band derogatory place names on official maps.

Harriet Staton married Rev. John Broadaway (1811-1870). According to files from Wadesboro, North Carolina, it states John was the grandson of Old William and Martha Morris. John had 9,000 acres of land, obtained by Grant, which he willed to his adopted son, William Canny Staton. Canny was the first son of Uriah Staton and (first wife) Elizabeth B. Lee, daughter of Rocky River Bill Lee. Harriet and John's home place was seven miles from Uriah's house. The Broadaways lived near Brown Creek Baptist Church.

William Canny Staton (1837-1906) was only two days old when his mother died at the old Staton home. William was adopted by Harriet and John Broadaway and received all of the estate, plus three ¼ acres of land and a Mineral Spring at Ansonville, North Carolina. In addition, he received twenty-five dollars from his grandfather, William (Rocky River Bill). William Canny served as Lieutenant in the Civil War.

He enjoyed riding horses. W.C. was trained early by his mother. W.C. and his young wife, Roxana Huntley (1852-1938) owned a store. Their first child was named John Broadway Staton; the third child was named William Cannie Staton; and the tenth child was named James Marcell Staton. Those names repeat in the family. Earlier in 1857 William Staton received a grant for thirty acres of land in Anson County on the waters of Lanes Creek which runs with the Staton line.

Ennis Staton (1798-1885) married his third wife, Betty Broadaway. Betty was the widow of Mr. Turner. Ennis and Betty are buried in the Ennis Staton Cemetery in Union County, North Carolina. The location is three miles northeast of Fairfield Baptist Church.

STATON AND BROADAWAY SLAVE AND LAND OWNERS

The wife of John Broadaway, Harriett Staton, was a possible slave owner before John Broadaway to our Great[3] Grandfather James Broadaway. Harriett was from a family of slave owners and big land owners. Her father was Captain Frederick Staton. Additionally, John Broadaway was an ambitious man who became a slave owner and a huge land owner, too.

According to the 1960 Staton History book "Every Staton We Could Find in the World", John Staton of 1666 arrived in Pennsylvania from England. Most of his family had sons and many of them used the same names. A few of his descendants were James, Thomas, Jesse, and Frederick Staton. Interesting enough Maniza Staton of 1812-1859 married a cousin, James Staton of 1802-1858. James worked as an apprentice of Frederick Staton for seven years.

Original land grants were obtained by the Statons in Annapolis, Maryland (Land Grant Office). During the 1700's the land tracts were classified by given names. Some examples of names used for tracts of land were Staton's Adventure, The Meadows, Delight, Vienna Town, Staton's Folly, Lott, Staton's Lott, Hazard, Good Neighborhood,

Patuxent Fishery resurveyed, First Addition to Patuxent Fishery Resurveyed, Lotts Addition, Puzzle, End of Division, Worchester Co., and Staton's Necessity.

One of the earliest Staton land grants was by James Staton in 1715 for 663 acres. Others who received land grants during the 1700's were Walter, Solomon, Joseph, and Thomas Staton. Additionally during the 1800's, land grants were acquired by Authur, Frederick, James, John W, John, Walter, Uriah, Ennis, William, J.A., Reuben, Walton, and William Cannie Staton. According to the Staton book, it shows a land grant was acquired for as little as 1 ¾ acres by J.A. in 1879 in Henderson County for 12.5 cents per acre to as much as 685 acres during 1761 by James Staton of Northhampton.

Statons who eventually owned more than 1,000 acres each were James (1,300) of Northhampton County and others who were all of Anson County, Ennis (6,000), Frederick (1,500), Uriah (1,000) and William Cannie (W.C.) Staton (9,000). William acquired land on his own and eventually inherited the land of Uriah his father and John and Harriett Broadaway, his uncle and aunt.

John Broadaway had over 9,000 acres and willed it to William Cannie Staton who was also the adopted son of John and Harriett Broadaway. Evidently, John learned the land trade quite well. Could some of that knowledge been acquired by ancestors James and Marshall Broadaway? Did James Broadaway, after slavery, ever own land?

We know Marshall and Silvia owned land in 1874-1884. But for whatever reasons, they were not able to hold on to the land in North Carolina. Were they tricked out of it? Did they owe a debt? Did they have to leave town in a hurry? Were there racial issues? Why did William Cannie Staton buy the land? Or were they moving away from their past for better opportunities?

JOHN BROADAWAY – AN INDENTURED SERVANT

John Broadaway was an indentured servant for seven years for Frederick Staton. Owning indentured servants was a practice during the 1800s. An indentured servant was typically a laborer or tradesman, under contract with an employer for a fixed period of time, typically three to seven years, in exchange for their ocean transportation, food, clothing, lodging and other necessities during the term of their indenture. An indenture was a legal contract enforced by the courts.

Many immigrants arrived in Colonial America as indentured servants, which usually involved their new master paying the ship's captain for their transatlantic voyage. Most were young men and women from Britain and Germany, under the age of twenty-one, whose service was negotiated by their parents.

Many plantation owners welcomed the tradesmen with skills of blacksmiths, watch-makers, coppersmiths, tailors, shoemakers, ship-carpenters and caulkers, weavers, cabinet-makers, ship-joiners, nailers, engravers, copperplate printers, plasterers, bricklayers, sawyers and painters, also schoolmasters, clerks and book-keepers, farmers and laborers. John Broadaway started as an indentured servant, but later became a slave and land owner.

FORMER SLAVE OWNERS

Getting a sense of where Great[3] Grandfather James, Great2 Grandfather Marshall, and the former slave owners were in the timeline was a revelation, just five years after the abolishment of slavery.

During 1870, former Broadaway slave owners, John and Harriett Broadaway and William Cannie Staton lived in the same household in Burnsville, Anson County, North Carolina. John and William C. were farmers and Harriett was the housekeeper.

Also during 1870, living as neighbors to John Broadaway in Burnsville, North Carolina were Black laborers, James, Marshall, Margaret, Jane and Mack Broadaway. James was about fifty-five years old and Marshall was about seventeen who worked on the farm.

James was also head of household. Since they were listed immediately after John Broadaway's White sixteen year old laborer, Harington Ellis on the 1870 U.S. Federal Census, it can be assumed they were still working for John Broadaway. Margaret and Jane were listed as domestic servants. Mack had no occupation listed.

The following is a detailed chronological list of Broadway (Broadaway) slave owner(s) and key people in the lives of our Broadway ancestors. The information includes the slave owner's name, U.S. Census year, age, birth and death year and supplementary information.

JOHN BROADAWAY, PARENT OF BROADWAY SLAVE MASTER

- **1750** born (1750); white slave master and farmer; his wife, Lehai, born in 1750
- **1790** 40 (1750); lived in Person County, North Carolina.
- **1812** 62 (1750); volunteered as private with Russells' Separate Battin MTP Gunmen in Tennessee.
- **1820** 70 (1750); slaveowner of 7 in Staton, Anson, North Carolina
- **1830** 80 (1750); slave owner of 9 in Anson, North Carolina
- **1840** 90 (1750-1840); died 1840

REV. JOHN BROADAWAY, BROADWAY SLAVE MASTER

- **1811** born 1811, another White John Broadaway was born
- **1850** 39 (1811); farmer, Meltonville, Anson, North Carolina with real estate value, $1,000
- **1855** 44 (1811); married Harriett Staton
- **1837** adopted William C. Staton, nephew, as a son
- **1860** 49 (1811); farmer in Diamond Hill, Anson, North Carolina. The value of his real estate was $5,000 and personal property value was $20,000.

- **1866** 55 (1811); received a Confederate Presidential Pardon. He was living in Anson County, North Carolina.
- **1870** 59 (1811-1870); John was still farming with a real estate value of $2,500 and personal property of $4,000. He was living in Burnsville, Anson, North Carolina.
- **1870** 59 (1811-1870); died in Burnsville, North Carolina. He was buried at Brown Creek Baptist Church Cemetery, 4 miles northwest of Wadesboro, North Carolina.

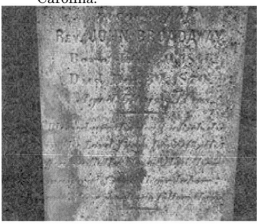

REV. JOHN BROADAWAY **(1811-1870)**
picture by Julious.Burr@windstream.net on 7/28/2010

HARRIETT STATON BROADAWAY, SLAVE MASTER'S WIFE
- **1850** 34 (1815); White, housekeeper, Meltonville, Anson, North Carolina
- **1860** 45 (1815); White, housekeeper, North Carolina
- *1870* 54 (1815); White, housekeeper, Burnsville, Anson, North Carolina
- **1880** 65 (1815); living with William C. and Roxanna C. Staton, Burnsville, Anson, North Carolina
- **1887** 72 (1815-1887) Harriett died 1887. She was buried at Brown Creek Baptist Church Cemetery, 4 miles northwest of Wadesboro.

HARRIETT STATON BROADAWAY **(1815-1887)**, WIFE OF REV. JOHN BROADAWAY *picture by Julious.Burr@windstream.net on 7/28/2010*

WILLIAM C. STATON, ADOPTED SON AND NEPHEW OF JOHN & HARRIETT BROADAWAY
- **1850** 13 (1937);
- **1860** 22 (1937); farm laborer, value of real estate $700
- **1870** 30 (1837); farmer, Burnsville, Anson, North Carolina; with his real estate valued at $400

- **1872** 32 (1837); married Roxanna C. Huntley Staton 20 (1852-1938)
- **1880** 42 (1837); farmer, Burnsville, Anson, North Carolina; 3 kids (ages 7,5,2); mother Harriett Staton Broadaway living with them 65 (1815-1887)
- **1885** 48 (1837); farmer, Burnsville, Anson, North Carolina; purchased land from Marshall & Silvia Broadway
- **1888** 51 (1837-1906); Register of Deeds document appeared; Marshall & Silvia Broadway sold 133 ½ acres of land in the Big Brown Creek area to W.C. Staton for $450 on March 21, 1885.
- **1906** William Cannie Staton died. He is buried at Brown Creek Baptist Church Cemetery, 4 miles northwest of Wadesboro.

CAPTAIN HAMPTON BEVERLY, FAMILY OF THE PERSON WHO SOLD MARSHALL BROADWAY LAND
- Birth Unknown
- Death April 1865, killed and buried at Eastview Cemetery Wadesboro, Anson County, North Carolina, 4 miles northwest of Wadesboro

JAMES BEVERLEY, ALSO LIVED IN WADESBORO, FAMILY OF THE PERSON WHO SOLD MARSHALL BROADWAY LAND
- 1870 66 (1804-1896), White, Wadesboro, Anson, North Carolina and buried at Salem United Methodist Church, Wadesboro, Anson County, North Carolina

SUSAN THREADGILL BEVERLEY, ALSO LIVED IN WADESBORO, FAMILY OF THE PERSON WHO SOLD MARSHALL BROADWAY LAND
- **1870** 56 (1812-1883), White, Wadesboro, Anson, North Carolina; 5 children and buried at Salem United Methodist Church, Wadesboro, Anson County, North Carolina

CHARLES WESLEY BEVERLY, FIRST TO SELL LAND TO MARSHALL & SILVIA BROADWAY
- 1847 00 (1847-1919) born Nov. 12, 1847
- 1919 died June 11, 1919 and buried at Salem United Methodist Church, Wadesboro, Anson County, North Carolina. C.W. Beverly and Charlotte played a critical role in the Broadway family's lives because they were the first to sell land to Marshall and Silvia Broadway.

CHARLOTTE CARPENTER BEVERLY, WIFE OF CHARLES WESLEY BEVERLY
- 1849 00 (1849-1934) born Dec. 3, 1849
- 1934 died Nov. 12, 1934 and buried at Salem United Methodist Church, Wadesboro, Anson County, North Carolina

JAMES MARSHALL BROADAWAY (J.M. BROADAWAY)

(Note: Broadway ancestor (unknown relationship) used the same name, lived in the same area, and likely attended the same church)

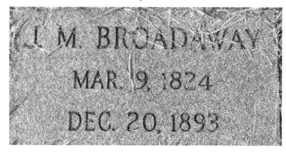

Cemetery Record
- 1824   00 (1824-1893), White, Anson County, North Carolina, Mar. 9, 1824
- 1893   69 Buried at Rocky Mount Baptist Church Cemetery, Dec. 20, 1893

picture by Chris Curley ccurley100@hotmail.com on 9/18/2010

URIAH STATON, FATHER OF WILLIAM CANNIE STATON
- 1807   00 (1807-1888) born May 5, 1807 in Anson County, North Carolina
- 1888   died Nov. 23, 1888 in Anson County, North Carolina and buried in Red Hill Baptist Church Cemetery in Ansonville, Anson County, North Carolina

Captain Frederick Staton, father of Rev. John Broadaway's wife
- 1772   00 (1772-1864) born Tarboro, Edgecombe County, North Carolina
- 1812   Frederick Staton was a Captain in the War of 1812
- 1882   died Jan. 29, 1864, buried in Fredrick Staton Cemetery, Burnsville, Anson County, North Carolina

The Fredrick Staton Cemetery is located next to the old Staton home place. The area is now forest and access to the cemetery is difficult, going over rough forest roads. The forest was timbered in the early 2000's. (Peurifoy, 2009) The Cemetery was surveyed by Dr. John Staton in the 1960's. A monument was erected by the Staton descendants. To the right of the monument are located a number of unmarked slave graves. Most of the stones are overgrown with ivy, placed by the family in the 1960's. As of 2009, the land is fenced off and inaccessible.

A WILL KEEPS IT IN THE FAMILY
Even back in the 1700s and 1800s, the Statons and Broadaways believed in making wills. A will is a desire, wish, choice, preference, or a command of what is to happen in the event of a person's death.

The two families owned a lot of land and seemed to have developed a system to keep the land in the Staton family. Rev. John and Harriett Staton Broadaway, slave owners of our ancestors, had a will. This article will show the emphasis and importance the Statons and Broadaways placed on a will.

According to "Staton History", Jesse Staton drafted wills during 1740s through 1813s. Starting on page 99 of the Staton's history book, it states Jesse willed his

1. Wife, Rebekah, 120 arces of land, one Negro man named Pompy and one Negro woman named Charlot and Charlot's son, Stephen, plus any increase.

2. Son, Frederick Staton, one Negro man named Rueben which he had already.

3. Son, Thomas Staton, after the death of my wife, one pair of firedogs to him and his heirs forever.

4. Daughter, Sarah Manning, $10 to her and her heirs forever

5. Daughter, Lovey Andrews, after the death of my wife, lend one Negro woman by the name of Charlot and her son Stephen and all her increases, and after heirs, and if she dies without an heir the said Charlot and her son Stephen and her increase is to be equally divided among my three sons: Frederick, Thomas and Bythel to them and their heirs forever.

6. Son, Bythel Staton, lend to his disposal, the land and plantation I am now in possessed with (except my wife's part I have lent to her) the remainder part of my plantation, and after the death of my wife, and if dies without a lawful heir begotten of his body for the said property to be equally divided between Frederick and Thomas, but if Bythel Staton should have an heir to him and his heirs forever.

7. Wife, Rebekah Staton, two bee hives, and my will is three men be chosen to fix on them together with provisions of all kinds for one year and she have the fowls of all kinds to her and to her heirs forever.

Executors for the will were Miejah May, Thomas Staton and Bythel Staton. Jesse Staton's last will and testament was recorded October 8, 1812 in Edgecombe County, North Carolina and signed by Jesse Staton. Additionally, it was proven by William Bargell and James Staton and witnessed by Miejah May and Thomas Staton.

Preserve the Staton Name. Jesse was dead in 1813 and the home place in Edgecombe County went to Bythel Staton. Frederick was in Anson County, North Carolina and had purchased 235 acres of land in Anson on February 17, 1801. Thomas had purchased 314 acres of land in Martin County. These guys had wills because they had a lot of land and their obligation was to preserve the Staton name through their heirs.

Frederick Staton kept excellent records. He was born in Edgecombe County near the Tar River in 1772 and died in Anson County in 1864. Frederick received a good education. Also, he was a business man, rounding up wild horses from Edgecombe, training, and selling them to people in Anson County. There, it is believed over 30,000 acres of land passed through Frederick's hands. Additionally, much of the land was gifted and willed to family members.

Families Move to Anson County. During the same time Frederick moved to Anson County in 1796, it is believed the following families arrived: Ross, Coburn, Allen,

Martin, Morris, Benton, Broadaway, Turner, Waddell, and Davis. They appeared to always be near each other in the early days. You will see them marrying into each other's families; they witnessed each other's wills; and some of them attended church together.

A Church with Slaves. According to Rev. Edgar book, "History of Rocky River Baptist Church" where Frederick's son, Uriah Staton was a deacon and Elder Joseph Magee was a White minister. Within Magee's will, Ralph Freeman, a colored man, had been freed and was sent for to preach McGee's funeral. This church sometimes allowed slaves and freed colored ministers to be members during the 1820's. Magee willed Ralph an additional $50, a fine horse, overcoat, and Magee's Bible.

Content of a Will. Another example of a will was from Frederick Staton who was born 1772 and died 1864. Frederick's will provide for the following:

1. His just debts to be paid.
2. Son, Ennis Staton, 700 acres, tract of land on Niggerhead Creek and Gourd Vine Creek, Negro named Vilet, her increase and Negro girl named Ann. Third wife of Ennis Staton was Betty Broadway. His first wife was a Ross and his second wife was an Allen. Ennis was born 1798 and died 1885.
3. Son, Uriah Staton, all land on East side of Lanes Creek also a tract of land of 300 acres (Yarbrough lands), also land between Lanes Creek and Cribs Creek except Taylor tract. Will Negros: Ellick, Charles, Linda and her children and future increase. Pay $400 annually to lawful heirs of Temperance Smith after my decease.
4. Son, Reddin Staton, all lands on Richardson Creek (Austin, Sharps, and Thomas and Nance Land), 5 Negros named Willis, Tom and Ann, Jo and Sam.
5. Temperance Smith, Negro boy named John, girl Jane, girl Caroline with her children except the oldest named Frona.
6. Lawful heirs of daughter, Maniza Staton, all the land where James Staton lived and died, also a tract known as Taylor land, also, three Negros named Nancy, Calvin, and Laura.
7. Daughter, Harriet Broadaway and the heirs of her body, a tract of land, adjoining John Broadaway, 250 acres, also a Negro boy named George. If the said Harriett Broadaway should decease without a lawful heir of her body, then her property would return to their surviving heirs.
8. Granddaughter, Theatus Staton (daughter of Ennis), one Negro girl named Frona.
9. Wife, Rhoda Staton, Negro boy named Dick. After Rhoda's death, willed to Uriah Staton.

The Last Will and Testament of Frederick Staton was drafted on July 9, 1859. The executors of the will were Uriah Staton and Miles W. Maske. Frederick signed and sealed the will in Anson County, North Carolina in the presence of H.M. Broadaway, D. Hyatt, J.W. Bennett, and R.H. Allen.

Deeding Land. Uriah Staton also had a practice of deeding land to his married children before his death, but still placing it in the will to show they were living on the land. If the child died, the will may provide for the widow and children. The children may have to wait until they turn 21 years or when they shall marry. But once the widow is deceased, the inheritance must go back to the Staton children. Uriah had over a dozen children. For example, according to his will, son, Baker E. Staton was willed Uriah's dwelling house and cotton gin. Daughter, Lilly F. Shankle, was willed 390 acres of land known as the Frederick Staton and Thomas Allen lands, except two acres for the family grave yard.

Inheritance. Harriet Staton, fourth child of Frederick Staton, was born June 25, 1815 and died May 25, 1887. She married Rev. John Broadaway who was born January 30, 1811 and died December 30, 1870. He lived near Brown Creek Baptist church. He served as a Lieutenant in the Civil War. Grandparents were William (known as Rocky River Bill) and Martha Morris.

Rev. John owned over 9,000 acres of land and willed it all to his adopted son, William Canny Staton who was also nephew of his wife, Harriett Staton Broadaway. William Canny's mother, Elizabeth Lee Staton, died when he was two days old. Harriet and Rev. John did not have any kids, so Uriah had them promise not to change his name from Staton to Broadaway and to will their estate to him wholly or partially if they had kids.

William Cannie Staton became a wealthy man once receiving his inheritance from Uriah Staton (grandfather), William Lee (grandfather), Rev. John Broadaway & Harriet (adopted parents).

William Canny Station named his first son "John Broadway Staton", born 1873 and died 1947, and son named his first son "John Broadway Staton Jr.", born 1906. W.C. is buried in front of Brown Creek Missionary Baptist church about four miles northwest of Wadesboro, North Carolina with good markers.

Maniza Staton (1812-1859) and husband and cousin, James A. Staton (1802-1858) died without a will. They had 9 kids and over 5,000 acres of land, but because they did not have a will, the estate was not settled until 1870.

The lesson learned from our former slave masters is to create a will to secure your family's inheritance.

SLAVES READING AND WRITING

Slave owners who were large land owners were usually well educated. During the early 1800's, teachers went from one large farm to another, and were paid by individual families who could afford this circuit instruction, as was the custom during that time. According to "Staton History", Frederick Staton, a slave and large land owner, received a good education during those times.

If a slave was fortunate enough to learn how to read and write, he or she was probably taught by the White children or learned at Sunday school. For example in

1818, Poplar Tent Church in Mecklenburg County, North Carolina was conducting a Sunday School for the Black people. (The African American Experience, 2010)

A get together, an election, or a political gathering was often an exciting occasion to the local slaves as to their masters. For example in 1822 Matthew Baine of Mecklenburg County wanted a law to prevent slaves' from attending general get-togethers and elections.

In 1826, a law was passed forbidding free Blacks to enter the state of North Carolina; and in 1835, they lost their right to vote, regardless of property holdings. Free Blacks were further barred from preaching in public, owning a gun without special permit, selling liquor, and were not allowed to attend any public school.

On one rare documented occasion, a master ordered his slaves be sent to school. In 1830, the General Assembly passed a law prohibiting anyone from teaching a slave to read or write. Since knowledge meant power, the masters wanted none of it. According to the African American Experience web page, "Lord, you better not be caught with a book in your hand," recalled Louisa Adams. "If you did, you were sold. They didn't allow that." After this law was passed, some slaves still secretly learned how to read and write.

Slaves, of course, were in the worst position. In 1830, state law prohibited anyone from teaching a slave to read or write; and the general legal position of Blacks eroded significantly during the pre-war years. Homicide of a Black person might go unpunished if committed by a White person.

Advertisements from various North Carolina newspapers, from 1838–1840, showed how Whites hired teachers to educate their young. In the antebellum period, North Carolina families who wanted their children to receive an education beyond reading, writing, and arithmetic typically sent them to private academies.

Although these academies were often in the same county where students lived, they were far enough from home in an age of horse travel that students typically boarded (stayed and ate with) with local families.

In 1860 a legislator proposed to fine Masters $100 if they gave their slaves permission to attend political meetings. In 1861, the General Assembly passed a law ensuring Blacks were unable to own or control enslaved people.

Even during the 1860s, slaves were generally not provided education and most of the owners did not want them to read and write, they would be punished if they were discovered reading or writing.

SECTION 3

SLAVE ANCESTORS FROM NORTH CAROLINA

THE NORTH CAROLINA SEARCH FOR ANCESTORS

The county where our ancestors lived was Anson County, North Carolina. The county consisted of several townships: Ansonville, Burnsville, Gulledges, Lanesboro, Lilesville, Morven, Wadesboro, and Whites Store. Please see a map of Anson County below from Wikipedia.org:

The post office was located in Wadesboro. Many ancestry searches have been made in those towns. Every township in Anson County has been looked at during the 1870 U.S. Federal Census to spot any Broadway relative.

1. Wadesboro had the largest population of approximately 2,400 with no Broadways spotted.

2. Ansonville had a population of about 1,900 with the head of households spotted: Relatives Robert Broadway, Sandy Clark, and Harry Broadway. Their race was listed as Black. It was noted that Ansonville had a lot of people with various occupations such as retail/dry good merchant, engineer from England, domestic servant, shoemaker (Black), physician, jeweler, and a boot maker from England. The merchant's real estate value was $10,000 and the personal property was $20,000. One of the physician's real estate valued $100 and personal property was $500; the other physician had real estate valued at $15,000 and the personal property was $8,000. So the physician was the wealthiest person in the town. Listed in parenthesis are age, sex, race, and occupation.

a. Robert Broadway (57, M, B, worked on railroad) was head of household. Living with him was his wife, Harriett Broadway (60, F, B, keeps house), Lydia Broadway (21, F, B, no occupation), Ellen Broadway (4, F, B, at home), and Harriet Broadway (15, F, B, no occupation). Robert is Marshall Broadway's uncle. Robert is James Broadway's (1820) brother.

b. Sandy Clark (21, M, B, worked on railroad) was head of household. Living with him was his mother, Hannah (49, F, B, keeps house), and Silvia Clark (13, F, B, worked on farm). Sandy Clark is Marshall Broadway's brother-in-law.

c. Harry Broadway (55, M, B, worked on farm) was head of household. Living with him was his wife, Eliza (45, F, B, worked on farm). Others included in his household were children: Adline Broadway (21, F, B, work on farm), Sam Broadway (13, M, B, work on farm), Marshall Broadway (7, M, B, at home), Julius Broadway (6, M, B, at home), Eliza Broadway (2, F, B, at home), Henry Broadway (5, M, B, at home), and Robert Broadway (1, M, B, at home). Harry is Marshall Broadway's uncle.

3. During 1870, *Lilesville's* population was about 1,750. No Broadways were spotted.

4. *White Store Township* had a population of approximately 1,450 people in 1870. Broadways were found.

a. A single male at the age of 16, Henry Broadway, was living and working on a farm in *White Store Township.*

b. *Alex Broadway* was also working on a farm. Alex was twenty years old and living with him and keeping house was Creacy Broadway at age forty. Alex is Marshall's brother-in-law.

c. Additionally, a White family was living in White Store, William Broadaway. He was a sixty-five year old small farmer. Living with him was Sarah (66) who kept house and had nine young folk ranging from ages three to seventeen. All the children were listed as working on the farm.

5. Lanesboro had a population of about 1,350 people in 1870. Spotted on the Census were two families of *Black Broadways.*

a. *George (35) and Harriett (20) Broadway* were in the same household. George worked on a farm and Harriett kept house.

b. *Sidney (35), Elizabeth (20), and John (4) Broadway* lived in the same household. Sidney worked on a farm and Elizabeth kept house.

6. *Burnsville* had the smallest population (about 1,050) in Anson County in 1870. This is the town where most of the Broadway ancestors lived.

a. *White slave owner, John (59) and Harriett (54) Broadaway,* lived in Burnsville. Living with them was their son, William C. Staton (30) and farm worker, Ellis Harington (16). Both John and William C. were farmers. Real estate value and personal property value for John ($2,500, $4,000) and William C. ($500, 0).

b. *Great[3] grandfather James Broadway,* a 55-year old Black male, lived in Burnsville and worked on a farm. In his household was Marshall Broadway (17, son, farm worker), Margaret Broadway (30, domestic servant), Jane Broadway (16, domestic servant), and Mack Broadway (10, no occupation).

c. Also in *Burnsville,* there was another Black farm worker, Albert Broadway who was 20 years old.

d. A close neighbor of Albert was Thomas Broadaway (White male) and family. He was a White farmer whose land was valued at $400 and personal property at $400. Living in the house with him was Michall (62, White, female); Hartwell (22, White, male, worked on farm); Dawson (20, White, male, worked on farm); and Sopmona H. (18, White, female, no occupation).

e. Another White family was James Broadaway (72, White male, farmer ($250, 4150) and Martha Broadaway (65, White female, keeps house).

f. Another Black family was spotted in *Burnsville.* Henry Broadway was listed as a 29 year old male farmer and his wife kept house. Adline was 25 and three children Walter (6), John (4), and Luvonia (2).

Broadway was just one of the Black families who lived in **Anson County.** Ten years after slavery, it was just interesting to find the Broadways who were still living in Anson County. Finding the Broadway ancestors, including James Broadway and his neighbors, was very interesting.

BIRTHPLACE OF BROADWAY SLAVE ANCESTORS

It was discovered earlier *North Carolina* was the birth state of the **Broadway ancestors.** The research started in 1982 and continued throughout the years by various family members. The *2010 Broadway Family Reunion* team passionately researched for two years to prepare for the *Broadway Generations* book that was presented at the family reunion during July 2010. The following North Carolina research trips were taken by part of that Reunion team:

TRIP 1 TO THE BIRTHPLACE OF BROADWAY SLAVE ANCESTORS
Jerome Turner took a trip to Wadesboro (Post Office)/ Lanesboro, North Carolina in Anson County, the birthplace of our great grandparents, on November 19, 2009. He flew, rented a car and drove the rest. Jerome felt it was the time to visit, so he did it alone.

The Broadway ancestors lived in Burnsville Township, Anson County, North Carolina which is a neighboring town. Wadesboro, North Carolina in Anson County is about two hours from Charlotte.

Based on Jerome's research and the drive to the birthplace of our ancestors, he was overcome with a

sense of the times. He knew he was in the right place. Jerome's first stop was the old court house to check for birth records, but to his disappointment, he was told all birth records before 1913 were lost in a big fire. A new building was built in Anson County

STATE OF NORTH CAROLINA, ANSON COUNTY
DEED, JANUARY 1, 1875
CHARLES & CHARLOTTE BEVERLY TO MARSHALL BROADWAY & HEIRS

133 1/2 ACRES

359.

where death certificates and deeds from the 1800s could be found. He was able to find several Broadways.

TRIP 2 TO THE BIRTHPLACE OF BROADWAY SLAVE ANCESTORS

Others just had to see the birthplace. A trip was organized to North Carolina by Eugene Broadway taking his wife, Shianne, and three Broadway cousins: Mary Booker, Jewell Farley and Lolita Foxworth.

This group traveled from Atlanta to North Carolina. Eugene took with him descendants of the sons of Marshall Broadway. Taking in every site of the trip were descendants of Oliver, John, Senior, and Morris Broadway. While there, the group visited Statons and Broadways who were residents of Burnsville, North Carolina and whose race was Black. They had an opportunity to be guided to and through the slave graveyard by a distant relative, Delores Broadway-Hammond, who is pictured below.

The trip was very successful not only because of the tours, but because they made the find of the times. The group discovered the land deeds where Marshall Broadway had purchased the 133 ½ acres in North Carolina during 1874. The team was so excited!

TRIP 3 TO THE BIRTHPLACE OF BROADWAY SLAVE ANCESTORS

After extensive research, another trip was made to North Carolina by first cousins, Jerome Turner and Eugene Broadway. This trip made it all worth it. Touring the town, talking to the residents and town officials was very informational. The highlight of their trip was locating and touring the grounds of the Broadaway Plantation site.

A significant find was another slave graveyard. Broadways were buried there, but many of the graves were merely identified with various sizes of stones with unreadable marks. Knowing slaves could not read or write, nor were they allowed,

the cousins understood why many of the graves were nameless.

First cousins, Jerome, and Eugene are pictured at left at one of their many stops.

DNA THOUGHTS

James Broadway, born 1820 and was the father of my great^2 grandfather, Marshall Broadway.

James Broadway was a slave; he may have been owned first by Frederick Staton, then by John Broadway (1811-1870) and Harriett Staton Broadway (1815-1887). Frederick had many slaves. James was thought to have been given to John and Harriet as a gift from Harriet's father, Captain Frederick Staton. Harriett married Rev. John Broadway before 1838. They produced no children but adopted William Cannie Staton. James was born a Mulatto, a person with one White parent and one Black.

SLAVES IN THE FAMILY

James Broadway and his brothers, Harry (Hany) and Robert and son, Marshall were born into slavery. They were all born before 1865. James's daughter was Bellie who was a slave also as a little girl. James Broadway was born and lived in slavery until he was forty-five years old. Marshall was about twelve years old when he was freed. The Broadway family has said through the years that we were a mixed people. Our ancestors were said to be Black, White, and Indian.

EUGENE BROADWAY'S DNA AND FAMILY DIALOG LINEAGE

Tracing his Great[3] Grandfather James Broadway's lineage has become very important to Eugene Broadway. He traced his ancestors back into slavery. Once in the slave house, Eugene's research ran cold. Broadway began to look at DNA. His hopes were to find something that had not been taken from his ancestors. His ancestors were property that was bought and sold. No detailed records were kept. So, Eugene began ordering different kinds of DNA tests. He first ordered the Paternal Lineage DNA test from Ancestry.com and then the Family Finder autosomal DNA test from AfricanDNA.

PATERNAL LINEAGE DNA TEST FROM ANCESTRY.COM

With Ancestry, Eugene submitted a DNA cheek-swab. The Paternal Lineage DNA Y-46 test promised to identify the DNA handed down from father to son through generations which helps a person connect with genetic cousins. Ancestry continues to match the genetic cousins to grow a person's family tree. If one participates in DNA Groups, Ancestry compares levels of relatedness.

Ancestry found that Eugene Broadway belong to the haplogroup E, specifically E1b1a, the Language People. The test was completed on 12/1/2009. This haplogroup is found in west and Sub-Saharan Africa with a very high population in Cameroon and Benin. Eugene's ancient ancestors were instrumental in developing the rich bank of languages known as Bantu, which represents over 400 different ethnic groups in Africa, and literally means "people". Swahili, Shona and Zulu are a handful of the more than 500 Bantu languages.

FAMILY FINDER AUTOSOMAL DNA TEST FROM AFRICAN DNA

A new form of autosomal DNA testing is Family Finder. This test checks your autosomal chromosomes which are the other twenty-two pairs beyond the sex-linked X and Y chromosomes. The test can find matches in ANY branch of your family tree. It is not limited to just the narrow paternal or maternal lines. This new autosomal DNA test only works when people share relatively recent ancestors. The test evaluates matches and calculates probable relationships of close relatives.

The Family Finder can tell which specific races are in your lineage; female mtDNA will only show her female line; Y-DNA is only passed-on through the male line; and it is the Y-DNA which is used for the Family Finder test. With the Family Finder test, you may extend the power of genetic genealogy to all of your ancestors. You can discover connections to descendants of all sixteen of your great-great-grandparents!

The Population Finder program determines your biogeographical ancestry by comparing your autosomal DNA to that of our world DNA population database. Population Finder results consist of up to four out of seven continental groups: Africa, America, East Asia, Europe, Middle Eastern, Oceania, and South Asia.

Eugene took a painless cheek swab. The process is a bit like matching fingerprints on CSI. A match between his DNA and the DNA from a person from Africa means that Family Finder DNA have possibly found someone with whom Eugene Broadway shares a common ancestor.

Results of the Family Finder autosomal DNA test were received by Eugene Broadway during August, 2011. According to the AfricanDNA, Eugene is approximately 77% West African. Know that, according to Professor Gates, "About thirty percent of all African Americans have White male ancestors." And Eugene is no different. He is 23% European. See the table below shows the results of the Family Finder autosomal DNA test.

CONTINENT (SUBCON-TINENT	POPULATION	PERCENTAGE	MARGIN OF ERROR
Europe	French, Orcadian, Romanian, Russian	23.42%	+/-0.16%
Africa (West African)	Yoruba	76.58%	+/-0.16%

However, by comparing Eugene's results with results from research databases, Family Finder test looked at the tribal information of those who have the same results. In this way, they told what tribes, regions, and populations Eugene shared common ancestry. Additionally, African DNA updates this comparative analysis whenever new results are added to the database as research and testing continue.

Enough DNA testing samples were taken from the native populations. It was discovered that the tribal origin and region for Eugene Broadway is Yoruba. The general geographic area, Yoruba, is located in West Africa in the lower Sahara Desert with the closest large body of water being the Atlantic Ocean.

The Yoruba people live on the west coast of Africa in Nigeria and can also be found in the eastern Republic of Benin and Togo. Because the majority of the slaves brought to the Americas were from West Africa, Yoruban descendants can also be found in Brazil, Cuba, the Caribbean, and the United States. There are also many Yoruba currently living in Europe, particularly Britain, since Nigeria was once a British colony.

The Yoruba are one of the largest cultural groups in Africa. Currently, there are about 40 million Yoruba world-wide. The Yoruba have been living in advanced urban kingdoms for more than 1,500 years. They created a strong economy through farming, trading, and art production. Their outstanding and unique artistic traditions include woodcarving, sculpture, metal work, textiles, and beadwork.

In 1960 Nigeria became an independent country. Ten million Yoruba were known to live in Nigeria at that time amongst many other ethnic groups. Today, the Yoruba still continue many of their traditional ways of life. Many Yoruba live in large towns and cities, and many towns are still based on the extended family dwellings in compounds. Lagos is the largest city in Nigeria and over ten million people live there, including a large Yoruban population. Many Yoruba today are still employed as carvers, blacksmiths, farmers, weavers, and leather workers. Today, the Yoruban people still make some of the world's greatest works of art.

According to various family dialogs, the following ancestors of Eugene Broadway were said to be part Indian. Great Grandfather Oliver Broadway's mother, Silvia Clark Broadway was part Cherokee; Grandfather Sam Broadway's mother, Dora Reese Broadway, was part Indian; and Daniel Broadway's mother, Nazaree Hansberry Broadway, was also part Indian.

Yet, none of the DNA test classified Eugene as part Indian. It is possible that Eugene needs to have testing done on the maternal side of the family. Most of the family members were women who were identified as part-Indian.

Some of Eugene's ancestors who seemingly had White ancestors were labeled as Mulatto at least once on a United States Federal Census. The Mulatto ancestors were Great[3] Grandfather James Broadway, Great[2] Grandmother Silvia Clark Broadway, Great Grandfather Oliver Broadway, Great Grandmother, Dora Reese Broadway, Grandfather Samuel Broadway, Grandmother Nazaree Hansberry Broadway, and Father Daniel Broadway would have been labeled a Mulatto if the terms were still used. The Family Finder test labeled Eugene as approximately 23% European (French, Orcadian, Romanian, and Russian).

Lastly, Great[2] Grandfather Marshall Broadway was always listed on the United States Federal Censuses as Negro or Black. Additionally, the picture of Marshall appears that he was African American. The DNA test specified that Eugene Broadway was approximately 77% West African (Yoruba). *(See Table next page: Eugene Broadway's Bloodline.)*

62

EUGENE BROADWAY'S BLOODLINE

Eugene Broadway	Shianne Carter, Wife
Daniel Broadway, Father	Lee Esther Smith, Mother
Sam Broadway, Grandfather	Nazaree Hansberry, Grand-mother, a Mulatto
Oliver Broadway, Great Grandfather, a Mulatto	Dora Reese, Great Grand-mother
Marshall Broadway, Great² Grandfather	Silvia Jane Clark, Great² Grandmother, a Mulatto (Cherokee)
James Broadway owned by Frederick Staton Great³ Grandfather, a Mulatto. Then owned by Harriett Staton & John Broad-away	Slave, Great³ Grandmother, ?
Slave Master, Great⁴ Grandfather, White English Descendant	Slave, Mother, Black African Descendant

COULD SARAH BE JAMES BROADWAY'S MAMA?

Could Sarah, the slave of Frederick Staton, have been James Broadways' mama? If so, Sarah is James's mama and Frederick Staton is James daddy. Frederick was big in the church and he was the big-money man. She named her baby and used Frederick Staton brother's name, James. Frederick was also a kind hearted man. Frederick Staton had a lot of deeds in Anson County and other counties where he bought property and slaves.

It was told Frederick's slaves worked basically six days a week, but on Sundays they would go to church. So the slaves attended the same church Frederick and his family did. You would also find them on Sundays going by Frederick's house to watch Frederick and his family play music and dance, they would be singing all the way up the hill talking about what a good boss they had. And the boss was better than others in the County.

It is believed Sarah is James's mother and possibly Frederick Staton is his daddy. (1) James was a slave of Frederick and Frederick had a brother named James so it is believed James may have been named after Frederick's brother. (2) James is listed in the 1880 U.S. Census as a Mulatto which meant he had at least one White parent. (3) It is also believed James may have been slave property of Frederick's. So when Frederick's daughter, Harriet, married John Broadaway, James may have been given to them as a wedding gift. (4) James was very loyal to John and Harriet Broadaway. Even after slavery was abolished, James and his son Marshall and family lived near John and Harriet Broadaway.

SECTION 4

BROADWAY SLAVE COMMUNITY

SLAVE MEMBERSHIP IN *1828* AT ROCKY RIVER BAPTIST CHURCH

If you are wondering if slaves attended church back in the early 1800's, they did in North Carolina at the Rocky River Baptist Church according to Rev. Edgar Brook's "History of Rocky River Baptist Church." This was one of the churches where slaves attended the same church as their masters but with separate services. (Brooks, 1828)

Slaves were basically a religious people. They firmly believed one day God would deliver them from bondage. They viewed themselves as a people of faith-the Lord's people. Many slaves' compared themselves to the Israelites who had been Jehovah's people in biblical times. They had kept the covenant and had been delivered from bondage. Thus, when emancipation occurred, many viewed this as the unfolding of God's plan.

Listed below are colored people who lived during slavery and worked on plantations that were owned by White church members of Rocky River Baptist Church. According to the way they were listed in Brook's book, the slave master's first or last name which was followed by the male slave name. The following were the colored male members of the church in 1828:

- Hany Clark
- Dortor Soloman
- Legrand's Thomas
- Lillie's Jack
- Dumas's Moses
- Lanier's Toney
- Capel's Jacob
- Steel's Joe
- N. Hearn's Bill
- Ingram's Davey
- Staton's Mack
- Rusel's Abraham
- Wyatt Nance's
- Watson's Daniel
- Benjamin (apparently free, perhaps a minister)

Back then, Colored people were given freedom if they were ministers, and Uriah Staton, who was a White deacon of the church, freed two slaves.

Please note in 1828, James Broadway, a slave, was only about eight years old. He could have been the son of one of the slave women of Frederick Staton or Uriah Staton, Frederick's son.

Notice the women were listed separately but have some of the same masters. The slave owners who had both male and female slaves were: Lillie, Lanier, Ingram, Staton, and Ingram. The Colored female members at Rock River Church were as follows:

- Candice
- Lillie's Judey
- Hogan's Sally
- Nance's Lucky
- Lanier's Nelly
- Hough's Pleasant
- Genny Freeman
- Mendingal's Ginna
- Boggan's Darkes
- Daragan's Cate
- Voluntine's Hannah
- Threadgil's Cassle
- Randol's Judith
- William Lee's Rose
- Moses's Vilet
- Ingram's Presilla
- Elibeth Davie's Aely
- Mask's Lucida
- Lucy Ingram's Molly
- Bro. Uriah Staton's Betty
- Frederick Staton's Sarah
- Uriah Staton's Mariah

The older Staton family possibility was the previous owners of our ancestors before John Broadaway and Harriett Staton. If so, our ancestors may have been Statons before Broadaways.

James Broadway was born a slave about 1820 in the same neighborhood as the Statons. Also, John Broadaway, who was born 1811 worked as an indentured servant for Frederick Staton. It is believed that is where John met Harriett.

REACQUIRE BROADWAY LAND THROUGH CHEROKEE INDIAN ANCESTRY
Why not reacquire Broadway ancestors' land by following the Silvia Clark's ancestry

of being a Cherokee Indian. Since the land may have been taken from Silvia Clark and Marshall Broadway in 1885, a case might be made. Statues and laws of the United States may be so one cannot obtain the land because it has been so long ago when the land was taken. Marshall and Sylvia were both United States citizens. But in addition, Silvia Clark Broadway was a Cherokee Indian. The United States government laws towards Cherokee Indians are different than just ordinary United States citizens.

THE CURSE OF THE "X"

We go through life taking a lot of things for granted. All my life I have taken for granted the reason headstones are unreadable. I originally thought it was because slave graves had gone through so much weather the names had been weathered away. I did not really put it together until I visited the Slave Graveyard in Burnsville, North Carolina where my great[2] grandfather was from. I was reminded it was against the law for a slave to read and write. I then came to the realization the headstones never were written on for most slaves. The headstones before 1865 were different shapes, sizes, and locations to know who they were.

Another moment of realization came to me was about the "X" signature. Most legal documentation entered into by the ex-slave was mostly signed with an "X" and witnessed by someone who could write which usually was someone "White". Although some ex-slaves could read and write, nevertheless, they were afraid to let this be known for fear of repercussions of how they or their families would be dealt with. One example of this is of great, great grandfather, Marshall Broadway, when he purchased land.

In my research, Marshall Broadway bought property in North Carolina in 1875 and signed with an "X". He allegedly sold his property in 1885 to W. C. Staton and signed with his signature. The deed was registered in the Register of Deeds office in 1888 supposedly signed by Marshall Broadway with his signature M. B. Broadway and an "X" by his wife, Sylvia Broadway. All other deeded documents entered into by Marshall Broadway after 1884 were signed with an "X".

This really makes me wonder. Was Marshall afraid to let the White man know he could read and write? Was it because W.C. Staton already knew Marshall could read and write and allowed him to sign his name? Or just for whatever reason, W.C. Staton signed the deed for him.

Let's face it according to Staton History, Marshall's slave master was known to be good to his slaves and tried to educate some of them. Additionally, W.C. Staton's name is William Cannie Staton. Marshall and Silvia named one of their sons William Cannie Broadway. I feel if Marshall thought he had been wronged with land deal in 1885, he would not have named his son after the man he sold the land to when he left North Carolina.

W.C. Staton was the slave master's nephew. At two days old, slave master John and Harriett Broadway raised W. C. Staton. Did he sign or did W. C. Staton sign Marshall's name? You be the judge. It is well known the southern states had a problem with "40 acres and a mule" and having any Blacks own land. President Johnson came up with the idea of land grants where the person would stay on the land for a while and then the land would be sold to them for a small amount of money. The problem for the Whites was the land could be owned by Blacks. However, what they had on their side was most Black men could not read or write. Consequently, he had to sign with an "X".

The Whites constantly conspired to retain and reacquire land. The conspiracy theory the "Curse of the X" could have been something like this. "Make out the collateral deed to reflect being sold to a White. Wait until the said owner is dead and acquire the land. Who at the time would contest a legal document?" Remember, we did not talk too much to one another or family about financial matters because we were afraid.

MULATTO BROTHERS

The 1880 Federal Census Book Number 13 and 14 were used to spot these brothers. Everyone during the times of the 1880 and 1900 Federal Census who were "high yellow" Black folks were listed as Mulattos. Ancestor James Broadway was list as one of the Mulatto brothers.

A Slave Deed (1790-1830) of John Broadway, who lived in the Burnsville's Staton community in Anson County, showed seven slaves were in his possession: three boys under age ten, two females under the age of ten, and two females under the age of twenty-six. These two young slave ladies were assumed to be the mother(s) of those kids who included the three Mulatto Broadway slave boys: Robert, James, and Harry.

All the males who were listed on the Slave Schedule were not old enough to father a child. No males who were old enough to father a child are listed on the slave schedule. If the kids were fathered by someone from another plantation, then the parents must have both been Mulattos or the father was White because these three boys were listed as Mulattos. Another scenario is someone else was permitted on the plantation or the master fathered these children. No father is listed.

Robert Broadway, brother of James and Harry, lied about his age. He passed for White. He claimed he was White on the 1870 Census. Robert was listed ten years later as a Black in 1880. He was married to Harriett, an older lady.

James Broadway, brother of Robert and Harry, was also listed as a Black in the 1880 Census. James is also listed as the father of Marshall Broadway, our great^2 grandfather.

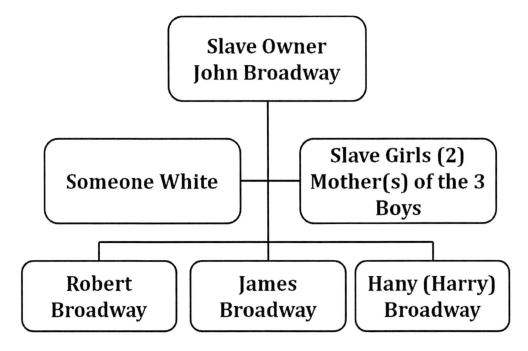

Additionally, Hany (Harry), brother of James and Robert, was listed as a Black in 1880. Hany (Harry) was listed on his son, Sidney Broadway's death certificate as Cannis B. Harry was married to Eliza. Thus, our light-skinned heritage began. See the following chart.

SLAVE GRAVEYARD

The slave graveyard is located near a go-cart track and a huge stone is at the entrance in Burnsville, North Carolina. Many of the graves are there did not have headstones, but some did. It was assumed the many stones of different sizes represented the headstones. Not forgetting slaves weren't allowed to read or write, therefore slaves placed distinctive stones with identifying marks on the stones at the grave.

Jerome Turner tipped-toed through a bed of leaves and vines as he followed Eugene Broadway. As steps were made, the ground became soft. He was sinking. Jerome called for the Vietnam Veteran, Eugene Broadway, who had experience with going through the thickets. Jerome then jumped to a log for fear of going six feet under. To his displeasure the tree crumbled. He caught his balance and continued checking out the graves with Eugene.

Also, according to the Anson County, North Carolina Genealogy Services, there are several former slaves buried at Bethlehem Cemetery in Ansonville, North Carolina. One of them is Elder Ralf Freeman who died about 1838. According to historical records, he was a forceful and useful Baptist preacher. His freedom was purchased by the Bear Creek Association. There is a historical marker honoring Elder Ralf which stands by Highway 52 South at the entrance to Bethlehem Cemetery.

THE EFFECT OF SHERMAN'S ORDERS ON THE BROADWAYS

According to Quintard Taylor of www.blackpast.org on January 16, 1865, Union General William T. Sherman issued Special Field Order No. 15 which generally stated lands were reserved and set apart for settlement of the Negroes now made free by the acts of war and the proclamation of the President of the United States which was President Lincoln. (Taylor)

The affairs of the Negroes would be subject only to the United States military authority and the acts of Congress. Negroes were also encouraged to join the military as a payback for the favor of passing this order. Vengefully, President Lincoln was assassinated; consequently President Johnson took the opportunity to revoke the orders.

Earlier, Sherman did not believe Blacks should be held equal. He did not want them to fight in the military with Whites. However, after many life experiences and having met in Savannah with Secretary of War Stanton and some Black leaders,

General Sherman was characterized as a friend and gentleman by some Black leaders in 1864-65 because his military campaigns freed many slaves. The Black leaders wanted something out of the deal, too. They knew Sherman needed their help to win the war. Later in his life, he came to disapprove of slavery. The Blacks needed forty acres and a mule to make a "sound start" for a farming family.

Historically, Arkansas Broadways were slaves of John and Harriett Broadaway and before that some of the same slaves were owned by Frederick Staton of North Carolina. Ironically, the North Carolina slave owner's Staton was John Broadaway's in-laws. Also the Broadway family's slave ancestor Frederick Staton was killed by Sherman's raiders. It was guessed slave James Broadway was gifted to John and Harriet Broadaway by Frederick Staton.

SECTION 5

FREED BROADWAYS

FREED BROADWAYS

LIVING FREE IN NORTH CAROLINA

Freed Broadways may have missed out on an opportunity to own 40 acres for six months in 1865, but ten years later, Marshall and Silvia purchased 133 ½ acres from Charles Beverly. Plus, Marshall and Silvia Broadway owned the land for ten years before the Broadways surprisingly and abruptly sold the land to W. C. Staton and his heirs. Then, shortly after they moved to Arkansas and purchased more land to make a "sound start" for their farming family.

BORN FREE IN NORTH CAROLINA 1865-1885

Some of Marshall and Silvia Broadway children were born free in North Carolina. Broadway children Oliver, John O., Annie E and Mary F. were born free. Of course, Marshall Broadway was born a slave. The research team's job was to locate Broadway ancestors immediately after slavery was abolished? The following articles offer a picture of where and who they were.

BURNSVILLE NEIGHBORHOOD IN 1870s AND 1880s

Neighborhood population in Burnsville, North Carolina during August 1870 included many Blacks and Whites as categorized by race on the 1870 U.S. Federal Census. There were many White families with the last name of "Staton" and a couple of Broadaways. Also, there were a few Black families with the last name of "Staton", "Broadaway", and "Clark." These are some of the family names according to census believed to be related to the Broadway family.

The Statons are thought to be the former slave owner for James Broadway. Uriah Staton (1807-1888) was a brother of Harriett Staton-Broadaway. Other White "head of household" Statons during 1870 were Roda (66), Alexander (42), Elizabeth (75), Mary (20), Mack (46), and Marshall (25). They were all farmers and the real estate values were calculated. However, there were many Black farmers who owned their farms and there were those who sharecropped. A couple of Clark families were farmers: Thos A., Mack (27), and F.A. (40) and one Broadaway, Henry (29) were farmers. All the Blacks were listed as laborers. Not one of the Blacks had a value listed for real estate, nor personal property. Was it because they were new owners or former slaves? The wives' occupations were all listed as housekeepers whether Black or White.

During the 1880 U.S. Federal Census, there were more Black land owners, along with Marshall Broadway. The Blacks who were farm laborers seemed to live near their former slave owners same as with James and Marshall Broadway in 1870. Occasionally, one would find the slave owner sold and gifted land to the former slaves. That was not the case with the Broadway ancestors. James did not own any land. Marshall purchased land from a White neighbor; then later sold the land back to the slave owner's adopted son, William Cannie (W.C.) Staton.

Puzzling, Jane Broadway (14, 1856) was a young girl who was documented as living in the household as a servant with James Broadway (55, 1815-1884), head of household, and Marshall Broadway (17, 1853) in 1870 in Burnsville, Anson, North Carolina. Marshall was listed as James' son and as a farm worker. Additionally, two other people were in the household: Margaret Broadway (30, 1840) was a Black female servant and Mack Broadway (10, 1860) was a Black male who did not have an identified occupation. Mack (42, 1858) was seen again in the 1900 U.S. Federal Census in San Hill, Moore, North Carolina.

Then in 1880, Jane Watson was listed as married with her two children who were Benjamin Watson (4, 1876) and Nellie Watson (2, 1878). She was listed as a Black female who was 25 years old. Jane was listed again as a servant and being a part of the household. Marshall now head of household was listed as a farm laborer in Lanesboro, Anson, North Carolina. Other members of the household were Marshall's wife Silvia, their four children and Marshall's sixty year old father, James Broadway who was a farm laborer and widower. Why was Jane labeled as the servant when she was the daughter of James and the sister of Marshall Broadway?

Close neighbors of James and Marshall were Alexander G. (29, 1851-1924?) and Isabella (28, 1852) Broadway. They were listed as farmer and housekeeper on the 1880 U.S. Federal Census report which most likely signified Alexander owned the land in Lanesboro, Anson, North Carolina.

Bellie Broadway (53, 1847-1929) was seen again in the 1900 U. S. Federal Census in Hampton, Lee, Arkansas. She was listed as widowed after twenty-five years of marriage. She also had five children living with her: Jim (18, 1881), Ellis (1882-1949), Ellace (14, 1886), Arlander Lane (13, 1886-1949), Susie (10, 1899-1902)

According to the Anson County, North Carolina Genealogy Services and Anson Times issue of May 19, 1881, Polkton, North Carolina, "A number of Colored citizens met in the Academy at 3pm to organize a prohibition society for Lanesboro Township & the following Colored men were elected as Vice Presidents; Wyatt Hamilton, Rev. Randal Bennett, Arthur Horne & Sidney Broadway. Also, a colored prohibition society was organized at Mt. Zion Baptist Church through the influence of Sidney Broadway." (Times, 1881) Sidney and the following Black Broadways were noted members of North Carolina and Arkansas:

NOTABLE TIMELINE OF MARSHALL BROADWAY (ALIAS M.B. OR ROBERT BROADWAY)

- 1854   Born in Burnsville, Anson, North Carolina into slavery
- 1865   Emancipated from slavery at age 11
- 1870   Burnsville, Anson, North Carolina; farm laborer; age 16
- 1874   Burnsville, Anson County, North Carolina; purchased land; age 20
- 1874   Burnsville, Anson, North Carolina; a son was born, Oliver
- 1876   Burnsville, Anson, North Carolina; a son was born, John O.
- 1879   Burnsville, Anson, North Carolina; a daughter was born, Annie Ella, died young
- 1880   Burnsville, Anson, North Carolina; a daughter was born, Mary F., died young
- 1880   Lanesboro, Anson, North Carolina; farm laborer; age 24
- 1885   Hampton, Lee, Arkansas, Farmer; age 29
- 1900   Hampton, Lee, Arkansas; farmer; age 48
- 1910   60 (1854-1921); Hampton, Lee, Arkansas; farmer; Silvia, wife 58 (1852); 6 kids: Marshall 18 (1892), Albert 14 (1896), Hermond 12 (1898), Annie 9 (1900), John (1880), Mary (1901)
- 1920   65 (1955); Hampton, Lee, Arkansas; farmer; in household Mary L 20 (1900), Senior 22 (1902), Lula 21 (1899), Othiler 1 (1919)
- 1926   died; Chicago, Cook, Illinois; laborer; age 72

NOTABLE TIMELINE OF ALEXANDER BROADWAY

Alexander Broadway

Alexander Broadway was born 1851 and he was sighted in the U.S. Census many times

- 1851   00 (1851-1924); born
- 1870   Lived with mother Creasy in Whites Store community
- 1880   29 (1851-1924); Lanesboro, Anson, North Carolina; farmer;
- 1894   39 (1855 – 1924); Lanesboro, Anson, NC; married Mary 25 (1875); Son, Elijah 1(1899); Boarders: Mary Polk 30 (1870); James Polk 11 (1889); Manly Polk 8 (1891)
- 1900   45 (1855 – 1924) Lanesboro, Anson, North Carolina; wife Mary 25 (1875)
- 1910   55 (1855) Lanesboro, Anson, NC; wife Mary L. 38 (1872) with 7 kids: William C. 10, Andrew R. 8, Aleandria 7, Walter 5, Mittie O. 4, Mary R. 2, and Francis A. 1.
- 1920   65 (1855) Lanesboro, Anson, NC; wife Mary 42 (1878); kids: Eliza C. 1900; Andrew b. 1902; Walter L. 1906; Mittie 1907; Mary O. 1909; Francis A. 1911; Booker W. 1914; and Fletcher 1916.
- 1924   73 (1851-1924); Lanesboro, Anson, North Carolina; farmer; age 73

NOTABLE TIMELINE OF BELLIE BROADWAY

- 1847   00 (1847-1929);
- 1880   28 (1852-1929); Lanesboro, Anson, North Carolina to Arkansas; housekeeper, wife of Marshall C. Broadway; had 2 children: Robert (5) and Charlotte (3)
- 1900   53 (1847-1929); (Hampton, Lee, Arkansas; farmer; owned home, but mortgaged; widow, head of household; had 11 children (5 alive): Jim 19 (1881), Ellis 18 (1882), Ellace 14 (1886), Hylander 13 (1886-1949), Susie, 10 (1889-1902)

FORTY ACRES AND A MULE
by Marie Broadway-Toms

Freed slaves who were farmers in the area of South Charleston to St. Johns River, Florida were allowed to settle on 40 acres and given a mule to plow land by Sherman's Order on January 16, 1865 according to Wikipedia's free encyclopedia. They did not want former slaves to benefit from this so they revoked the orders and made sure no slaves could benefit.

Incidentally, the orders were short lived; President Lincoln was assassinated and President Andrew Johnson revoked Sherman's orders. By June 1865, the former slaves were ordered to return the land to the original White owners who had abandoned the land. But revoking would help reestablish a labor force for Whites; thus sharecropping was born. Sharecropping was where Black families would rent small plots of land in return for a generous portion of the profits.

Land. Twenty years after slavery, Marshall Broadway and family took a wagon train which used mules/horses he had learned to care for. They traveled from North Carolina. Then they settled in Arkansas and immediately Marshall and Silvia Broadway purchased land thus making a "sound start" in farming.

Even during the 1940's and 50's, owning 40 acres and a mule was considered making a good start. According to Lee County's Deed records, Marshall is noted as owning eighty acres; black horse; three mules; white/black cow; one red yearling; and a two-horse wagon was reprocessed through Marianna, Arkansas courts in 1898 because of a note for "$281.28 which according to county records was for balance due on account up to the date with interest to Oct. 15, 1898 and $110 was for supplies to be advanced that year.

That did not stop the Broadways, they continued to buy land. Land was still a sound choice for a Black farming family. Ocie Broadway and his siblings were and are good examples of successful farmers who owned and farmed their own land.

Mules. Historically, the mule far outshines the horse in its usefulness.

1. The mule's greatest value remains its versatility. They can plow a field, carry a heavy pack or be ridden in comfort with very little care required. Many North American farmers with clay soil found mules superior as plow animals; By the way, a mule is a cross between a female horse and a male donkey. They were bred to be superior. Mules were originally brought from Europe by President George Washington and later bred in North America.

2. However, horses were cheaper but were not as versatile as mules. Horses were faster. But it is believed ancestor Marshall and his crew used mules for the long trip.

Owning a mule worked for a while until tractors were invented along with a plow which could be connected to the tractor. Cousin Frank Miller teased Sam Broadway who owned a tractor in the early 1950's that his single-plow with tractor could not disc land any faster than a person with a mule paired with a single-plow.

Lenner Broadway owned a pair of mules before owning a tractor. He was known to take care of his property and equipment. Parlee said Lenner was very attentive to his mules and he took very good care of his property and equipment.

SECTION 6

LIVING FREE IN ARKANSAS

FREE BROADWAYS IN ARKANSAS

The land below was purchased from Charles and Charlotte Beverly, a White couple and neighbors of Marshall Broadway. The Beverlys and Broadways were listed on the 1870 U.S. Federal Census in Anson County, North Carolina. Marshall and Silvia Broadway purchased the land in 1875. They proudly owned the land for ten years. Marshall and Silvia may have agreed to sell the land to W.C. Staton before leaving North Carolina because the deed was dated March 9, 1885. At any rate, the ownership was not finalized or transferred until 1888. The deed stated Marshall and Silvia were given $450 for 133 acres. It is unclear how this transaction transpired but perhaps an agreement was struck and the monies helped finance the Broadways move and trip to Arkansas.

Direct decendants of the Broadways, Marshall Broadway purchased the family's first acreage of land. See the deed listed below.

STATE OF NORTH CAROLINA, ANSON COUNTY
DEED, JANUARY 1, 1875
CHARLES & CHARLOTTE BEVERLY TO MARSHALL BROADWAY & HEIRS

133 1/2 ACRES

359.

A FREEDOM MOVE

1870 Neighbors in nearby, Ansonville, North Carolina were Hanah Clark's family and Robert Broadway's family. Working on the railroad was Robert Broadway at age fifty-seven and Sandy Clark at age twenty-one.

During 1873, Marshall got married to Silvia Clark and they had four children, two sons: Oliver (5) and John O. (4); also, two daughters: Ann E. and Mary F.

By 1880 U.S. Federal Census in Lanesboro, Anson, North Carolina, Marshall Broadway who was about twenty-seven years old became the head of household and his father was living with him. Marshall's father was a Mulatto, a farm laborer, and a widow.

Also living in the house was a married woman, Jane Watson and her two children: Benjamin Watson (4) and Nellie Watson (2). Jane was said to be a servant. During the 1920 U.S. Federal Census, Jane Watson, a Black widowed woman, was about sixty-five years old. Grandson of Jane was John N. Watson (1909) who owned his own farm. In addition, John N. was Benjamin Watson's son.

AN ACT OF FREEDOM

During slavery and after slavery was abolished, the former slaves were Broadaways. It was not until a large number of Black Broadways moved to Arkansas did they completely feel it was time to separate themselves from the slave family and completely acknowledge freedom and independence by changing their name to Broadways.

DEBT SERVITUDE ISSUES

Not only did sharecropping encourage indebtedness to the landowner, but purchasing the supplies to start a crop for the next year for the landowner became a debt servitude issue.

Even during the 1950's and 1960's, many of the land owners still owed annual mortgages on their land; they also owed for seeding and 'non-harvest season' groceries. When the harvest time came, land owners and non-landowners found themselves in debt. Most of the time, the balance had unknowingly increased and the Black borrower seemingly had no way out. Many of the Blacks could not read or write and if they could, they were still fearful of letting on they knew how to take care of their business for fear of gaining a reputation of being an "uppity Negro". This may have caused them to not qualify for a loan as well other troubles if perceived as one.

Supply and demand happened naturally; but the prices to buy and sell were set by the "White powers that be". Whether it was a good or bad crop, Negroes were bound to just break even or end up in more debt. If for some reason, the "White powers" didn't take everything, they would raise the grocery prices. Remember too, they did your taxes. Wow, what a trap! "Not only that", the quality of products sold to Negroes were inferior to what was sold to Whites.

Different strategies continued to indebt the Negro farmers to the point they could lose their land: denial of FHA loans, insurance companies not fairly settling claims, or FHA suggesting farmers stop farming because they were unsuccessful, etc. If the FHA deemed a farmer as unsuccessful, they would stop lending money to them to start a crop. The action pushed a lot of little farmers out and paved the way for only the big 1,000-plus acre farmers who were White. According to the 2000 U.S. Federal Census, the average acreage for a farmer in Lee County was 1,000.

Additionally, homeowner's insurance was paid but 'the powers that be' ran that too.

If a claim was submitted for a damaged roof, the insurance company would only pay to replace that portion that was damaged, thus promoting mismatched shingles. Most business dealings were arranged to favor the Whites and the insurance industry was no different.

BROADWAY LAND OWNERSHIP

Many folks believed Arkansas looked like a promised land with economic opportunities greater than the states they came from. They had heard of the towns that were viewed as progressive and commercial centers. They were built near railroads in Marianna and Brinkley. The Broadways were no different.

They pulled up stakes in North Carolina and traveled by wagon train in their move to Arkansas. They first purchased land in Hampton, Lee, Arkansas in 1885, thus becoming a Black farm owner. According to the History of Lee County, Arkansas by Lee County Sesquicentennial Committee and by 1905, the Broadways had become a part of the approximately 240,000 Black farm owners, comprising nearly 16.5 percent of all southern land owners.

The following are a few of the Broadways who owned land during the late 1800's and early 1900's. The summary includes some land purchases of members of Marshall and Silvia Broadways family:

James Broadway. Former slave, James Broadway, is not known to have owned land. Even though, land was recognized as a tremendous asset according to Frederick Staton and John and Harriet Broadaway who were former slave owners. James Broadway (Juin Broadway, 55, male, Black, worked on farm) is listed on the Schedule 1 – inhabitants in Burnsville Township in Anson County, North Carolina on August 5, 1870 at the Wadesboro, North Carolina Post Office.

In James Broadway's household is listed Marshall Broadway, Margaret Broadway, Jane Broadway, and Mack Broadway. Living in the same area and listed on the same schedule are former slave masters, John Broadaway (59, male, White, farmer, $6,800 value of real estate owned) and Harriet Broadaway (54, female, White, house keeper).

Additionally, William C. Staton (30, male, White, farmer, $300 value of real estate owned) is the person who Marshall and Silvia Broadway sold their land to is listed on the same schedule. When James was found in the 1880 Federal Census, he was a widow living with his son, Marshall Broadway in North Carolina. By 1880, James was not head of household and still did not own any land.

Marshall Broadway. Marshall Broadway was twenty-one years old when he first purchased land. He acquired 133 ½ acres of land from Charles W. Beverly on January 1, 1875. The land was located in North Carolina, Anson County, Big Brown Creek, adjoining the land of James Boggan and C. Staton which was SW ½ E T 115.1.5 for

$566. Silvia and Marshall were married in 1874; so I can imagine how excited they were when they signed on the dotted line with their signature or with an "x". I can also imagine how nervous they probably were since it was just 10 years after slavery was abolished. But something happened quickly because approximately ten years after, Marshall and Silvia sold 133 1/2 acres of land to W.C. (William Cannie) Staton and then headed for Arkansas.

Perhaps the land was poor and nonproductive, plus maybe fertilizer had not been developed. So imagine, Marshall and Silvia took their best horses, mules, plants, seeds, and plenty of supplies and equipment (including guns and fishing equipment) and bade their friends and family "good-bye" and started west. Whether they knew where they were going is not known. Or could it have been something like what Marie Broadway said,

"I believe they knew what they were doing. The laws in North Carolina prevented them from comfortably living there and they wanted a brand new start with distance between their slave state and them. I believe they had heard about the fertile land in Arkansas and purposely made that trip. If they thought W.C. Staton had forcefully taken the land, why would Marshall and Silvia name one of their sons after William Cannie Staton, the man who purchased their 133 acres of land in North Carolina."

Once in Arkansas in 1885, Marshall located eighty acres that they laid claims on W ½ SW ¼ Sec 27 T 2N R 1E. The land was purchased through the State of Arkansas Homestead Act and officially registered in Little Rock, Arkansas on April 4, 1887. Land was about $1.25 per acre, so the proceeds from the sale of land in North Carolina was enough to pay for the land, build a house, and buy and grow the necessities needed to survive.

Early 1900, the eighty acres and a black horse, mule (1 yr), mare (16 yr), bay mare (6 yr), white/black cow, 1 red yearling, and a two-horse wagon was officially signed over to Lessor & Company on April 9, 1900. The indebtedness of a $391 debt was fully secured by this conveyance. Between 1902 and 1921, the interest rate was 10% if issued credit. Marshall still had forty acres that had not been taken.

According to the Federal Censuses, by 1900 Marshall Broadway was forty-six years old and still farming. He owned his farm but still had a mortgage. Marshall was using the name James Broadway. He and Silvia had given birth to fourteen children with ten of those living in 1900 and six of those children were living at home: William Cannie, Julia Lessie, Senior, Julius, James Morris, and Mary E. (Mary L.).

Two daughters who were born in North Carolina and listed in the 1880 Census were: Ann E. (1) and Mary F. (3M). Mary F. stayed in North Carolina and Ann E. came to Arkansas. According to the Thirteenth Census of the United States: 1910 Population, Department of Commerce and Labor Bureau of the Census, Marshall (60) and Silvia (54) had the following children in their household in Hampton township,

Arkansas: Marshall Jr., Albert, Hermond, and Annie. The 1910 Federal Census showed Marshall and Silvia had twenty kids and five were still living. It also stated Marshall was a general farmer originally from Alabama who owned land. Yes, this is our Marshall in 1910 but according to our research much of the data in 1910 was not consistent with 1880, 1900, 1920 and 1930.

Oliver Broadway. According to the 1880 Census, Oliver and John were born one year apart to Silvia Jane and Marshall Broadway in Lanesboro, Anson, North Carolina. They were four and five years old in 1880. Their sisters Ann E. and Mary F. Broadway were one year and three months.

Living in the same house was their grandfather James Broadway and Aunt Jane Watson and her two kids Benjamin and Nellie. Oliver is seen in the 1900 Census with his wife of one year, Dora, in Hampton, Lee, Arkansas. Oliver was twenty-five and Dora was sixteen.

Oliver is listed as owning his home; however, the farm was mortgaged. By 1910, Oliver was thirty-six; he and Dora had four children: Samuel, Nathaniel, Green, and Marshal. On the WWI Draft Registration Card of 1917-1918, Oliver is listed as James Broadway at forty-three years of age, born June 11, 1875. He is listed as a farmer in Moro, Lee, Arkansas. The person who was to know his whereabouts and his nearest relative was his sister, Mary Broadway. James signed with an "X".

By 1920, he was listed as owning his home and being able to read and write. James Oliver had two additional kids: Cynthia and Joe (Pheobia) plus Samuel and his wife, Nazaree were staying with them. Dora died in 1921. Before Dora died, she and Oliver supposedly agreed to receive advances on their crops (loans) because a deed was drawn up that stated they owed $2,100 evidenced by the account books of the third party and they had to pay $525 per year by January 1922, 1923, 1924, and 1925 with 10% interest or the eighty acres of land (E ½ SE ¼ Sec 28 T2N R1E & SE Sec 28 T2NR1E) would be deeded to The E.J. Beazley Co. Then in 1925, Oliver lost that land.

By 1930, Oliver at age fifty-five had a new wife, Mary Ivory Abernathy Broadway (39) and they lived in Dixon, Monroe, Arkansas. Living with them at the time was Mary's sister-in-law, Amy Abernathy (18). Oliver was a general farmer and he owned a lot of land at one time. According to Dora Miller Word, Oliver lost the last of his land when someone came by and said the land was heir land and they took it.

Oliver was first married when he was twenty-two to Mary Ella Gilbert and Mary was first married when she was sixteen. Oliver died in Lee County August 1950 at the age of seventy-six, born 1874. Cousin L.C. Broadway's wife, Dorothy Dampeer Broadway, died the same year, July 11, 1950.

John Broadway. During the 1900 Census, John Broadway lived in Spring Creek, Lee, Arkansas at the age of twenty-three (Nov 1876) with his wife of three years Eady, one child John Jr., and cousins Ellis Broadway, age eighteen and Calvin Clark, age nine. According to the 1910 Census, John was thirty-three years old with five children and wife, Edie who lived in Hampton, Lee, Arkansas.

Additionally, John Broadway was forty-five and was listed as being born December 14, 1872 in North Carolina on the WWI Draft Registration Card of 1917-1918. He lived in Thomasville, Lee, Arkansas with his wife Edie Broadway.

He was a farmer who owned some land. John was still in Arkansas according to the 1920 Census and he owned his home, plus, he had ten kids with oldest being eighteen and the youngest two. John's age was listed as forty-three and born in 1877.

On a 1920 U.S. Federal Census, John's oldest son, John Broadway Jr. is eighteen and married to Odel with one child, Ethel B. living in Hampton, Lee, Arkansas. They were renting their home.

William Cannie Broadway. Also, during that Draft Registration, William Cannie lived in Marianna, Lee, Arkansas. He was born August 12, 1883 and was thirty-five in 1918. He farmed for George Lee in Marianna, Arkansas and was married to Lizzie (Elizabeth Stephen) Broadway.

No picture has been found of William Cannie, but according to his Draft Card in 1918, he was medium height, stout build, brown eyes and black hair. He was also listed as a Negro.

Cannie was a farmer and he could read and write. His signature is shown on the Draft Card. Later in life, Cannie owned his own land and most of his children owned land and became successful farmers and entrepreneurs.

Julia L. Broadway. Julia L Broadway was born October 1887 in Hampton, Lee, Arkansas to parents Robert and Silvia Broadway who were originally from North Carolina. Julia L. sometimes called Lessie was Marshall and Silvia's second child who was born in Arkansas. During the 1900 Census, Lessie was twelve and during the 1910 Census, Lessie Broadway (Lessie Beasley) was a spouse to Adolphus Beasley (Uolford Beasley) from Tennessee.

It is assumed Adolphus still had the 160 acres of land he purchased in 1890 (Sec No 12 2N 1W Lee Co) before he married Lessie. He also had purchased 120 acres of land (S ½ NE ¼ & NE ¼ Sec 5 T2N R 1E) and asked to reserve one acre for burial grounds when he was married to Bettie Watson in 1904.

Plus Adolphus bought and sold land on numerous occasions in Lee and Monroe counties. By the 1910 Census, Adolphus and Lessie were married with maybe one child and three step children in the household. Lessie was twenty-two at that time. Adolphus had moved from Monroe to Hampton, Lee, Arkansas.

During the 1920 Census, Adolphus and Lessie (Lizzie Beasley) were married with seven kids. Adolphus was born about 1856 and was sixty-four in 1920 then died March 25, 1927 in Lee County.

Lizzie (Lessie) was born about 1888 and was thirty-two in 1920. She married Sandy (Samuel) Wilson after Adolphus died. Sandy owned his home and was a farmer according to the 1920 Census. It is believed some of the Beasley's and Wilson's land is still owned by the families.

Morris James Broadway. Morris James Broadway was born October 1886 in Hampton, Lee, Arkansas to Robert (Marshall) Broadway and Silvia. In the 1900, Morris was three years old and living at home with five other brothers and sisters.

Sometimes before 1920 Morris and Josephine owned forty acres of land (SW ¼ NE Sec 21 T217 2N R). The Lee County, Arkansas land deed shows the land was sold on November 18, 1919 for $400. The money was to be paid to them at $100 per year and was paid in full by December 1924.

By 1920, Morris was married to Josephine with three kids: Maggrosy, Lizzie B. and Osbie Broadway. They were renting their home in Arkansas in 1920. According to the 1930 U.S. Federal Census, Morris and Josephine had moved to Chicago, Cook, Illinois. Morris (34) and Josephine (33) had seven kids living with them: Mary (15), Osebie (11), Alfred (9), Charles (5), Susie Lee (3), Dorothy (1), and Dona Lee (1).

Then, according to the U.S. WWII Draft Registration Cards in 1942, Morris lived at 1007 South Damen Ave. in Chicago, Illinois with Claudia Broadway who he said should always know his address. He worked at Chicago Steel Foundry Company. Morris stated he was born July 29, 1893. He was five feet six inches tall, weighed 198 pounds, dark complexion and had a distinguishing scar on his upper lip.

Morris and his family were known entrepreneurs in Illinois. Their family members owned a moving company, cleaners, beauty shop, and a non-profit organization.

Julius Broadway. Julius Broadway, another brother, was born August 6, 1894. He was twenty-two at the time of the Draft Registration of 1917-1918 and married to Annie B. Broadway with one child, L.A. Broadway. According to the 1920 Census, he had another child, Hattie Lee.

He was a farmer for his brother Oliver and rented a home. Later, Julius did own land. At his death, and according to Georgia Mae Welch, Julius owned land and willed land to his children.

Senior Broadway. During 1920 Census, Marshall was a sixty-five year-old head of household and found in Lee County off of Springfield Road with his son, Senior and wife and child. Senior was born October 30, 1896 in Arkansas. He worked for his brother, Oliver Broadway.

At that time, Marshall still owned the house where they were staying. Additionally, Mary L. Broadway was also living in Marshall's house. Marshall's wife, Silvia, had died in 1916. During the 1917-1918 World War I Draft Registration, Senior, did not own land. The Draft Registration Card also stated Senior was twenty-one years old, lived in Thomasville, Lee County, Arkansas and worked in the same area. Senior was married to Lula Williams on July 23, 1916.

90

Mary E. Broadway. Mary E Broadway was a one year old baby daughter of Marshall and Silvia during the 1900 U.S. Federal Census. She was born March 1899 in Hampton, Lee, Arkansas. Comparatively, Marry L Broadway was a twenty year old single daughter still living at home with Marshall during the 1920 Census.

Marshall was sixty-five and Silvia had died. Mary Broadway was also named as the nearest relative of James Oliver Broadway on the World War I Draft Registration Cards, 1917-1918. The card was dated September 12, 1918 where James Broadway signed with an "X".

The Arkansas County Marriage Index 1837-1957 states that Mary Broadway married a Harvey Collins on November 6, 1920 in Lee County. They lived in Thomasville, Lee, Arkansas. Records have not been found where she had kids or own land. One record stated Mary Broadway died on September 16, 1946 and it was rumored she had no kids.

LAND SUMMARY

Children of Marshall and Silvia who were known to have purchased land in Arkansas were Oliver (120+ acres), Morris (40+ acres), Lessie/Adolphus (120+ acres), John (60+ acres), William Cannie (120+ acres), and Julius (120+ acres). They were farmers and successful entrepreneurs during the 20th century. Those who began farming and found that was not their cup of tea were Morris, John, and Senior who headed north to better their situations.

FREEDOM – DID OUR BROADWAY ANCESTORS FIND IT?

In 1865, some freed slaves packed up and left the plantations with very little thrown across their shoulders. They headed for freedom. However, most stayed very close to the place where they were slaves because of familiar countryside. Things happened to keep freedmen from knowing what freedom was like. For example:

1. Opposition from their former masters to regain control of the South's Black population.
2. Not giving them their land as promised (forty acres and a mule) so they could take care of themselves. The White man preferred to hire us or starve us as they pleased.
3. About 40,000 former slaves got a hint of what freedom was like from January 1, 1865 before President Johnson ordered that lands be returned to pardon former Confederates.
4. Hard pressed to find Whites to sell land to Blacks, most former slaves had no choice except to return to work for their former masters.

Black codes were legislation passed to control the labor, migration, and other activities of newly freed slaves. Whites intended to secure a steady supply of cheap labor and continue to promote the inferiority of freed slaves.

With African-Americans migrating north searching for prosperity and freedom, I would say they did not find total freedom. Freedom only lasted as long as it took for White America to pass laws to limit African American success.

A FAMILY'S DEMAND TO THE UNITED STATES GOVERNMENT
Submitted by 1990 Hansberry Reunion Family, Jackson, Mississippi

The inhuman condition of slavery, discrimination, prejudice, inequality and injustice describe the historical relationship between the majority White society and African Slaves and their descendants in the United States.

The first Blacks were freemen. By the end of the 1700's, most Blacks were trapped by a White racist society that has never afforded them equal status guaranteed by the 13th & 14th amendment of the constitution.

At the end of the U.S. Civil War, Blacks began a long journey to achieve integrity, dignity and equality, a journey that today is not fully realized. Although Blacks were freed they were ill prepared to deal with their new found destiny as free citizens. The Slave became of "no value" to White society since he could no longer be worked for free. He was never recognized as a citizen by White society.

If White society had accepted ex-slaves as citizens then the White society could no longer justify the brutality it had heaped upon the slaves. White society continued to think of the ex-African slaves as sub-human, childlike and deserving of abuse. Therefore, White society continued to abuse, mistreat, cheat, rape, and lynch. Blacks were barred from voting under the threat of death and property lost.

During the Reconstruction (1865 to 1877), the federal government for a short time made a feeble attempt to prepare Blacks for the new status. But Blacks lacking and denied education, land and other resources (were programmed for failure), they were forced once again into second-class citizenship. In the aftermath of Reconstruction, despite guarantees of Civil Rights such as equal protection under the law and the right to vote, as provided in the 14th amendment of the constitution the South returned to "home rule".

The United States Government failed to protect the freed African citizen, therefore, is liable for serious damages. The United States Government failed to return kidnapped Africans to their motherland, Africa, with reasonable haste and liable damages to both the bereaved motherland of Africa and the kidnapped African.

The United States Government not only failed to return the African to Africa, it also failed to educate and guarantee land parcels to help ensure a good beginning and allowed Southern States to pass Jim Crow Laws to nullify the 13th & 14th amendments.

The United States Government failed to crush the KKK, one of the most devastating organizations to further terrorize the Blacks by brutally lynching, tar and feathering, raping and robbing Blacks of self esteem, hope and dignity. The KKK members saw to it that monetary and educational gains were nil. Sharecropper systems were hybrid systems of slavery. Blacks were not accepted as full citizens in the North, they were denied civil rights and segregated in public schools and public places from the turn of the century until the 1940s.

The United States Government failed to setup special skill schools and to make education "very" available, education being the speedy key to success, recovery and development. None of the expertise that supported slavery of the African went into the recovery of the African ex-slave...

Much time has passed. The United States Government must now face the liability of having failed to right a hideous wrong to a people who did not choose to come to America but were kidnapped and brought here against their will for profit. A people, who have suffered untold agony and horror, yet have worked to overcome, without basic skills and tools, the worst human terror the world has ever seen.

Listed are twenty-two counts of human depravation against the African American, for which the United States Government is liable:

1. Kidnapping and enslaving the African American.

2. Perpetuating lost of culture. (Culture being the back bone of self-esteem)

3. Separation from family. (Child from mother and husband from wife)

4. Failure to educate. (If a slave was caught with a book, he was blinded, killed or lost his hand or foot)

5. Failure to secure the right to vote.

6. Taxation without representation.

7. Failure to compensate.

8. Failure to provide safety.

9. Failure to create a nurturing environment for redemption.

10. Failure to provide "catch-up" programs for the freed slave; jobs education, recreation, housing, financing for small businesses and health care.

11. Failure to provide free first grade, second grade and advanced education.

12. Failure to stop the motion picture industry and other media from constantly portraying African Americans in negative demeaning roles that have prejudiced people around the world against Black people.

13. Failure to stop law enforcement nationwide from beating, arresting and killing innocent Black youth and men. The despondence of African American men in jail speaks to this abuse. So damaging to the African American community is this abuse that young Black women are hard pressed to find someone to marry. Police brutality nationwide represents the worst hazard to the Black family.

14. Failure to prevent rape of the pure African Slave women, especially the Mandingo (one of the finest human specimen on earth). Rape, introduced degenerate white blood cells carrying disease, mental illness and all the genetic frailties suffered by European descendants. The mixing of foul White blood has had long range debilitating effect; some Blacks experienced self-hate, "the passing for White" madness, some children of those unions felt bastardized, others as Creoles were deluded into believing they were somehow superior to pure Blacks when in fact the opposite was true. The French are not and never have been superior to the African and especially the Mandingo's Royal bloodline.

15. Failure to punish law enforcement officers, sheriff deputies and judges from jailing innocent African American people and giving them excessive jail terms and even executions and subjecting the innocent to the horror and festering inhuman conditions in overcrowded jail system and road gangs throughout the nation.

16. Failure to review the total prison system and the despondence of Black young men incarcerated by a racist White society.

17. Failure to cease and desist, discrimination, segregation and inhuman brutal treatment which has resulted in down-line "Getho Madness" of self-destruct and genocide.

18. Failure to protect the share cropper, farm land, real property, oil and timber land from being confiscated by local city, state and federal agencies and officials particularly the IRS "Gestapo" tactics.

19. Failure to remove J. Edger Hoover from the FBI, who directed terrorist acts against African Americans, including wiretaps, infiltration of Black organizations, assassination of leaders and civil right activist, covert activities, lifting of passports, creating illegal files of surveillance and intimidation and discrimination against Black FBI Agents.

20. Failure to guard our Black national treasure of music developers and artist, (many of whom had no education or access to legal counsel) from abuse and theft by agents, music corps and record industry. Most of the great Black musicians died without benefiting from their great work and were subjected to untold hardship on the road, "one night stands" and not being able to eat or sleep in the very hotels and clubs where they spent hours and hours playing wonderful music the world has come to treasure…Many times the musicians were cheated out of even their pay.

21. Failure to compensate and care for African Americans driven insane by the day to day horrors inflicted by a racist White society.

22. Failure to apologize. (African Americans suffer the hurt and insult of Bache so called reverse school and job discrimination litigation in the courts). How dare they?

The Liability of the United States Government for having failed to carry out the humanitarian responsibility to the African American Slave, hence the African American community causing said community to endure the second class status while other communities have flourished and prospered in this democratic society.

We the descendants of James Broadway 1820-1884, William Hansberry 1819-1894, James Smith 1835 and Perry Carlton 1840, (African American Slaves) demand damages and liability of $62 billion. We the descendants demand that these funds be distributed to all descendents of James Broadway 1-820-1884, William Hansberry 1-819-1894, James Smith 1-860-1931- and Perry Carlton 1840-

GENEALOGY
As Told by 1990 Hansberry Reunion Family, Jackson, Mississippi

Genealogy: An account or history of the descent of a person, family or group.
Since the beginning of history, lineages have been kept for various reasons. Sovereign ruling families kept careful family records for obvious reasons. Many nations of the East, particularly the Arabs and the Jews, kept careful family records at a very early date.

The Books of the Bible include many genealogies. Two books are Matthew and Luke describing the ancestry of Jesus. Matthew 1: 1-19 was written to prove to his fellow Jews that Jesus was the long promised Messiah and traced his ancestry back through King David, to Abraham, the founder of the race. Matthew also wanted to show that Jesus was the Son of Joseph and the he had a most respectable Jewish ancestry.

Luke, a Gentile of Greek background, traced the lineage back to "Adam, the son of God." His purpose was to present Jesus as a Universal Savior for all races of men, Luke 3:22-38, a total of forty-two generations. The experiences of Alex Haley, Roots, in search of his ancestry influenced many families to have family reunions in search of their roots.

Traditionally, family reunions have been emphasized primarily in the South, but now, in every section of the country, these festive gatherings are on the increase. This is a time for the elders to share their memories of important events in the life of the family and old stories are given new life that captures everyone's imagination. And the younger generation more deeply understands its responsibility to the future of the family.

Reunion: The job of being together in fellowship and love.

SECTION 7

MEMOIRS OF EUGENE BROADWAY

MEMORIES

Earliest Memory. My earliest memory when I was a young boy was being held by my brother while my mother and father were in the fields working. There were mice or should I say rats crawling through the wall paper in a little shotgun house we lived in. I can remember distinctively my brother taking me in his arms and holding me near the stove to console me.

The next memory I have was during Christmas time. I remember my brother and I got some toys, he received a tricycle and I got a red wagon. I remember my brother pulling me around in the wagon.

Another memory, when I was little and we were visiting someone, I needed to use the restroom and my mom sent me to the toilet by myself. I think I was

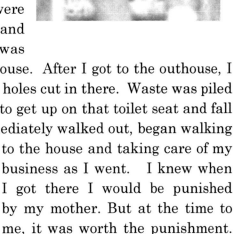

around three or four. The restroom was an outhouse. After I got to the outhouse, I opened the door; looked in; there were two big old holes cut in there. Waste was piled a mile high; it just frighten me to think if I were to get up on that toilet seat and fall in, I would drown in all that mess. So, I just immediately walked out, began walking to the house and taking care of my business as I went. I knew when I got there I would be punished by my mother. But at the time to me, it was worth the punishment. So that is when I learned to accept responsibility for my actions.

Living in Moro, Arkansas. I also can remember living in Moro at an early age. Keep in mind, this is before about four or five, I can remember my Dad would have us go to the pump and pump water. We would then carry the water to the house. I can remember one night he had us bring in stove wood from outside.

Of course, mosquitoes were outrageous in Moro, Arkansas. I believe they are still that way today. I can remember crying to my daddy, "The mosquitoes are biting me."

And my daddy being hard like he was saying, "I am going to bite your ass if you don't get out there and get the rest of that wood."

Moving to Little Rock, Arkansas. Then at about five, I can remember moving to Little Rock. We left this old shotgun house and moved to Little Rock. We moved to Granite Mountain. It was a nice housing project in Little Rock.

We had three bedrooms, a living room and a kitchen. Being young, I can remember getting lost in the apartment. I remember the white bathrooms. In that house, I used the bathtub for the first time because before then, we used those little round tubs to bathe in.

Also, I remember we did not have a chimney. It was very confusing to me on how Santa Claus was going to get to us. The room next to the bathroom had a wooden

compartment so in my mind, since everything else was brick; I assumed that was how Santa would get in.

First Grade. In first grade, one of my memories was my teacher Mrs. Hill. As a kid, we used to play and someone would always ask for candy. They would say, "Are you going to let me have some of your candy?"

We had the habit of spelling and saying, "No!" I remember learning my ABC's in the first grade and then we would learn to spell. The first word I learned how to spell was "No". The teacher went to the black board and wrote the word, "No" then asked what does that spell.

I was somewhat reluctant to answer. I remembered the little game we used to play. But going to the board and writing it and being asked what does that spell and realizing that "n-o" spelled "No." I was never reluctant to spell any word again whether I was wrong or right.

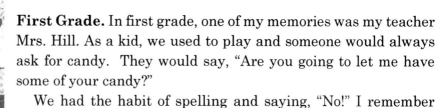

Second Grade. Second grade, my teacher was Mrs. Robbie Lile. Nothing really significant happened that year. I just had lots of fun being in her class.

Third Grade. Third grade was Mrs. Daisy Smith, one of the best teachers I ever had. Danny (my brother) was in the fourth grade. My mother was very sick. I remember Mrs. Smith took me to her house for a couple of weekends and Danny would go to his teacher's house, Mrs. Birtch because my mom was very sick. The younger children were living with different family members in Moro. Danny and I stayed with my father in Little Rock.

Fourth Grade. Fourth grade, Mrs. Crump was a teacher I will never forget. I thought she wasn't a real good teacher. She told a lie on another student and me. This was the first time I was brought to the principal's office. I was sitting in her office afraid to death.

The principal assured me she had a reputation of being able to give real good whippings. She told me if I lied, she was going to beat me to death. And of course, I told the truth, but in telling the truth, it implicated Mrs. Crump had done something wrong. I will never forget, a couple of days later Mrs. Crump visited our apartment in Granite Mountain. She told my mom I was outside and put my hands down some little girl's pants. It sounded so appalling and distasteful to me at the time. I cried and told my mother I did not do that. She listened, but beat my butt anyway, because the teacher was always right.

Fourth grade also, was the first time I encountered my best friend in life, Ronald Smith, known as Smitty.

Fifth Grade. Fifth grade, Mrs. Perry was considered to me somewhat of a lazy teacher. She had dentures and they would always clap together. She had a habit of sitting behind her desk and eating Mr. Goodbars all day long.

Sixth Grade. Sixth grade, Mr. Woods was probably the most exciting teacher I have ever known. Mr. Woods put us somewhat on the fast track. My brother, Danny, had dyslexia or I don't know what. Danny was in Special Education; Mr. Woods took Danny out of Special Education and put him in our class. Danny started making "B's" and "C's" in school. I always loved math. Mr. Woods would challenge us by giving us math problems. He introduced us to Algebra and word problems. He would challenge us and whoever could win would get a quarter.

A quarter was like a $100 dollars in those days. I was the one who pretty much always won the quarter. Also, I took on the responsibility of trying to help my mother by working at the community store, (Duncan Store) after school. I did different jobs around the store. Matter of fact, I worked there about two years.

Seventh Grade. Seventh grade, Junior High School, I had the same homeroom teacher seventh through ninth grade. I was a pretty good student. That year was my first run for a student body position as vice president of the student counsel, in which I lost.

Eighth Grade. In eighth grade, a student teacher encouraged me to run for student body president. I was a student from the ghetto and most of these positions always went to students whose parents were affluent in the community. For some reason, the masses got together and I was voted Student Council President.

How great that was! I can clearly remember having to receive my winning. I needed black pants and a white shirt. Since we were poor at the time, I remember my mother going to Kent dollar store and they had two types, one two little and the other too large. I wore them to school. I was so embarrassed; I stood behind the podium to hide the pants and accept my position.

Afterwards my best friend, Smitty and I played hooky for the first time. Of course, we got caught. My mama beat me and the teacher at school beat me, too.

That summer, my mother would send us to Moro for the summer because she did not want us to get into any trouble. In the projects, people would get into trouble and go to jail or worse. She did not want us around the projects with nothing to do.

We would go to live with my Uncle John. Uncle John always got us by to see our other relatives on my Dad's side. Grandpa Sam, Mama Minnie, Uncle Lenner and I also got a chance to meet Marie and other cousins. I was always impressed with Uncle Lenner. I felt he was the hardest working man on earth.

Anytime I visited Moro, if it wasn't a Sunday, Uncle Lenner would always be working "Always working, Always working".

After the summer of the eighth grade, I was somewhat reluctant to go back to Little Rock. I was afraid of my position of president of student body. Somehow I did not feel worthy. Mom made me come back home.

Ninth Grade. After being in the ninth grade, my position as president of student counsel wasn't quite as bad as I thought it would be. I was able to interact with the principals and teachers. The lower class students (underprivileged class of students) were very, very proud of me.

First time an underprivileged student was able to win this position. I was instrumental in getting a school flag for the first time. Also I can remember being approached by my homeroom teacher, Mrs. Darzel, who was trying to get Black students to attend Central High School in 1967.

Mrs. Darzel asked me if I would attend Central the next year. She said they were looking for students who would set a good example for Black people and make a good impression. That is probably the main reason why I went to school at Central High School in 1967.

Tenth Grade. In my tenth grade year, I attended Central High School from 1967 to 1968. It was a major, major shock for me. This was the first time I experienced racism to the point of just being blatant racism. Me being me, it caused me to rebel. Also during this time, I had survived my mother and father going through a divorce.

My father lived in the west end of town; it was closer to Central. I tried to make things easier for my mother; I moved in with my father, so I could walk to school every day. But living with daddy, Daddy was kind of street. Daddy really was not a nurturing person like Mama. There was really no discipline.

I can remember Daddy telling me one time he did not mind me going. It bothered him when he woke up and I was gone and he didn't know where I was. So he told me, the only thing I want you to do is let me know when you are going. So it got to the point I could wake up at 2:30 a.m. and something mischievous was going on, all I would do is say, Daddy, I am gone. Dad would say, "Ok Gene."

Eleventh Grade. Eleventh grade was very traumatic for me. This was during the time Martin Luther King was killed. Also during this year, we had a big basketball riot between Horace Mann H.S. and Little Rock Central H.S.; Central being the predominantly white school and Horace Mann being the Black school.

I remember trying to get involved and a friend girl of mind was afraid. I was asked to look out for her to keep her from being beat up. Our photographer for the school and journalism department took all kinds of pictures of the riot. The next couple of days, we had all kinds of students being brought to the principal's office.

They were being expelled because they were caught on film fighting in this riot. That was a pretty rough year. Quite a few Blacks got kicked out of school for the rest of the year. Some totally expelled and some had to go to other areas, like Sweet Home and Wrightsville. And some moved away. I survived the aftermath because of Phyllis Strong, "Thank you, Phyllis."

Twelfth Grade. My twelfth grade year, even more involvement, but by this time I had turned pretty much into a militant. I had the attitude these White folks didn't care 'nothing' about me,

I didn't care 'nothing' about them, so as far as their homework was concerned, they could forget themselves. I am not going to take any books home, get their homework and take it back to them. I was sharp enough to be able to attend a class, listen to the lecture, and be able to make a "C" or "B" on the test.

Being young and not guided, one of the crucial mistakes I made was not to do homework. I was a member of all kinds of school clubs. We had this Black Vice Principal, one of the few Blacks who were brought onto the staff. I think his job was pretty much to try and control us Black students.

I was caught a couple of days being late for school. My Vice Principal, the Black guy, approached me and told me if I was late another day for the detention hall, which started at 8:00am, he was going to expel me from school. He was very convincing, so I believed him.

And me being my own man, the next day trying very hard to get to school on time for the 8 o'clock detention hall, I can remember distinctively it was February, 1970. I ran to the detention hall getting ready to go in. Low and behold, "who did I see?" Mr. Powell, the vice principal. So I knew it was over for me.

I knew I was going to get expelled, so I decided at that point I was going to go join the military. I immediately started walking down the hall and while walking, the vice principal came out of the door and hollowed "Broadway, come here."

I had made up my mind and I knew what I was going to do. I was so angry at him for being an Uncle Tom brother. I felt like I was pretty much his size; if push came to a shove, I could beat his butt. I turned around, walked straight up to him, looked him straight in the face and gave him one of the worst cursing I have ever given anybody in my life.

Boot Camp. Two weeks later, I was in boot camp. Ooh, boot camp was one of the biggest nightmares of my life. It was the first time I wished for my mother, knowing my mother couldn't do anything, but it was just the idea. For some reason if I had Mama there everything would be somewhat better. Boot camp at the time was a big ordeal, but I made it. It was twelve weeks; I made it graduating PFC in my class. That was somewhat of an honor. We had five people graduate with this honor. Having this honor, I was selected to be a "Sea Duty Marine."

A "Sea Duty Marine" is one of those marines who go around on these big ships for the Navy. They are also guards at embassies all over the world. This was a top notch position. Second of all, we had to go to infantry training. After all that training, we were supposed to have been going home on leave. I was pretty home sick as it was, but we found out the Sea Duty school was starting earlier than expected.

So I wasn't going to get a chance to go home on leave. Well, being me, I got in the formation with the rest of the troops. I went on the airport base to buy a ticket. I bought my ticket and went home. Basically, I went A-wall. I stayed thirty days and then went back to the Marine Corps base. After I came back, I was knocked out of the program to go to Sea-Duty school. I was then given orders to go to Vietnam.

Vietnam. I was somewhat fearful of going to Vietnam. It was thought this particular group of Marines may not have to go. They were saying Vietnam was slowing down. I got my orders which were for Camp Butler, Okinawa.

I called my parents and they were all excited because I did

not have to go to Vietnam. When I got to Okinawa, all those Marines were jammed in a big room at the U.S. Air Force base. Sergeant Major came out and said, "Some of you might be glad and some might be sad but all of you are going down south," meaning Vietnam.

Of course this was a shocker to me. One of the biggest fears I had was we were going to be flying to Vietnam on commercial planes and none of us had guns. What if they shot us down? After I got to Vietnam, one of the first things I remember is being assigned to my unit and going out looking at the place.

Man, I'm not going to be able to deal with this. No matter what, I learned within two weeks time, a person will learn to deal with it. Vietnam was pretty much the nightmare of my life.

Looking back on it was also a blessing. My experience in dealing with adversity, in dealing with rough crowds, Granite Mountain and fighting at school, somewhat prepared me for Vietnam. No, I won't say prepared me for Vietnam, it prepared me for survival in Vietnam. My Vietnam experience was a nightmare.

Camp Pendleton. After Vietnam, coming back to Camp Pendleton, I came home on leave. I had problems adjusting back into the world. After returning to the base, I started playing football for the Marine Corp and was injured. I had surgery in December 1971.

My Brother. Low and behold, January 10, 1972, I received a phone call and I was told to call home. When I called my brother Bobby's voice had changed; he had come into manhood. He shared with me this is something your daddy needs to talk with you about.

He gave the phone to my Dad who shared with me that about eight guys had come to our house and called my brother Danny to the door. They shot him in the head; shot up the house and he was killed.

To this day, no one knows who killed him. My brother was very, very close to me. We always ran together. I don't know if it was Vietnam or my brother's death but it created a situation in me that I didn't really run around with anyone anymore.

It was as if this killer of my brother could very well be amongst my group of friends. I did not want to give them that distinction of being around them and thinking I was totally in the dark about it.

About three and half weeks later, February 4, 1972, I was discharged from the U.S. Marine Corps. I came back to Little Rock in order to live with my mother to try to help her out. They say there is always good and bad in stuff. One of the things transpired in my brother's death, it brought my mother and father back closer together.

They eventually remarried and moved from Granite Mountain. Those were the years that led from one through twenty years old.

Adjusting to the Real World. After being discharged from the military and not having a debriefing, my brother being killed, coming back to the ghetto (keep in mind these were the 70's) we still had a lot of racism going on. It seemed in a sense, I had a hard time. But I was determined after quitting high school; I made a promise to myself that I wasn't going to let the White man have the last laugh.

Higher Education. I would eventually finish high school and college. While in the Marine Corp, I took correspondence courses from Army Navy Academy. I received a GED, also a diploma from Army Navy Academy of Carlsbad, CA in 1972. When I was released from the Marine Corp, I did have my high school diploma. I enrolled in Philander Smith College during the summer of 1972. From the time of 1972 to 1985, I went from Philander Smith College to Arkansas Baptist, Shorter College, University of Arkansas at Little Rock and eventually returned to Philander Smith College and graduating from there. Throughout those twelve to thirteen years, I acquired 250 plus hours and only needed 124 hours to get a college degree. After changing majors often, in May of 1985 I finally graduated from Philander Smith College with a Business Administration degree.

My Children. March 29, 1973 was one of the proudest days of my life, my first child was born, Shuanta. Shuanta had a profound effect on me. I had never really known love like I experienced love in having a child. Realizing today, the effects of Vietnam, the turbulences of being in a young marriage, Karen and I were divorced in 1975.

The next proudest moment of my life was August 26, 1976, Danny was born. Karen and I had married again when Danny was born. This time around, Karen and I tried to work at it real hard, but by October 28, 1981 we were divorced again.

Of course, I went through life and another proud moment, May 15, 1981, Jhane' was born in Dallas, Texas. After her birth, I went to Dallas, Texas and met my daughter, Jhane'. On February 4, 1982, I married Valerie Kennedy and June 21, 1983 another proud moment of my life, Michelle was born.

On July 3, 1984, another proud moment in my life, my twin girls, Crystal and Cocoa were born. During these times, dealing with four children, my step son and three daughters at home, it was very hard times in supporting a family.

I went through some trying times, made some mistakes in life, but one of the joys that came out of this was April 23, 1986, my daughter April was born and what a precious child. I got a chance to meet her when she was less than one year old and again at three years old. April was made aware that who she thought was her father, was not her father.

She communicated with her grandmother that she wanted to meet her biological father

which her Grandmother Bee communicated to me. Grandmother Bee got in touch with me and shared this dilemma she was having. At the age of seven is when April and I met again. It has been a beautiful relationship from then on.

New Found Sister. March 1984 was a big thing for me. I don't know exactly when Roots, the movie, came out but it had a profound effect on me. The little girl we always admired in a picture hanging on my parent's wall was our sister Carol Jean, born nine years before me in 1943. I started researching to try to find her.

This was the first time I started trying to research my family's history. This was

a great experience for me in finding my sister, Carol Jean. Carol was forty-two years old at the time. What a glorious reunion and after that Carol came to Little Rock to meet her father for the first time who she thought was dead.

Post Office Career. After retiring from the U.S. Post Office in 1988, I felt like I was grown. I had no one telling me what to do, with a chip on their shoulder, mad at their wives and taking it out on me. All the while, I was putting up with it because I had a family to support. For about a year, I pretty much did what I wanted. Then it became very boring and I had a desire to do something else in life.

Barbershop Career. I was always interested and amazed in the barbershop. I used to like just hanging out at the barbershop. I loved listening to older people talk. People come to the barbershop, (Doctors, Lawyers, etc.) and you learned all kind of information. When men come to the barbershop, they pretty much wore the same hat. This was a very, very rewarding career for me.

From forty to fifty years of age, I was pretty much doing my barber thing. I got so involved and I advanced rapidly. I got my master barber license. I went on to cosmetology school. I got my cosmetology license. I went back to barber school and became a barber instructor.

After that, I was awarded a teaching position. I was the second Black in the state of Arkansas to become a barber inspector for the barber board which was very rewarding.

My Dad and His Dad. The year 1992 was a very significant time in my life. My father was pretty ill; he had heart problems and my Grandfather, Sam Broadway, died. My sisters Naz and Geraldine, my nephew Yancy and I made the trip to Chicago to attend our grandfather's funeral.

My job was to record the funeral so my father could see his father's funeral, which we accomplished. I met cousins like Jerome Turner and others. This was the first time I remembered meeting Jerome. When Jerome and I hooked up in 2009, I had an opportunity to view the funeral again and a lot of significant things came out of that weekend at the funeral.

The sermon that was preached talked about Daddy Sam being such a humble man, a great family man and he wanted his grandchildren to keep his legacy going and keep in touch with each other. It's been almost ten years since Daddy Sam passed away and that sermon has more meaning today for me than ever.

On September 3, 1999, my father died. The significance of September 3, my sister Gerri brought to my attention and played us a song by the Temptations, "Poppa was a Rolling Stone." In this song, it speaks of my father. "On the 3rd of September, that was the day, my daddy died."

Traveling Around the World. Between the years of 1995 and 2000, I was living a life of going back and forth to Little Rock. I was trying to support my kids in school and their endeavors. Teare, my wife, was a flight attendant. This afforded me the

opportunity to travel free. During this time, I had an opportunity to travel pretty much all over the world. Life comes in again and Teare and I were divorced.

My Love, Shianne. The year 2003 was when I met my current wife, Shianne C. Richardson. Shianne and I attended the same church. One never knows how life will play itself out. I distinctively remember being in church, always looking forward to this little pleasant lady walking around the corner. Some days she wouldn't make it and it was a little disappointing for me. But always, always, I looked forward to this little lady coming around the corner. One day she visited a business next door to where I was working. Of course, I approached her and kidded her a little bit and asked for a Turner Chapel hug, that was a practice of our church. At church, the visitors would be introduced and they would ask the members to give the visitors a Turner Chapel hug and after that, people would hug each other.

I distinctively remember one day in particular Shianne and her daughter were sitting near me and we were asked to give the Turner Chapel hug and I hugged her and it was just something about the hug. Well, today, it's history. December 2007, Shianne and I were married. So far, we have lived a happy life.

One of the things I learned about life in my current situation, people with similar cultures are more apt to co-exist for longer periods of time and it makes transitions in life much easier.

Broadway Mission

In 2009, I hooked up with my two first cousins, Marie Broadway-Toms and Jerome "JT" Turner, known as "Superman". Jerome expressed they were putting together a Broadway Family Reunion and my sister, Naz, being like she is, volunteered me to help with them. Jerome was somewhat reluctant to call me because at one particular time in our lives, Jerome had tried to contact me about a family reunion and he got no response. With me living my life, I wasn't living in the location he sent the letter to and he got no response, so he was somewhat reluctant to call and ask me.

But when he called, he got an immediate "Yes, I'll help out." Things went from there. And I must say hooking up w

for me.

I was somewhat ashamed being a grown man; I had always felt I did not know what my true purpose was in life. But after I hooked up with these two cousins, it made me realize what my true destiny is. My true destiny is to find my family and let them know who they are.

SECTION 8

LIFE JOURNEY STORIES - OTHER BROADWAYS

MEMORIES

Many of the Broadway family members wanted to tell stories about their life journeys; I have included those stories.

1. LIFE WITH MY SIX SIBLINGS
by Naz Pride

I can honestly say it was funny, educational, patience, lots of imagination and extreme love that got us through those years. Our story started in Moro Arkansas where the first five were born, the fifth being Nathaniel, the baby boy better known as Skip. Then we journeyed to the big city of Little Rock. I can imagine it was like, when the Clampits move to Beverly Hills. But NO, we did not discover oil.

I was the only girl for about seven years so you can say at that time I had lots of attention from Daddy and my Mom was grooming me for womanhood. But I happen to have had some pretty competitive brothers, Danny, Mr. Disciplinarian. He saw to it every order was carried out from Mom. He was like the second daddy but Eugene saw to it he was not a part of it.

They put me through many test to see just how tough I really was. I was dared so much to do things and yet I met every challenge. I climbed trees in dresses; I even out ran all of them. I fought and wrestled as well but that is one I can't brag on. They shut me down on that one; my brothers wanted me to be able to defend myself; they were very protective of me.

Before my seventh birthday, my life changed! My first sister was born as Lil Miss Linda Dianne. A beautiful ball headed little princess came into my life. After a few years, her head was filled with locks and locks of big jet black curls. She loved to eat!! I remember her trips to the fridge at night. She tried to sneak; but for some odd reason she always had to hum some type of song. And yes we would all sing out in unison, "Mom Ma Linda in the refrigerator." Then it was on.

That was one of our fun times, watching each of us getting a beat down by Mom. Then we would impersonate them the next day or right after, if the coast was clear. "I whipped you because I love you." How many times have I heard that one! There were so many days I just wanted her to dislike me for a while.

I got my fair share, trust me, especially when that last little demon came along. Lil Geraldine was named after my Dad's oldest sister. She could do no wrong; she got away with murder. She reported everything she saw or heard and it was ok for her to repeat it verbatim. She was small, quiet and sneaky. She would be somewhere watching, but you never saw her until it was too late and all I could say was, "old my God"! I knew I had to prepare myself for my walk with the belt.

One day I went to my brother Eugene because he seemed to have been able to master things of this caliber. I asked him how I can take a better whipping. DUH!!!! He said; Naz when she start whipping you, just don't cry and it won't last long at all, but my mother was tough. The saying, so---- you are not going to cry, huh? And it got worse; that's when I invented my famous beat down dance. I think that's really what helped me. I was jumping and moving around so fast she couldn't keep up with me not to mention me causing the belt to hit her several times. That belt was long so I stayed close as possible to her. She gave up fast. So I had the answer to my crazy question all alone. But, when someone was about to get a beat down all siblings were summoned. They were like the WWE (WORLD WRESTING ENTAINTMENT). Mom was the superstar and the official so you can see it was a fixed event.

I think my Mom started the buddy system back before Uncle Sam. All of us were assigned a buddy, mine was Bobby. We were the official dish washers. We had three meals a day, breakfast, lunch and dinner. Don't mention holidays and big family gatherings, we would be in the kitchen for hours. I had to come up with a workable system that would make this job bearable.

I put job assignments in a bag and Bobby and I would pull and work the kitchen like we were in a factory; it made sense at the time. Then I started with the calendar, I posted our job duties by the month, therefore we knew where we stood. Because the job was there, nothing could keep us from it. Sickness, injuries, mad, homework, NOTHING. I made a pact with my brother; we could hide the pots and pans in the oven and go to bed. And Mom would take care of it for us.

I remember her coming to check on us when we were supposed to be asleep. She would smile at us and say; I'll do it they're sleeping so peaceful. But I blew it for us; I was overheard plotting. And the very next time we pulled that one, she entered the room snatched the cover off of me; need I say more!!! That was one of the worse culture shocks you could ever experience. Bad idea! But in spite of it all we truly had a loveable childhood. We loved each other so much, to the point when we fought; we made sure each was not seriously hurt. We walked to and from school together in the neighborhood.

We invented games and puppet shows by cutting out people from the newspaper and magazines, each character had a name. We made slides, skateboards, and bow and arrows. We played jacks, marbles, hide and go seek, four square, dodge ball, soft ball, and school. We even made up a little business selling popcorn balls, candied apples and donuts; we were very resourceful, and it was all done around our little small yard.

Our foundation was the love of family and the love of God. We were brought up in Church. We went to Sunday school, morning service, BTU, revivals, and you name it, we were there. We were there when the doors opened. My Mom always made sure of that.

Proverb 22:6; Train a child in the way he should go and when he is old, he will not turn from it.

2. LETTER OF LOVE TO MY BROTHER EUGENE
By Carol Jean Broadway Martin

One day when I turned forty years old, I got the biggest surprise of my entire life. I had gone over to my mothers, on a break from my part time job at Montgomery Wards something I had rarely done. But she lived really close.

So we were having lunch and the phone rang. My mom answered. And after a few minutes she got a really different look on her face. She then said you know I do not have time for jokes; I could tell she was getting mad. So she continued talking to the person on the other end of the phone. She was telling whoever about herself growing up. I was very concerned as to whom she was talking to, as she was telling them things about herself I didn't even know. Then she started talking about me.

She then said Carol Jean is right here; she seldom comes over like this from work. She gave me the phone and said here, someone wants to speak to you. So I took the phone and said hello. The gentleman on the other end of the phone said to me, "Hi I am your brother Eugene. I have been trying to find you for a long time. I told him I do not have a brother Eugene, just Calvin.

Then he told me, "Yes you have a brother Eugene, and other brothers and sisters." He said, "I am Daniel Broadway's son." And I said that is my dad's name but he is dead. He then said, "No he is not dead; he lives in Little Rock Arkansas." He told me how there was a picture that always hung on my Dad's wall of a little baby girl." He said, "When we asked our dad who she was, my dad said that is Carol Jean, she is your sister." My brother said he and my other sisters and brothers had always asked about me. But my dad told them he did not know where I was, as we had moved from Kansas, where he last saw me.

My brother said he was very curious about me. So he decided he was going to find his sister. Like Roots he started to trace me. He started in Herington, Kansas where my dad last knew where I was. He said he finally got in touch with a lady there that knew my mom. She told him my mom had moved to Colorado due to illnesses.

My brother said he went through the phone book in Colorado and sure enough my mom and step-dad were listed. He knew all kinds of things about my Mom and Dad's Broadway younger years. Those were the things he was talking to my mom about.

What was such a miracle was my grandmother Leona Pitts and my Uncle Leon V. Smith, always said they did not feel my dad was dead. My grandmother said one day before you die you will see your real father. Though, she did not live to see it or my uncle; I so wish they had. It was the happiest day of my life to hear he was alive.

The last time he saw me I was three days old. He and my mom were getting married; then he was going into the military. He went partying before he reported in and got a little intoxicated. He missed the ship off. All the guys in the unit were killed my brother said.

So, therefore, that is why we were told he was missing in action. So, I never heard anything else about my dad until my brother Eugene got in touch with me. What a miraculous day for me. God is so good. I truly was blessed my brother took such time, patience and love to find me.

The greatest gift of all in my life continues. How my brother found me continues: now after the blessing I had received of finding out my dad Broadway was still alive through my brother Eugene Broadway. I received even a better gift. My brother and I of course kept in touch with one another. One day I received a letter from my brother Eugene that he was going to come to meet me and my family here in Denver. I was so excited.

He came and I picked him up from the airport. It's like I knew him immediately, as he favored my picture I had of my dad for over forty years. He spent real quality time with me and my family here in Colorado. It just seemed like I had known him forever. My family adored him, especially my mom.

We took him all over Denver and he saw all kinds of new places he had never seen, as it was his first time to Colorado. I took him to meet all my family and friends. It seemed as though every day was a big party while he was here. I did not want to let him go home. But I knew he had a family in Little Rock.

After he was here, even though I was desperately afraid of planes I decided I needed to see my Dad and the rest of my family in Arkansas. I did not have a lot of money. But a good friend of mine wanted me to go; so he bought me a round trip airline ticket. I called my brother and told him I was coming. I too spent quality time with my new family there. My Dad and my brother Eugene met me at the airport. I knew my Dad the moment I saw him; it was like looking in a mirror. They treated me like I was a princess. I had never been to Arkansas. My step mom cooked and cooked and cooked. I bet we ate five meals a day. She was a fantastic cook.

Me and my Dad had special times making up for lost time. He took me to meet my aunts and I even got to go out to Moro and meet my Grandfather Sam, whom I had never met. He was so much fun; he was so funny.

The first day I was there I met so many family members. They were all so sweet. We ate and chatted about everything. So many of my family members there looked just like my family here. My Dad's sisters looked just like my mom. I felt I had a family made in heaven.

My sisters and brothers took me to show me all around Little Rock. We went somewhere different every day. I could have stayed for ever; I felt so at home and loved there. The time went by entirely too fast.

I only got to see my Dad a total of three times. The day he passed away was a devastating day in my life. I felt I had just found him and got to love him, then God took him away. But just the blessing of knowing I did have him, still meant the world to me. Now, my family and I, my step mother, brothers and sisters, aunts, uncles, cousins, and friends, are always in touch. We now have a Broadway Heritage Website with over 4,000 family members and we all are in touch with one another always. Thank you' Lord, for my beautiful extended family. I am so blessed.

3. GIVE ME A NICKEL
By Linda D. Broadway

As a young girl between the age of four or five, I had one sister and four brothers who were true born hustlers. Our apartment was the neighborhood grocery store, #9 Richmond Lane. My sister and brothers sold pickles, popcorn balls, candy apples and loose candy. Cause back then, Gene worked at Duncan Store. They knew how to make money even though we were poor. So they would make their money from us or our neighbors.

We had this old kitchen sink that I could fit under perfectly standing up. When we had company, I would get my hustle on because I loved to eat. As they would come to clean their plates I would come out from under the sink and say "Give Me a Nickel"....... Because, when I wanted something sweet, I'd ask for the nickels so I could buy something sweet to eat.

4. LOSS OF CIVILITY
By Eugene Broadway

When I was growing up in Little Rock, Arkansas and within a Black family, we were always taught how to do and say things with politeness, good manners, courteousness, respect, graciousness, and consideration. We were taught to extend those courtesies to everyone; it did not matter who they were.

I don't hear children and young adults saying things like "Yes Sir" and "No Madam" any more. I don't see parents and older adults schooling young folks on what to say or do like telling them to practice "After you," "Be kind to everyone you encounter," "Don't cause a commotion in public," "thy shalt love thy neighbor as thyself," "don't get too big for your britches," "always ask, never tell" and address as "Ladies and Gentlemen". For children, one has to practice what to say or do. I believe families have lost their civility.

Children have to be repetitively taught civility and with consistency. When taught and practiced, you will later see children repeating what you say and do. Some of the things that children were taught when I was growing up were: politeness – "Excuse me" and "Please"; good manners - ; courteousness – "Thank you" and "wave to greet"; respect – "add Mr. or Mrs. to their first name" and "May I?"; graciousness - ; and consideration – "No, you first" and "Is it OK if I".

Additionally, how we dress and what is appropriate to wear depicts civility. It did not matter how expensive or inexpensive, we were taught to wear with pride. Boys were taught how to tie a tie. Girls were taught what was tasteful or not.

We were also taught how to act in certain situations: dinner table, accepting gifts, asking for money, accepting charity, begging, hiccups, belching, telling a person he/ she is a lie, writing thank you notes before playing with or using it, doing a job for no pay, chewing gum, couple walking on the street, opening doors, standing when someone enters room, dinner etiquette, not to curse in the presentence of an adult, yawn, cough, or sneeze without covering your mouth, entering a room where people are gathered, when someone hands you something, phone manners: identify yourself, "Mom is unavailable right now." If unavailable, "Yes, she is right here, would you hold a moment please?"

Eye contact: teach children to look the adult in the eye and speak clearly, shaking hands and say "nice to meet you", Never Interrupt when someone is speaking, never wear a hat indoors, best to say "Hello Judy," or "Hello Mr. Smith," excuse yourself from the table or room when blowing your nose, never speak with your mouth full of food, keep your elbows off the table and your hands in your lap when not in use, turn off cell phones before entering a restaurant, and wait until your entire party is seated and served before eating.

I feel one way to bridge the gap or neglect, especially for men is to teach these traits to young people beginning at infancy. I think this can link people. Wherever they come from and wherever they go, they would know the proper thing to do and say. Civility will be reconciled.

5. ABOUT MY TWO FATHERS
By De'Shondra Me'chelle Broadway Smith

The Best Day of my Father's (Daniel Broadway Jr.) Life...
My name is De'Shondra Me'chelle Broadway and I was born November 1, 1971 to Daniel Lee Broadway Jr. and Lynda Robinson. You see I was only two months and ten days old when someone murdered my Father. So, therefore, my memory of him is of faded pictures and glimpses of him in my dreams. Through my dreams my Father lives!!!!

Let me see if I can explain better to all who don't know the day my Father was taken from our lives. I was with my Auntie Naz and Mother Lynda at a baby shower when I started cutting up as sometimes babies do. I was told they tried changing me, feeding me and even coddling me (nothing worked). I believe this was my way of letting them know something was VERY WRONG!!! Soon they (my Mother and Aunt) received a phone call that turned their life into a living hell.

My Mother's fiancé and Aunts' brother was shot and killed by a group of men. This is when they figured out exactly why I could not be consoled; my Father was being murdered at that very moment!!! Everyone in my life said my father loved me like no other father ever could; I was his everything and I could do no wrong in his eyes.

As the story goes I had the best of everything, dresses, toys and more. He believed all I would accomplish would be tremendous too. My Daddy said often "You are the most beautiful little girl on this earth and you are going to be Miss America."

In reality that didn't happen but I am a very fortunate child because you see, I have two wonderful fathers in my life (the one that has passed on and another still here to this day) helping and taking care of me as if I was his flesh and blood. His name is Darrell L. McDaniel, the man my Mother eventually married.

MY EARTHLY FATHER IS DARRELL MCDANIEL.

My mother always says "You feel like he does no wrong." I guess to some degree I do. My father has been exceptional to me. I thank God for allowing him to be here on earth in my life. But I am also grateful for my biological father in my dreams. I dream of my biological father throughout the year and definitely always on his birthday.

I believe my Father is and always has watched over me all of my life. Unlike most, the Lord has blessed me with a father much like the one I was born to. My Dad also thinks I can do no wrong.

I am both Daddys' sunshine and they have and always will be mine. I also want to let everyone know that despite all that happens in the world, God is a good and an awesome God. What the world took, God gave me an awesome man to continue to love and raise me. He has been and will always be my Daddy in life.

To Mr. Darrell L. McDaniel, although my biological father is no longer here on this earth; I've been spoiled just the same. I've had an abundance of influential people in my life who have helped to shaped me. Most importantly, thanks to my Granny Lee Ester Broadway for taking on responsibilities that my Father would have done and more.

Also, thanks to a host of Aunties and Uncles. Thank you all for helping me to be the person I am today. I Love You Always and Forever Will, my two Daddys.

6. AN EXTRAORDINARY WOMAN
By Olaf Lacy Tweedie

Tears wail up in my eyes, whenever I think of my Mama Rose Broadway Harrison. Yes, I miss her that much. She was kind, softhearted, charitable, courageous, joyful, and peaceful. Those are just a few choice words that describe her. If it wasn't for this awesome woman, I would be lost as a bachelor. She taught me how to cook, clean, and sew; she just taught me how to survive.

Whenever I needed her, she was there with open arms. When I was born, she was there. When my brother was born, she was there. And when the house almost burned down, she saved us by putting the fire out by herself. When my aunt and uncles got sick, she was there. Her whole life, she was always giving, never taking. In fact, our house was a daily meeting place for the farmers, my uncles, and my grand daddy. And if there wasn't enough food, she would make more, never complaining. Nobody was left hungry.

I used to love to just sit on the porch with Mama Rose and help her shell peas. She would talk to me; she would tell me I was a child and to enjoy my childhood. I not only owe her for her guidance but also her knowledge. She touched so many people in so many different ways. People would come from all over and visit Mama Rose. They all shared stories of how Mama Rose touched their lives.

I remember that I loved ducks; Mama Rose helped me dig a pond and make a pen for the ducks. We went and bought two mallard ducks and two Peking ducks. The next day two were dead; so we went and bought two more. The next day two were dead, again. And off we went to buy more ducks.

This went on for a week, before we figured out our dog was killing them. She never spoiled me but she would give her last and never complain. Yes, Mama Rose was a gem as flawless as a diamond. She had all the ingredients of an extraordinary woman. I love you Mama Rose and think about you every day. I know you are still an angel in heaven and thank you for watching over me.

7. ME AND MY MOTHER
By Olaf Lacy Tweedie

My Mother is my heartbeat.
I love her more than I love myself.
I care about what she thinks and has to say.

I would easily give my life to save hers.
Yet every day I strive to stay alive because losing me would kill her.

I'm my Mother's first born and we are closer than skin is to flesh. Without exchanging words, I know many of her thoughts. Sometimes I have to leave her presence to avoid being swallowed by them.

I wanted to be the best son possible,
Not only because I'm the oldest, but because she deserves it and I respect her beyond anyone else.

My Mom doesn't change her mind every few seconds, minutes, or months. She is steady. Her love and loyalty are forever. Her friendship is something you can count on.

She is also down to earth, a hard worker, but always pleasant. She is smart, and so unselfish. Even when she criticizes, she is accurate, but soft and always sweet.

The best thing is her certainty and belief in my Lord and Savior. You can see it in her every action everyday without her preaching a word of it.

I love you Mama, you deserve happiness, and a companion that treasures the ground you walk on.

8. FAITHFUL IS OUR GOD
By Deborah Hall Milliken in Memory of Her Mom, Mattie Medlock

God is so faithful; He's always been faithful to me. From childhood to my present life, I have always trusted and had faith in God. Even in my stormy times of life, I've always called on "Jesus" to be with me. God promised in his Word that he would never leave us or forsake us. And the LORD said, "Unto Moses, I will do this thing also that thou hast spoken: for thou hast found grace in my sight and I know thee by name." (Exodus 34:17)

This parable is about me as a senior high school student:

When I was in the tenth grade, I decided I wanted to be a Registered Nurse (RN). Not realizing how tough nursing school was I ventured into the nursing field. During my senior high school year, I attended Metropolitan High School. I would attend school the first half of the day; then I would leave school about 1:00 pm to go to my part time job which was at Saint Vincent Hospital. I took training courses for a period of one year. After I graduated from high school I ventured out to other job opportunities for better pay and experience.

At the age of twenty years old I started working at Arkansas Children's Hospital pursuing my career in nursing. My mother, Ms. Mattie Medlock worked at Arkansas Children's Hospital's Burn Unit for thirty-one years. My mother was very well known and had contact with all the doctors and nurses. She was also well loved by the children. I was hired and worked as a nurse's assistant. During my two year period at the hospital I became very excited about my career, I became close with the doctors and the nurses, and especially close with the children.

One of my experiences was working with a sick child by the name of Edward Broadway. He was eight years old and was from Marianna, Arkansas. Edward was in the hospital for a burn injury. Mattie Medlock, a Scrub Technician from the Burn Unit, provided assistance to the doctors and nurses with burn patients that had been burned, or needed to have surgery for burn injuries over their body.

My experience as a student nurse was that I loved children and did everything I could to help and make the children feel better. A burn injury is very painful and the healing process takes time. As a nurse I tried to bring love and comfort to the children when they needed it. One evening after returning from work I spoke with a friend that I went to high school with, his name was Eugene Broadway.

I told Eugene about this young child in the hospital that had gotten burned, and had burn injuries over his body. I asked Gene if he was related to this family because they had the same last name and spelled the exact same way. Gene informed me that he had family from Marianna, Arkansas but he did not know if he was related to that family or not.

Years passed, and the subject was never bought up again. In March, 2011 Gene and I were talking about his past years as a teen-ager and as an adult. Gene seems to have a good memory; he could remember things I couldn't. After Gene shared some of his past life experiences with me, I asked him, teasing him...do you remember the little boy that I told you about years ago from Marianna, Arkansas. This little boy was in the Arkansas Children's Hospital. Gene paused and stated: Yeah!!! Deb, I do remember. I met Edward Broadway about two years ago at a Family Reunion.

Gene states: I need to call him to let him know that you and your mother were the ones that took care of him when he was sick and in the hospital. Wow!!! This is very exciting and I can use this experience in my book that I am writing.

Gene contacted his cousin Edward to tell him about my mother and myself. Mother was a Scrub Technician; she provided assistance to the doctors and the nurses when performing surgery on burn patients.

When Gene contacted his cousin to tell him that I knew him and I remembered him as a child, Edward was tearful, very astonished and did not know what to say. I told Gene if Edward wanted my phone number it was okay to give it to him. Edward was in shock and could not believe Gene knew me personally.

Edward asked Gene if he could have my phone number because he wanted to contact me to talk to me. Gene gave Edward my phone number and I received a phone call from Edward around 11:30 pm on March 27, 2011. Edward called and asked to speak with me; I answered the phone not knowing who was calling me so late at night. Edward explained that he was sorry for calling so late but he had to speak with me. He told me who he was and he had spoken to his cousin Eugene Broadway. Eugene had explained everything to him.

In talking with Edward he told me when he got old enough he returned to Little Rock to Arkansas Children's Hospital. He tried to contact me and my mother. Edward stated that he wanted to "Thank Us" for the love and support we showed him during the time of his storm. Edward stated that he felt God sent him two guardian angels to take care of him and to be with him throughout his illness. Edward goes on to tell me that he wanted to thank me and my mom so many times but had no way of contacting us. I was amazed that Edward remembered me; he was only eight years old.

I remember an incident one day when I was at work, working a total of eight hours a day. After my shift had ended for the day it was time for me to go home. Little Edward cried and cried, he did not want me to go home. I did everything I could to stop him from crying. The nurses had to slip me out of the room to stop little Edward from crying. I gave Edward a picture of me, telling him to keep this picture with him. I was sad for Edward and did not want to see him cry. I bought him a picture of me, to remember me by. A few days later Edward was discharged from the hospital.

In our conversation Edward told me about the picture I gave him. I did not remember what I looked like on the picture. He told me I had a small afro and I was wearing a black dress. The black dress really surprised me because I had a black dress back in the day, which I really liked. I was very impressed and happy to know that Edward remembered me and my mom. After talking with Edward I told him that my mom passed away in October, 2010 but she would have been so excited and happy to know he's doing well.

We have made arrangements to someday meet here in the Atlanta area. I would like to meet Edward now that he is older, to let him know that God never changes and neither will I. My heart belongs to God; therefore I will strive to all love. I loved Edward on yesterday; I will love him on tomorrow and will love him the day after.

My mom Mattie Medlock passed on October 28, 2010 in Mansfield, Texas, due to illness. However, mother would be so pleased and happy to know that Edward Broadway is doing so well today and he is married with three children and a wife. I told Edward that I was married, three children and lived in Villa Rica, Georgia. I also told Edward God has been good to me and my family. We've had our storms but God was in the mist through it all.

9. OUT OF TOUCH IN TOUCH
By Ed Broadway

Being raised up on a farm meant working at practically all times all year 'round. In the Fall of 1971 in Moro, Arkansas during harvest time, my brothers and I had to go to the fields every evening after school to work. It was work, but at our age, it was more like playing. At this particular time we were harvesting cotton and my oldest brother would come home, pick us up and take us back to the cotton field.

As our father would pick cotton with the "one-row" cotton picker, when the hopper or large basket would fill up with cotton, he would dump it over into a forty to forty-five foot open trailer. Our job then was to spread the cotton out over the trailer and trump or pack it down so that our Dad could dump another load until the trailer was filled to the top with cotton.

The autumn evenings and nights would many times get very cool outside. We would many times lie in the cotton and cover ourselves up in the cotton to keep warm. On one particular evening after school when my older brother had come home to pick us up to take us to the fields, I observed a cigarette lighter underneath a chair as we were leaving out the door.

Picking up the lighter, in my mind I said, "I am going to take this lighter and make a small fire in the cotton to keep warm tonight." After Dad had dumped a few loads of cotton and my brothers and I had spread and packed it down, I decided to make a tunnel in the cotton. After I made the tunnel, I pulled out the lighter and while lying down in the tunnel of cotton I lit the cotton and the cotton began to burn quickly nearly like gas would ignite and burn.

I immediately got out of the small tunnel and stood up; by this time, almost the whole trailer of cotton was on fire. I saw two of my brothers get out at one end of the trailer. So, I started trying to run towards their end to get out. But this seemed farther than the opposite end which had a built on ladder to climb out. Since, I was getting weak due to the fire about to consume me; I figured I should turn around and get to that end to climb down the ladder. By the grace of God, I know now, that I was able to make it to the ladder. But instead of climbing down, I fell down because I was now in nearly unbearable pain. The fire went out on its own, or rather, God put it out because I didn't know then that you are to roll on the ground to extinguish the fire. (Don't ever play with lighters or matches).

My oldest brother drove me home to pick up our mother then we went to the hospital there in Marianna. I was in unbearable pain and couldn't bear even the wind blowing on me. In the Marianna hospital they wrapped my arms with some type of bandage (later found out this was a bad thing to do).

I threw up everything until there were only a small volume of fluids left in me. I overheard the doctors say that I might not make it. But I had a praying mother who had a straight line to Jesus. I was taken by ambulance to Little Rock's Children's hospital very early the following morning.

As soon as I arrived at children's hospital, the doctors began to remove the bandages that the doctors in Marianna had put on my arms. As they were removing the bandages my burnt skin was peeling off as well, talking about pain, this eight year old fellow was experiencing it!

A few days later the doctors at Little Rock Children's hospital told my mother that they needed to do skin graft and it would come from my thigh. The skin graft went as planned. My thigh pained and itched for some time but I could not scratch it because it was covered with cast-like bandage.

The days or weeks later were some of the most painful days of my life after the skin graft. There was a salve or healing cream they rubbed over my skin graft area. It had to be washed daily or every other day. The nurse would place me in the shower and spray my arms off. I would yell, cry, and beg her not to do it. But she knew it had to be done. She took her time and took much patience with me because she also knew this was very painful.

I asked her to allow me to clean it on my own. But I couldn't put myself through the pain. Each day it seemed, after this painful experience, there was another nurse or assistant by the name of Deborah who would talk with me. She would nurture and play games with me to help take my mind off the pain and everything I was experiencing.

I was in the hospital I believe for over three months. The first two months were nearly too much for me to bear. I recall one day as Deborah was playing games with me, I asked her to give me a mirror so that I could see my face. This was after about two months in the hospital; I had never seen the burn scars on my face.

She gave me a mirror and I observed the scar tissues on my face. I was somewhat saddened by my appearance. Nurse Debra noticed my sadness but she hugged me and kissed me on the forehead and told me I was good looking and handsome.

Those four words coming from her carried me through to my adult hood because I thought she was a beautiful nurse so it didn't matter what anyone else said about me.

I believe if she had not spent time with me, played games, showed me the ice cream and orange sherbet freezer, and showed me love, I believe I would have lived a somewhat defeated life until God showed me otherwise. But God placed her there at that moment, for such a time that I was experiencing, to see me through it.

After I left the hospital I was out of touch with Nurse Deborah. I went on to finish grade school, graduated from high school and then I went to college in Little Rock in the Fall of 1981. I went back to the Children's Hospital to try to get in touch with Nurse Deborah. I wanted to personally thank her for being my nurse and helping me through my hospital experience.

When I got to the hospital they told me she no longer worked there and they had no other information. I looked up Debra Hall in the phone book but I couldn't find her. After I graduated from college, moved to Texas and got married, I tried another time during one of my visits back to Arkansas to find her but still fell short on finding her. I gave much thought to hiring a PI to locate her but I did not follow through on it.

In July of 2010, we had a "Broadway" family reunion in Chicago, Illinois where I met one of my cousins whom I only heard about named Eugene Broadway but had never met. I heard about him because there were two Eugene's along about the same age. We chatted a few times at the various functions that we had for the family reunion weekend and through emails leading up to the reunion.

In March of 2011, Cousin Eugene e-mailed me asking me if I knew a Deborah Hall from Little Rock, Arkansas. I cannot describe what I felt as my mind zipped back thirty-nine and half years to the time I spent in the Children's Hospital. I couldn't believe that someone who knew me also knew Nurse Deborah Hall, as well. I replied back to the e-mail with my telephone number. Eugene called me back that night telling me that he knew the nurse Deborah Hall-Milliken.

Also, she had asked him if he knew me. After he made a call to her and contacted me back with her number he encouraged me to immediately get in touch with her that night. After forty years, the Lord God allowed me to personally tell Nurse Deborah Hall-Milliken thank you for allowing God to use her as one of His angels.

She planted confidence, self-esteem and love down into my spirit. It helped shaped me into who I have become today! She told me that the other nurse that helped me and cleaned my painful burn scars in the shower was her mother.

The Lord God answers prayers and he yet blesses folk with the desires of their hearts. As Psalms 37:4 says, "Delight thyself also in the Lord and He shall give thee the desires of thine heart."

Thanks Eugene for listening to the Spirit of the Lord and allowing him to use you to unite friends and families all over the country.

I almost forgot to add to my story; I am now a volunteer chaplain at the Parkland Hospital Burn Unit in Dallas Texas, encouraging the burn patients just as I was encouraged. May God Bless you!

10. CHILDHOOD STORY
By Nathaniel Broadway

I would like to share my childhood story of how I got so involved with football. My father would sit us down and we would watch the Dallas Cowboys. He would tell us about Bob Hayes the fastest man in the world who was playing wide receiver for the Dallas Cowboys, at the time. Shortly after, I would go out in the streets or someone's back yard and play football with my friends. I developed many good and long lasting friendships that way. As I grew older, I started really following the game and learned from some of the best football minds you could come across. I learned the informative parts of the game from my brother-in-law at the time, Yancy Hooks.

He also taught me about other sports as well. I learned techniques from my brother Eugene who taught me the proper way to play defensive back and how to be physical at the line of scrimmage. To this day, that's why I like the defensive side of the ball. I learned the art of quarterbacking from my brother Bobby. Even though he is a lefty, I learned the proper form and how to throw. I passed that along to all the younger guys that I got a chance to play with.

When I started working in high school, I had a friend that we would take the game to another level and play for money. We would take the winnings and buy the guys' burgers and shakes. We did this for a while and it was a lot of fun. Just seeing the young guys' faces and how they competed to win, this kind of competition got a lot of guys interested in playing for their perspective schools. I was proud of them for that.

I have many people to thank for my knowledge of the game that I love to this day. I would like to thank them all for helping me along the way. I have tried and hope I succeeded in helping pass that along to others as well. I'm very proud and fond of those childhood memories.

11. CHOICE
By Mary Booker

Have you wondered what it would be like if you never crossed a path that was not meant to be? I came because I had no choice; I am here because I made the choice and I made decisions because it was my choice. When my time is up, it will be His choice.

When growing up the questions have been "what do you want to be", "where will you live", "how many children do you want?"Looking back, I wanted to be a lawyer but my parents felt it would take a lot of years. I believed them so I did not really pursue my real dream, being a lawyer. After many trials and getting myself ready, I became a teacher.

I have no regrets in this decision; because it was a path I had to follow and a choice that was made for me. The reason I said it was a choice made for me because of the things that I saw happening in the classroom. Children were thirsty for knowledge, and in a way, I put my sons in the place of those who were in need. I taught my children and felt that I could and did teach others. I was taught when a teacher asked you do something, (my parents and the "board of education") I had to do it. I am here now because of the choice I made. I wanted something better for my children and most of all, for me.

It wasn't easy pulling up roots to move to another state, leaving what you felt was all that you needed. For me, this was being an explorer in some sense. I never knew the other states except the one I grew up in and the area that surrounded it. Snow was all I knew and a few warm days were a pleasure. I was exposed to warm days in April and this was not from reading but from experiencing a warmer climate. Playing in the snow was a daily routine in the winter and bundling up to fight the cold was inborn.

My parents were middle-class folk and being hungry while living with them was not something I felt. Once I was out on my own, this was a different story. But the best part that was instilled in me was that I had to work in order to get fed. My choice was to work to eat or become whatever was out there and starve.

I chose to eat and work with the system to be somebody. I had a lot of bumps on the way and some that I was not proud of. But the best part was I made it. My mistakes were handled because I caused them and being unhappy was one of them. Once, a true friend was tired of hearing me complain. She would not assist me but only told me about the "steel melting." It took me a few years to understand her meaning, but when I did, I truly woke up to being me. I was able to be there for my family and learned how to survive.

While working for the Chicago Board of Education, I started off as a school secretary, went back to school and became a teacher. For the first two years, our monies were not prorated. During the summer, unless I worked, I had no income for three months. The money I did have was used and when it came time to pay important bills, it was not there. It was then that I knew some changes had to be made and fast. Choices were made and my children had food on the table. I knew a divorce was imminent for survival. I took it, the choice to get ready. I had no idea what the next day was going to bring but my answer came and I stepped out on faith.

When I moved South, I took a substantial cut in pay. My bills were few and I knew that my taxes would see me through should I need it. My teaching job was secure until we were told that we had to take the teaching exam to stay employed. The first time I took the test, I failed. I was told to take my personal things from the school I was assigned to because I was not "fit" to teach.

This was upsetting not knowing how I was going to make it. The Board gave me a year to pass the exam, gave me a tutor and on the second time, I passed. In my Bible, I had a prayer written down asking God to put the answers to the right questions. I was blessed and passed the exam and to me my score was not important only the word "congratulations." I taught until I retired.

During the interim, my oldest son was incarcerated. I was on the road every weekend and holiday for over twelve years putting my life on hold for him. I handled problems when he felt he was not treated right, made calls and trips to the Atlanta Pardons and Parole Board more times than I can remember. I joined an organization

"Coalition for Inmates" whose main purpose was to help those incarcerated. My son needed help and so many others that this was something I wanted to get involved in.

We met with the Parole Board, had meetings that the Parole Board members came to. It was always a well attended meeting because of the questions that were in need of answers. Through this organization, I started the Atlanta Consultant After Care, got my 501(3)© and continued to help those incarcerated.

Several inmates were released though this program and more and more came on to get help for their families and loved ones. This decision was in the making and became my choice.

The inmates started writing to ask questions. Because, I could not answer each one personally, The Liberty Bell newspaper was formed. We were able to communicate with the families. We offer them contact names, telephone numbers needed, solutions to the inmates' personal problems, their stories, and encouragement. I have had the opportunity to meet so many people who were in need of help, prayer, a hug or just a word to say all is well.

I could do this because I was involved and lived what they were living and went through what they were going through. Unless you have been there, you have no idea what that person is feeling. We all hurt and we all have to make choices. I would tell some family members that some of the inmates are Jonah. The whale swallowed them up because they would not go the way they were directed. They took a detour and when the whale spits them out, they will go the direction they were told to go. We all have a choice and decisions to make. When my time is up, it will be His choice.

12. SPIRITUAL JOURNEY
By Eugene Broadway

I believe meeting and working with family members and putting my heart and soul in genealogy work for my family is a spiritual journey for me. Looking back on my life, I truly believe I was prepared for my family's genealogical work. Moving away from Moro, Arkansas at a young age created a desire in me to know my family. For over thirty years, I played around with genealogy, thinking I would never find my family.

While growing up, I would go to Moro, Arkansas, most summers, to stay out of trouble. While there, my Uncle John Y. Smith would make sure I visited my close relatives on my father's side (Grandpa Sam, Aunt Fannie, Uncle Lenner, Aunt

Polly and my first cousins). I'm grateful for it gave me the foundation of knowing my immediate family. While growing up in Little Rock, I would meet family as they moved to or visited Little Rock. Meeting so many Broadways made things confusing for me because I did not know how they were all related to me. I attended a few family reunions but really did not know anyone but the immediate family.

God stepped in a little stronger on December 31, 2008. I had some heart complications and had to retire. I realized I was a workaholic. After retiring, I did not know what to do with my time. God was working through my sister who guided Jerome Turner and my cousin Marie Toms to get in touch with me to help plan a Broadway Family Reunion.

Immediately, the first part of the puzzle showed itself. I learned that my grandfather, not only, had one sister, but other brothers. Whoa!!! Things had gotten interesting already. It caused me to want to know more. I got so involved, I would dream about family. In my dreams, I would be given information. Low and behold, I would wake up and research the information that was given and it would be right.

Reflecting back on my Grandfather Sam Broadway's funeral, it was said that my grandfather loved family and wanted his grandchildren to stay in touch. I know a lot took place surrounding this funeral. My cousins, Marie and Jerome were there. Jerome and I communicated and took a picture together. I didn't remember the picture until he showed it to me years later at a family reunion meeting at his house. There is a feeling that Daddy Sam's spirit was involved in getting the reunion started.

There were times when the research had come to a dead end. The family's research team had no idea they were being prepared for something new and bigger. I must admit the tremendous findings would have been too much for my mind, if given to me all at once.

1. Lost family members
2. Lost Land
3. What was happening in Lee County, etc?

The way all the findings fell into place, in my eyes, was nothing but a 'Spiritual Journey.'

13. THE JOURNEY – THE TREES
By Shianne C. Broadway

My name is Shianne C. Broadway, wife of Eugene Broadway. I always tell Eugene I have found my soul mate in him and he is the love of my life.

Eugene and I met several years ago. We were and still are members of the same church. I remember the first time I visited Eugene at his townhouse. I was amazed at the beautiful artwork he had collected. There was one painting in particular that stood out to me and has always been my favorite, even until this day, "The Journey" by Danny Broadway.

Eugene and I have traveled to several cities and we have taken many pictures. During the summer of 2010, cousins' Mary Booker, Jewell Farley, Lolita Foxworth, my husband Eugene and I visited North Carolina. This was an important trip for Eugene and the rest of the family.

Since his retirement, he has become a genealogist and has done extensive research and gathered valuable information on the Broadway family history. This trip provided so much helpful information. We met Broadway family members, visited the courthouse and the library in Wadesboro, N.C. (Anson County). We were able to find deeds to land which belonged to some Broadway family ancestors. While we walked this land, we also took pictures. I really enjoyed taking pictures of the beautiful trees. One tree in particular stood out to me. It was breathtaking. It reminded me of the painting in Eugene's townhome when we first met. It was amazing.

We have visited Little Rock and Marianna, Arkansas several times. During the summer of 2010, we went to Moro, Arkansas and visited Marshall and Silvia Broadway's gravesites. There was another tree in particular that stood out to me. It also reminded me of the painting in Eugene's house. And of course, we still have that painting today which was painted in 1999 by Danny Broadway. It is a part of a collection of great artwork that Eugene has collected.

The painting depicts the Broadway ancestors' journey from North Carolina by wagon train to Arkansas. Danny Broadway painted the picture. He is pictured standing next to the painting below. The painting was used as the logo for the Broadway Family Reunion and the painting was on display during the family reunion event that we attended July 16 – 18, 2010 along with many family members. Danny's art display was available as a photo backdrop. Many of us took pictures within the art display.

What a wonderful time we had. This painting is now a part of Eugene's art collections in our home. It represents the journey of the ancestors who traveled to Arkansas on feet and by way of wagon trains.

I have come to realize the significance of the pictures we took of the trees in North Carolina and Arkansas to the painting we have in our home which is my favorite of all. They are symbolic because the picture that was taken in

- North Carolina is overlooking the land on the plantation of some of the Broadway ancestors.
- Arkansas is overlooking Silvia's gravesite.

The painting on the cover of this book represents the journey that the Broadway ancestors made from slavery through today. The book is entitled *The Journey* which came from a piece of art painted by Danny Broadway.

14. CONVERSATIONS AT THE BARBERSHOP
By Danny Broadway

I remember being a kid and spending time at the barbershop with my father. I always enjoyed sitting and listening to all of the conversations that went on.

There were always colorful personalities around. There was always someone coming in from the outside selling items like movies, pies, or clothes. It was fun! My Dad had lots of friends and people really liked being around him.

I learned a lot from those days. I was one of his main customers. I followed him all the way through Barber School. I watched the whole process of how to properly cut a fade. In fact, I now cut both of my boy's hair the same way; I remember seeing him teach it to others.

15. COUSINS
By Oneadia Kates

Now that I think back, I begin reminiscing when my cousins would visit us from time to time. We grew up happy and content. We felt really connected and proud. My parents would always treat our cousins like they were their own children. When it was time to eat dinner or other meals, our parents would make sure they ate just like we did.

We didn't have much but we shared what we had. Our Dad always provided good food and plenty of it. That was one of the qualities I looked for in a husband. I remember Eugene and his siblings coming down to visit us from Little Rock. We were proud of our Uncle Daniel's kids; that's what we used to say.

Edna, Bettye and their siblings, we were so crazy about our cousins. We called them Aunt Cynthia Burnett's kids. Flossie Miller and her siblings, we had so much laughter and fun growing up. Jerome Turner and his siblings, we were like sisters and brothers. They treated us just like one of their siblings. They were called Aunt Fleecie's kids. Carthina McKenzie and her siblings, we were proud of our Aunt Samella's kids. Janet Neely and her siblings, we also, had a lot of fun. Their mother, (Fannie) and I were like sisters.

Ramona Stedman and her siblings, we called them Aunt Bobbie Lee's kids. We long to see them growing up, knowing that was my Daddy's sister's kids. Our parents spoke of them a lot.

Elizabeth Broadway, we had a lot fun growing up as teenagers. I was so crazy about my cousin. Vonitha (TaTa), Aunt Vonitha Ward's daughter would visit us every day and we had fun. I could go on and on about the happy days I had with my cousins. These are just a few of the cousins that I grew up with.

16. DECISIONS, A REFLECTION OF TIME
By Leonard "Hanif" Toms Jr.

I have had time to really reflect and contemplate over my thoughts because I've done time. Many of these thoughts get or have gotten buried in the back of my mind because of the busy lifestyle that engulfed me. I asked myself how it got to the point where I was so busy, that it felt like I didn't even have time to think.

Reflecting on "how", it all fell back to the decisions made by me. This is not going to be a sad story about me having gone to jail, but something I want to share. This is my rejuvenated epiphany statement of sorts.

However, it is about reflecting over my decisions and admonishments and a reminder to myself! I pray that my reflections hinder me from making further bad decisions and awaken anyone who doesn't realize the value in good decisions.

I just turned thirty-three years old. I get it or I don't get it. Or should I say, I'm getting it. I'm talking about life. Not simply my life, but the way of life, and not just the way of life, but getting through life with success and the great reward of the hereafter.

I'm positive that the way of life for me is Islam. Yet I still have to get through life to receive the reward. Allah has referred to getting through life as "Siratal mustageen", aka the "Straight path". The part that complicates the straight path is us.

Being human, we have been given what some may call "free will." I'm going to call it what it is, "the ability to make bad decisions." This is what makes us special and eligible for the great reward if we make good decisions. But we can bring about pain, if we make bad decisions.

I remember when I was seventeen years old during the summer before my senior year in high school. My friend, Kirby Butler, was murdered in an alley on a Sunday night. We got news early that morning. I was so hurt and upset. Not only was he a close friend but he and I had just talked about how he was making changes in his life to do better. He had a son on the way, a job and all that.

I had seen violence and such. And for myself, I was straddling the fence of being a schoolboy and a hustler. But this incident was one that really hit a nerve. I had a summer intern job at a real estate company, plus football practice had begun. So my Monday was a cloudy day.

But I do remember a conversation I had with my father that Monday morning. He said, "You're about to go into your senior year. Son, you will be faced with many decisions; try and make the right ones." I was like, what! My boy just got killed and you want to say that. Reflecting on what he said, man he said a whole lot. I thank him for that. But I decided not to listen...

I don't know why that was my first recollection of decisions and me making them, but that came to my mind. I do remember thinking as a younger child while riding with my parents that when it comes to picking a direction to travel, if we might be lost, my mom makes the right decision all the time. "We should listen to her." That still holds true to this day. My mom is one of the best decision-makers, I know. She told me to do those taxes even if I didn't have the money to pay the IRS but I decided not to listen...

It amazes me the similarities shared between children and their parents. My mom and brother are so goal oriented and such calculated decision-makers. My father and I are both lackadaisical and impulsive decision-makers. But, both my brother and I want what we want, right then.

Also, I see so much of me in my son, Balaal, that it scares me. He takes risks and is impulsive among other things just like me and my father. I see this in him and he's only five years old. When he was not even two years old he was getting up in the middle of the night stealing cereal and snacks from the pantry or fridge or whatever he could get to.

One night, my wife and I were sitting at the table watching TV. As if we couldn't see him, Bilaal tries to slide by to the kitchen with his hands up over his eyes so he couldn't see us. In his head, he figured that if I can't see them, they can't see me! So

I'm going to go for it. Funny at the time, but thinking about it, it kept me up many nights thinking of how I can break that and teach him and all my kids to make better decisions than I have.

One day, I was in Wal-Mart's customer service line waiting to return something. It was very crowded and I was about the fifth or sixth person in line. In front of me was a thirty plus year-old White woman with three children. Her children, to say it nicely, were not well-behaved. She was calm and patient and spoke in a way that was almost surprising to me. The children were approximately nine, seven and five years of age. She said, "I've told you all to straighten up. You'll need to make the right decision." The nine and seven year-old almost immediately straightened up.

The five-year old continued on in a way that embarrassed me. She stayed calm and went over to him and said calmly but firmly, "Your behavior is not okay with me. Do you want to watch TV tonight or do you want to continue to behave like this? It is your decision, make the right choice." And she got back in line. You can see his little wheels turning. Then just like that, he turned into a well-behaved little White boy.

Needless to say, I was in awe. So I got the woman's attention and told her I really liked the way she dealt with that situation. She said, she was a teacher and had learned that technique in a workshop she attended. I called the wife and said, "Aye, I got a Jedi mind trick for the kids in hopes they will learn to make good decisions..."

There is really more than what meets the eye in making good decisions. Many variables are involved, such as education can play a big part, motivation, surrounding influences, and inexperience to name a few. As I reflect on some of my good and bad decisions, I can directly link them to some of the variables of decision-making. How do you have some type of variable control?

Just like the little White boy, take a little time and think about it before making a decision. Easier said than done; I know I must train my mind to slow down and think about it thoroughly before acting or deciding. Thinking does work with most things, even when asked a question.

Prophet Muhammad when asked a question, he would at least take a deep breath before answering the question. His pause would be so long at times, the questioner would repeat the question. When asked about that he said, "It is best that I thought about what to say before I decided to say anything..."

I could lose myself in the 'what if', or 'I wish I did' train of thought. Thank God, I understand there's no benefit in that. I do also understand that our Creator knows all. He has a plan for me and all my decisions are part of that plan. If it weren't for my decisions, good and bad, I wouldn't be who I am. I would not have my family, my religion, or my experiences.

My experiences haven't been all pleasant because of my decisions, but it is all in his plan. The purification for me is when I have patience with the hardships and gratitude when it's all good; then I know I am on the right track. So I thank God for the good and bad decisions. I pray that I continue to grow into a responsible man that makes good decisions for me and my family. Also, I pray that my children grow to be good decision-makers...

Knowing that I have a rough road ahead in starting part of my life all over, God has given me focus on the positive. Having served time has greatly benefited me. Time benefited me because I decided it would. I have written plans from A through Z. With time and God's help, I am training my mind to slow down with attempts to make better decisions. In time, I will be able to show progress in my journey of life. Good or bad decisions only show themselves over time. At times, persons are able to turn a bad decision into a good result. God willing, that's true for me.

This is me taking time to reflect about how decisions affected my life and how to bring a positive effect into my decision-making. I pray for guidance for me and for you. I pray for ease and comfort in this life and the next. I am sending a big thanks to all my family and friends for their support.

17. DON'T TURN AROUND
By Mary Booker

I talked to someone today who felt I was worthwhile and that I did not need to turn around to feel if someone was looking. It is hard to shape your thoughts into the action that being yourself is more important that wondering what someone else thinks about you. How many times have you turned around wondering who was looking at your face, dress, or hair and you feeling like a 'nobody' because you felt this was the way they were thinking about you.

Your thoughts always wondering did I say the right thing? Why are they angry at me? Should I buy them a present so that they will like me, or give them money if it would buy friendship? Always searching and never finding what was needed to satisfy that person, or was it my need?

Feeling like you will never amount to their expectations and trying forever to get their approval. This is a friend, you thought, you wanted to be like. You wanted to be included in the crowd, the dances, the get-togethers and most of all, to be noticed. How ashamed it was to be ignored or to have someone talk as if you did not exist or talk about you as if you were invisible.

Just ignore them, they are in the way. They can never be one of us, just look at him or her. Who would dress like that? Look at that hair, who told her/him that it looked good? Their clothes don't even match. Where did they buy that outfit, sure looks cheap, oh well, just act if they are not here. Along comes someone who can see yourself worth. They can see that you are a beautiful person inside and out; they can see the hurt in your eyes.

Now you wonder are they telling you the truth or want to use you like the other so-called friends you wanted to be with did? Which way should I go and how can I believe what they are saying is real. How can I tell if they are not someone who wants to rape my mind by telling me what I really want to hear?

What is wrong with me? I let myself go and talked to this person by trying to explain what is happening to me. I asked what did I do wrong that my friends do not want me around? I finally opened up and the tears started and I could not stop.

I heard a soft voice saying let it all out, felt a hug that was genuine, never injecting their feelings into mine, just listening. I was in a comfort zone of reality. I could talk about my looks, my clothes, the way I talked, how I was ignored when I tried to get into the conversations.

Nothing I said was oblivious to this person. They just listened. When I was able to control myself, they just sat quietly, hugging and patting me and saying, it's okay.

This person, told me to forget about what happened yesterday; don't look back and start feeling good about now. This moment is all that matters because it is what I am living now. Do not worry about what someone else thinks about you; worry about what you think about you. Then, love you, do for you, and be you.

If you feel that your clothes should be better, then look to see what it is that is missing and fix it. Your hair can be long, short, or no hair; this will not change the inside of you. Continue to smile; but you must be you.

Don't change for anyone and feel that this is what they want. Let your change be what you want. Because when you look in the mirror and see you, you must be satisfied and happy.

When you are happy, all those around you can feel the vibes and will be honored to have you as a friend. Be comfortable with your body and if you feel that there is need for a change, do it and don't turn back, go forward and be happy with you.

Remember, "You are today where your thoughts have brought you; you will be tomorrow where your thoughts take you." Don't turn around!

18. DRIVER'S LICENSE EXPERIENCES
By Parlee Broadway

What is it? A driver's license is an official document that I value. It allows me to operate a motorized vehicle, such as a car or truck on a public roadway. The driving license has become a standard form of picture identification for me in the United States.

The driver's license was issued to me after I passed a written and driving test. The tests were given to examine levels of competency consistent with safe driving habits and practices, as well as demonstrated skills and knowledge of laws relating to traffic safety.

I thought, "When was the first driver's license issued?" As automobile-related fatalities soared in North America, public outcry provoked legislators to begin studying the French and German statutes as models.

On August 1, 1910, North America's first driver's licensing law went into effect in the U.S. in the state of New York, though it initially applied only to professional chauffeurs. In July 1913, the state of New Jersey became the first to require all drivers to pass a mandatory examination before receiving a license.

I first received my driver's license in the state of Arkansas in 1993 after my husband died. I raised nine kids and all of them had acquired their driver's licenses. My husband taught all of them how to drive, even me. The only thing that he had not convinced me of was to take the driver's test.

I had to master the written test first. I went downtown Marianna and got a book to begin my study. I had not been in school in over forty years. My learning curve was tremendous, combined with my grief after recently losing my husband. I got permission to ride the senior citizen bus and walked over to the driver's license test office and took the test for the first time. The officer came out, called me and said "I'm sorry; Ms. Broadway but you did not pass this time."

I left with a sad face and decided I'm not going to let that stop me. I'm going to continue to study; I am going to pass that test. And then one day after taking the test, the officer stepped out of the door and called, "Mrs. Broadway, you passed the test!" I think we both were excited; they knew me well by then.

Now it was time to take the driver's test. I knew I wasn't ready to take the driver's test that day. So, I asked if I could come back later to take the driver's test and he said yes. I went home, made my schedule and began practicing parallel parking.

Parallel parking is a method of parking a vehicle in line with other parked cars. Cars parked in parallel are in one line, parallel to the curb, with the front bumper of each car facing the back bumper of the adjacent one.

Parallel parking requires driving the car in reverse gear into the parking space. I knew how to drive. I had driven many times in the fields and down the road to assist my husband in farming. But I had not driven in town; nor had I ever parked a car closely to another car.

So I decided to find two barrels and place them in my yard several feet apart. That was the set up that I used to practice my parallel parking. I waited until I thought I had mastered that before I went back to take my driver's test. The time had arrived to prepare to take the tests. I had to get someone to drive me downtown Marianna. I needed someone with a car to get down there because I didn't have a license to drive my own car down there. I took the test and made a left turn when it should have been a right turn. I drove carefully and looked in my rearview mirror.

I stopped at the stop sign. I parallel parked. I drove back to the police station and waited for the police officer to tell me how I had done. He said, Mrs. Broadway, you did well but you ran that stop sign.

I lost it! I forgot he was a police officer. He said when you get to a stop sign you suppose to make a complete stop, not a rolling stop. A rolling stop is a term used in traffic law to refer to when a vehicle fails to come to a complete stop. A complete stop is when there is no forward momentum and the needle on the speedometer is at 0.

In a rolling stop, the car wheels are still in motion and the car is moving at less than 5 miles per hour. Failing to come to a complete stop at a stop sign is a traffic violation governed by state laws, which vary by state.

The longer the stop, the more discernible it is to the naked eye, giving a motorist a better chance of avoiding a ticket. I thought I was going to get my driver's license anyway with that mistake, but he told me to come back again.

So I practiced some more and then went back again. I did it perfectly that time. When the officer and I got back to the station, he said, "Mrs. Broadway, You are not going to be driving to Little Rock are you?" I said "No I just want to drive to Moro, Brinkley and Marianna, that's all." Then the officer said, "Mrs. Broadway, you passed the test." I was so excited that I could've kissed him, but I didn't.

I realized recently that I was not the only one who did not have a driver's license. Men and women who had driven in the neighborhoods and towns had never acquired a driver's license. Furthermore, some people acquired their license without a test. Some paid to acquire them.

Others had the test examiner read to them, so they could mark the appropriate answers. And of course, there are some who never acquired a driver's license; they took their chances. Then just sometimes, it was all about who you knew and who they knew. Thanks to the Lord, I got my Arkansas driver's license and I am still driving at seventy-eight years old.

19. GRANDPA...TELL ME ABOUT THE GOOD OLE DAYS
By Wanda Broadway (Williams)

Being raised in Moro, Arkansas under the guidance of my wonderful parents Mr. L.A. Broadway and Mrs. Eunice Broadway, I must say those were some good ole days. On the weekends, there was always someone coming to visit from out-of-town.

There were young and old, men and women, and there was Cousin Daniel Broadway!!!

One could tell that he was a man who loved family. You could tell that by the way HE took the TIME to SPEAK and LISTEN!!

When I left home my Daddy told me to "look" my Cousin Daniel up when I got to Little Rock. And that I did. When my Daddy died, Cousin Daniel was at his funeral. He didn't say anything to me. He just looked and that look told me more than any word or words could ever say.

20. HIGHER EDUCATION AID DENIED IN 1970
By Marie Broadway

While talking with Mom about when she and Dad used to drive me to Jonesboro, Arkansas where I attended Arkansas State University in 1970, they thought there weren't any Black families in the area.

But after they visited me several times, they discovered there were quite a few. However, we were probably some of the first who attended college there in Jonesboro at the University. I remember when I started college in 1970; it was about 200 Blacks and about 8000 Whites on campus, so we really were some of the first few who attended ASU.

My parents were slightly afraid to send me there because of the rumors of prejudice. I had no idea being denied something I was qualified for because others were prejudiced would happen to me.

I only applied to two colleges for the 1970 school year: University Arkansas at Pine Bluff and Arkansas State University at Jonesboro. I received an ASU one-year full tuition scholarship because I was valedictorian of my Anna Strong High School class, so you see, I applied early.

My paperwork, test scores, and financial aid paperwork was in early. One of the community activist and my parents partitioned to get state and local scholarships but those scholarships went to the White high school.

I accepted the scholarship to ASU and was directed by the Finance department at ASU to apply for a loan and work study. I did just that. Through my own research, I found that my parents' income was at the poverty level during 1969-1970 and I should have qualified for a grant.

I submitted my second request to apply for financial aid (grant). I went by the financial aid office in person and requested an opportunity to apply for the grant for the next semester and if not that semester, then the next year.

THE JOURNEY | EUGENE BROADWAY

I was denied the opportunity to apply for that current year and the next. The reason given was that "you did not apply the first year, so that disqualifies you from receiving a grant." I never received a grant even though my parents were at the poverty level throughout my college days. I continued to work and get loans.

I promised that I would never let that happen to anyone else I knew. I educated others on financial aid procedures, paperwork and on the prejudices that can invade those procedures and paperwork.

Later, two of my sisters did attend college at the same university. One sister, Marilyn Broadway, graduated with a journalism degree and the other sister, Earma Broadway, attended ASU as a graduate student with a graduate Fellowship.

The journalism student received a scholarship, work-study and a grant. I was so pleased that the incident that happened to me did not happen to her. Not only was she financially and academically aware but she later became the first African-American to become Homecoming Queen at Arkansas State University.

21. THE POWER OF DNA
By Jhane' Broadway-Early

My name is Jhane' Broadway-Early and I am the third child of the astonishing Eugene Broadway. I must say that as a child well into my adult hood, I have experienced many unforgettable moments and in this brief story, I will mention three of those experiences.

Growing up in church was not unusual for me; my mother made sure that no matter what we did on the previous Saturday evening it was a must to be at St John Missionary Baptist Church on time for the 11:00 a.m. service. Although, I was the third child of my father, I was the only child of my mother Margaret Simmons-Ransom.

Because I was the only child she was known for being very over-protective. What I mean by being over- protective, my mother would never let me out of her sight. I was probably one of the only children who had to ride their bikes on the sidewalk. The sidewalk went from the front door of the house to the end of the curb right in front of our house.

At the tender age of four, I can recall meeting a beautiful young lady at church that I was drawn to for some unapparent reason. Every Sunday, I would beg my Mom to let me sit with her and to my surprise she would. This became a normal routine, Sunday after Sunday. While in the presence of this particular young lady, she would supply me with candy and gum against my mother's wishes.

Because of her generosity, I would look forward to our Sunday meetings at church together. Although, I can't really recall the exact moment that I came to the realization, as my father says "The Power of DNA."

I, later, realized that the young lady in question was someone more special than

I anticipated; she was my Aunt! All of this time, I thought that I was drawn to this person. All along, the lady that I only knew as Dana was actually Dana Broadway, my father's younger sister. The power of the "Broadway DNA" is more powerful than one can imagine.

22. UNCLE JUNE

By Jhane' Broadway-Early

On February 12, 1988, our lives would make a change forever. I was only seven years old and I attended Booker Magnet Elementary School. Because of the gang violence that was going on in the city of Little Rock, my mother made sure that my cousin Robin and I stayed together before and after school. We rode the bus together. I would go over her house after school until my mother picked me up.

Well, on this day things were different. My father, Eugene showed up at my school and demanded I leave with him without my cousin. Just days prior, there was a news special that encouraged all parents to create a secret password for their children to keep the kidnapping violence down, so my mother did.

When I asked my Dad for the password, he could not provide it, so I opted not to go with him. My Dad then began to explain to me in a stern voice that I needed to get into the car; that he was my father and didn't need a password because my mom gave him instructions to pick me up and I needed to go right then.

The look in my father's eyes showed me that he was serious and if I knew what was best for me, I better follow his instructions. I can remember the ride was long and quiet. My father had a look of hurt on his face and I did not know what was wrong. After pulling up to the house, my Dad sat me and my cousin Carlos down on the sofa in the den and he told us that my Uncle June had been shot to death.

My life changed at that moment. After the funeral, it was hard for me to sleep alone because I would always have nightmares about my Uncle's death. One night, my mother and I heard beating on our apartment door.

I don't remember much but all I can remember is my mother said it was a Caucasian male and he ran shortly after we would not open the door. This frightened me even more!

The following Saturday morning after our visitor, I received a visit of my own. I was watching cartoons as I did every Saturday while my Mom slept in. I saw a vision of my Uncle June leaning up against a motorcycle outside our patio door.

I was scared at first but I then received a calm feeling. Then I saw my Uncle's mouth move and the words I read were, "Everything is ok, don't be scared anymore." From that moment on, I never had a nightmare and I began to sleep in my own bed again.

23. A MATCH MADE IN HEAVEN
By Jhane' Broadway-Early

Boy meets girl; boy falls in love with girl; boy marries girl. On June 14, 2008, I would no longer be called Ms. Broadway, but now Mrs. Early. At the age of twenty-seven, I got married to the most wonderful man in the world (besides my father) Nicholas Early. It was a match made in heaven. I experienced what every woman dreams of. It seems only like yesterday.

My father, Eugene, for the first time was able to give his baby girl away to a man who had to now fill his shoes and care for his child. I felt like a princess, a queen even. Sometimes I wish I could turn back the hands of time to enjoy the experiences all over again.

You see, I was blessed to have not one but two fathers walk me down the aisle. I broke all traditions and stepped outside of the box. I had never seen it done before but I am known for doing things differently than others.

My father, Eugene Broadway, walked me down first, reminding me not to lock my knees because I would fall. Then he handed me over to my stepfather, Larry Ransom, whose hands were sweating like a river. Later, both gave me away to Nicholas Early who my life would begin and end with.

24. MORE THAN AN UNCLE
By Olaf Lacy Tweedie

My name is Olaf Lacy Tweedie. I am the oldest son of Elizabeth "Gidget" Broadway. For two years of my life, I had the pleasure of living with two of the most remarkable people I've ever known. That is Mr. Uncle Duke Broadway and Mrs. Rosie Broadway Harrison "Mama Rose." Living in Moro, Arkansas was some of the fondest memories of my childhood. I was a city boy with a country heart. I think it was because I loved the farm and all the attention that Mama Rose and Uncle Duke showered me with.

It was my Uncle Duke, who patiently taught me how to fish. He would say "come on boy" and I knew then to grab my cane-pole. I remember the first time I caught a fish; I jumped up and down with joy while the fish flopped and flopped and flopped back in the water. My uncle Duke just laughed. Sometimes he would sit with me for hours, because he knew I didn't want to go home empty handed.

My Uncle Duke also taught me how to drive when I was only eleven years old. On our first journey, I drove into the ditch, while I was turning off Highway 79. Even after my mishap, he still took me out daily, until I got it.

I also remember how Uncle Duke would dress up for a night at the Blue Goose. He would put on his favorite hat with the feather on the side, and yell, "I'm gone," and out the door he went. "I love you Uncle Duke; I miss you and I thank you."

25. NEW BROADWAY GENERATION

By Dr. Shuanta Broadway

I am Eugene Broadway's oldest daughter, Shuanta. I was born in 1973 when he was 21 years old. I have heard stories of how proud my father was of his first-born. I am sure he was excited to be a father. Two of his younger siblings and his older deceased brother had children the previous year. It was the beginning of a new Broadway generation.

I was always a little peculiar and markedly different from my first cousins. I learned to read at a very early age. While my cousins liked to watch cartoons and play outside until sundown, I would rather watch the local news and read obituaries in the newspaper. I called both of my parents, Eugene and Karen, by their first names. Understand, there was no disrespect intended. I just called them what I overheard everyone call them. Obviously, I was never corrected.

My family embraced and at the same time ignored my awkwardness. My cousins would tease me but would beat up anyone in the neighborhood who tried to do the same. My grandmother, who kept my cousins and me, would let me watch the news then put me outside against my will to get fresh air. I appreciate their toughness. It forced me to have some normalcy as a child.

It has often been stated by my older relatives that I was always an old soul, an adult in a child's body. I rarely wanted to play "pretend" or do any activities that were overly imaginative. I have always been a logical person that leans more toward fact than fiction. Knowing this about my personality makes this story about one night in my childhood intriguing to family members and close friends.

I vividly remember the night, December 24, 1980. I was seven years old. It was Christmas Eve and my brother and I were excited. We could not wait for our mother to come in our room, where we shared a bunk bed, to tell us to get up to come see our presents. You must realize that my mother was very strict and would not allow us to get out of our beds without permission. Also, our excitement was not about the arrival of Santa Claus. My father, who is also a realist, had told us years before that there was no Santa Claus and that our toys came from Service Merchandise, a now defunct department store. We were just excited to see what new toys we had.

So, as I lay in bed anxiously awaiting my mother to come get us, I saw a glimmer of light flicker in from the window. The tiny flicker of light looked like a starburst. I watched as the starburst floated in air. I initially thought my mind was playing tricks on me or that my eyelids had been closed for too long or too tight.

To visualize what I saw, close your eyes tightly in a dark room then open them quickly. If you see speckles floating.... this is what I am referring too. I rubbed my eyes and focused intently on the light. The tiny starburst started to grow. My heart began to beat faster as the light grew into a large, blinding, oblong, glowing presence. Inside the light I saw a figure of a person beckoning me to come to it.

I remember having a fear of losing my voice and not being able to scream if I were ever in danger. So, I hummed silently to myself to test my vocal cords. Once I knew I could make a sound; I screamed and screamed. It seemed as though I screamed for an eternity. Thinking back to that moment, I can only imagine the reaction my younger brother on the bottom bunk had to this blood curdling screaming.

My parents were separated at the time. But my father had spent the night; maybe because this would have been our first Christmas that we could remember without him. My father tells me that he remembers hearing me scream. He ran into the room to see what the problem was. In the act of rushing to our room, my father gashed his knee open. I believe he still has the scar to this day. I remember him coming into the room grabbing me from the top bunk to see if I was okay. I began screaming, "I saw Jesus!"

Needless to say the entire family was up at this point. I remember us going into the living room to open presents. I was not focused on the presents. I was still unnerved about what had just happened. I was not looking forward to going back to bed. It was in the wee hours of the morning and we usually went back to bed after opening Christmas presents.

I do remember one toy I received that Christmas. It was a life-sized Barbie doll head designed for little girls to practice their cosmetology skills. I rarely played with that doll head. I believe it was a reminder of that fateful night for me. In my mind the doll head was haunted. But that is another story.

After opening presents, as I feared, we were told to go back to bed. Once again I was inconsolable. My parents told me to sleep on the bottom bunk with my brother and they would leave the lights on so that I would not be scared. That was the first time I can recall staying up all night.

I remember the lights being on but the thing I remember most was the shadow on the wall that was waving goodbye to me. I was terrified. The first sight I saw that night was beckoning me to come; now the last sight is waving goodbye. However, this time I didn't scream. I just watched the shadow waving. I didn't scream because as I stated before, I have always been a very rational person. I had sense enough to know if I screamed either my mother was going to be very angry or my whole family would think I was crazy.

The next day was Christmas. I remember us making rounds to visit various family members. My nerves were still bad from the night before. I didn't want my parents to tell other family members about the incident, but they did. So part of our family folklore is 'Shuanta once saw Jesus'.

I believe most of my family believes I saw something that night. My mother's take on it was that it was a very hard time in our family's life. Maybe a bad spirit had infiltrated our lives. The figure was calling me to come to it. I remember an impulse came over my body; I almost gave in to go to the figure. My first instinct was to walk out from the top bunk into mid-air, not to climb down the ladder. I am sure that would have ended in some sort of injury. Some of my family members think a friendly spirit visited me.

Maybe it was a "friendly ghost." When I had the urge to go towards the figure, I remember a calm and peaceful feeling. And, I am sure some of my family thinks I am crazy. Despite what family members think, I know I saw something out of the ordinary that night. I have even had a few visits from "beyond" throughout my lifetime. And to this day, I cannot fall asleep in a dark room.

26. MISSED OPPORTUNITIES
By Bobby Broadway

There's always been a time in my life that opportunity came knocking but for unknown reasons within myself, I choose not to answer. I try to reflect back as far as I can to find out where this all started. It always seems to stop at January 10, 1972. I was a senior in high school, working a part-time job and nervously waiting to become a father at age seventeen.

This date, January 10, 1972 changed my entire life, completely. This was the day my oldest brother, Daniel Lee Broadway Jr. aka Denny was taken from me and my family. As the years have passed on, I feel I have built a wall of protection to prevent anyone from entering into my inner soul.

These ongoing changes have caused me a lot of missed opportunities in my life. Some of the missed opportunities have been: being a better son, husband, father, brother, grandfather and friend.

I feel to this day all of these opportunities I have missed are causing me to be misunderstood, health problems and happiness in my life. In closing, I must say I hope and pray this opportunity in life has not yet given up on me.

27. FASCINATION WITH OBITUARIES
By Marie Broadway Toms

Following in the footsteps of many of my relatives, I became fascinated with reading and studying obituaries. When I was asked to put together booklets for three family reunions during the early 1990's, I began collecting a huge binder full of obituaries.

I have acquired many hints from obituaries and death certificates. After reading them, I am able to expedite my research with family interviews, community cemeteries, and the website, Ancestry.com. Additional tools used to research and assemble family trees, photo booklets, and genealogy books are photo albums, Facebook.com, email campaigns, family tree software programs, and MyHeritage.com.

Eugene Broadway created and maintains the "Broadway" family tree on Ancestry.com and it has been a tremendous tool for the family. Once all the facts are gathered and documented, Eugene places the information on the tree; it is the best source the family has ever had.

Never in my wildest dreams did I know I was starting the journey to prepare me to write the "Peppers' Legacy" and "Broadway Generations" books. Since I don't live in the state where I grew up, Arkansas, my family continues to keep me informed of family deaths.

I also use the Social Security Death Index (SSDI) database of people which began about 1962. The first SS-5s forms were used in late 1936. The Social Security Administration has some records before 1936, a few more between 1940 through 1961, and the records are plentiful after 1961. (Beine, 2004-2011)

28. FOUND GREAT GRANDPA MARSHALL'S GRAVE IN CHICAGO
By Jerome Turner

Anxiously accepting the assignment to locate and verify the resting place of some of our Broadway family members in Chicago, Illinois; I began planning my trip there. My visit was to the Lincoln cemetery on the south side of Chicago.

On Friday, September 30, 2011, I journeyed to Lincoln cemetery. It was a windy and misty day. It had rained all week with winds at thirty to forty miles per hour. I traveled approximately twenty miles from my house to the cemetery. My mission was to search for our Broadway relatives.

Arriving there about 10:30 a.m., I was to meet with the funeral director at 11:00 a.m., but he was not there yet. I was early. So, I start talking with a receptionist and asked her if she had a listing of any Broadways burials that were in Lincoln Cemetery. At first, she seemed to be a little hesitate, but then she pulled out a list of name cards with all these Broadways, it had to be over twenty names. I asked her if I could copy the names and she told me I could. (Personnel, 2011)

As I started to go through the cards and see the names, I felt like I was going into a trance, spaced out or going off into orbit, just like going into another world. I thought, "We just had the Broadway Family Reunion last year during 2010." We had collected a lot of old photos; thanks to cousins Mary, Lolita, Jewell and many others. What was happening in my mind? What was I experiencing? I was able to put a face with the names on the burial cards. The adage "A picture speaks a thousand words" is true. It was like an out-of-body experience; it was like I was connecting with my kinfolks whom I had never met. Even though, they were deceased; I was still connecting.

Some had died many years before I was born. To see my Great^2 Grandfather Marshall Broadway's burial card which stated he died at Cook County Hospital, the same hospital that I was born at twenty-eight years later. I was feeling connected.

Then to see some of my great uncles: John and Morris plus their wives and some of John's children and cousins were buried there. None of those close family members had I met. I lived in Chicago all of my life and did not know that other family members were so close.

Additionally, some of our cousins who are also buried at Lincoln Cemetery are Horner and Horner Jr.; Alfred and Alfred Jr.; Josephine; Helen; Jean; Alice and others. Grandpa Sam Broadway's brother, Nathaniel Broadway, is buried at Lincoln Cemetery. Additionally, after collecting and seeing so many family pictures, I could identify them and somewhat identify their personalities.

I was trying to write as much information down as I could, but here comes the funeral director through the door. Awe shucks, it's about 11:00 a.m. and he is going to take me to the gravesites that I called him about. I wasn't ready to go; because I hadn't finished going through the cards. But I had to keep my appointment.

The funeral director and I got in his car; he took me where John, Morris, and their wives are buried. Then he took me to the spot where our Great^2 Grandfather Marshall Broadway is buried which is a short distance from his two sons, John and Morris.

Our Great[2] Grandfather Marshall doesn't have a headstone; he was buried in Lincoln Cemetery in 1926. I placed an America flag in the spot for now. I would like to go back and finish looking through those burial cards and visit more gravesites; but on my first visit, I did not expect to make such a tremendous find—our Broadway relatives.

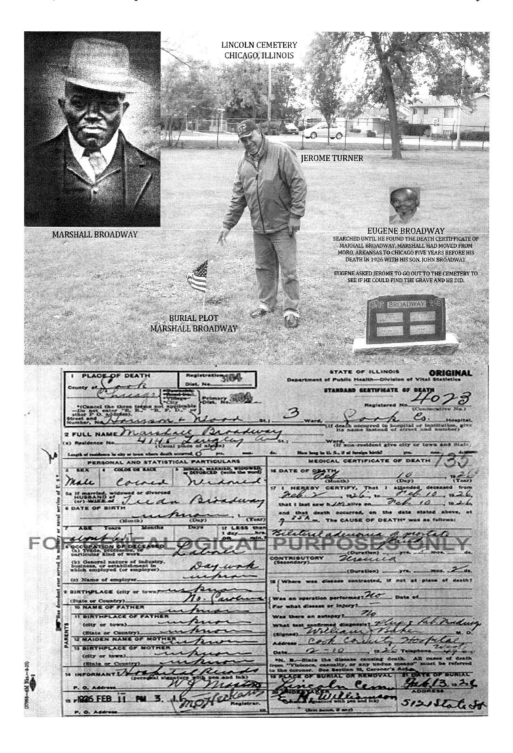

LINCOLN CEMETERY
CHICAGO, ILLINOIS

JEROME TURNER

MARSHALL BROADWAY

EUGENE BROADWAY
SEARCHED UNTIL HE FOUND THE DEATH CERTIFICATE OF MARHALL BROADWAY. MARSHALL HAD MOVED FROM MORO, ARKANSAS TO CHICAGO FIVE YEARS BEFORE HIS DEATH IN 1926 WITH HIS SON, JOHN BROADWAY.

EUGENE ASKED JEROME TO GO OUT TO THE CEMETERY TO SEE IF HE COULD FIND THE GRAVE AND HE DID.

BURIAL PLOT
MARSHALL BROADWAY

After thanking all the cemetery staff, I started my journey back home. I realized my mother Fleecy Mae Broadway – Turner and four of my brothers (Conel, Dwayne, Keith and Kevin) and my dad DJ Turner were less than three miles away at another cemetery, Restville Cemetery in Alsip, Illinois.

Additionally, my grandfather Sam Broadway is buried in the same cemetery. So I stopped by there to place flowers at their gravesites as well. As I stood gazing in the clear blue skies, I began sending up prayers to our heavenly Father that my family be comforted and be at peace.

As I left the cemetery to get ready for work, it felt like I had just left a funeral or that I was in mourning for my loved ones. I didn't bother to turn the radio on; I didn't want to listen to any music at all. My thoughts were all about my family. I was thinking about all the good times we had shared and the joy that my other family members had shared.

Always cherish your family. Keep fond memories of one another on the forefront of your mind. We may never know just how much history has been buried with our loved ones. We must pass as much history on to our children and their children as we possibly can. This is our Broadway family lineage.

29. THE AFRICAN-AMERICAN RACE
By Olaf Tweedie

This is the way Olaf saw it as a young man. He decided to tell the story in a poem.

The African-American race
has been laughed at and looked upon with distaste.
We've been raped, abused and considered human waste.
We've been beaten, murdered and even spit in the face.
But through it all, we stood proud and tall with grace.

Our journey begins the day we start to crawl,
and from that day on we're like a concrete wall---
stubborn and refuse to fall.

We were shipped to faraway places
and forced to live with unfamiliar faces.
They made us work in fields in our bare feet,
then tossed us the parts of the pigs they refused to eat,
not knowing that chitterlings were a treat.
But through it all we stood proud and tall with grace.

It was our women they loved best,
waking them up and disturbing their rest.
And we wonder why our women don't take no mess.

In 1793, Eli Whitney invented the cotton gin.
Years later our race began to win.
We went from living in shacks
to leaning in Cadillacs.

They thought we were people without knowledge.
Boy, did we show them when we started attending college.
But through it all we stood proud and tall with grace.

We roared through the 1900's like a clap of thunder,
showing off our skills, our talents and making the White folks wonder.
Are these the people we kept in captivity for so long?
But in their eyes, they could see no wrong.
Look at us now; we are running the nation,
and making fun of White folks on our own TV station.

So, my brothers and sisters, be all you can be.
Don't be afraid to share your testimony.
Remember we're the mighty African-American race,
and we will always stand proud and tall with grace.

30. CLOSER TO HEAVEN OR HELL - CHOPPING COTTON IN ARKANSAS
By Marie Broadway Toms

Chopping cotton was manual labor and Dr. Ivan R. Vernon tells it like it was. His article took me back to the days when I was chopping cotton. The weather was hot, dry, and dusty. The women especially looked 'pretty bad' with scarves, hats, and long loose fitting clothing to keep from getting sun burned or so dusty. De-weeding was a tedious job with the Bermuda grass being the hardest to get rid of. See a picture of what women looked like while chopping cotton. (Teske).

During May or June, many choppers glided across the field eliminating the extra seedlings and removing any weeds that had sprouted along with the cotton. Hoeing, chopping motion with a long-handled field hoe, was the second step to remove grass (Careless and Jimson) and broad-leafed weeds (Crab, Nut and Johnson) that had sprung up in the rows along with the cotton. Additionally, the only tools needed for chopping cotton was the long wood-handled, goose-neck hoe and a metal file.

A short school year was arranged around the cotton growth cycle. This called for school instruction only during winter and mid-summer. The children were in school only four or five months per year. Even during these periods, many families needed

their children to work even more by pulling cotton remnants off stalks after the regular harvest ended or de-weed the crop during the summer. (Vernon)

During the 1940s through 60s, the wages were $2.00 -$4.00 per day. During the later years, planters were trying chemicals to keep the weeds from growing. Then during recent years, farmers were chopping cotton again and paying approximately $100 per day.

ORIGINAL PAINTING BY DANNY BROADWAY

Even though it was thought that the cotton fields were closer to hell than heaven, I was born-again in the cotton field. A person ministered to me by the name of Minnie Miller. She was a neighbor and was hired to pick cotton for my Dad.

So for me, I became closer to heaven than hell. Pictured above is a piece of artwork named "Marie" which was painted by my cousin, Danny Broadway, a nationally renowned artist. Eugene Broadway was so struck by my love for my past experiences involving cotton that he commissioned Danny to create a painting "Marie."

31. THE COLOR OF OUR SKIN
By Dennis Jerome Turner

The experiences growing up in the North (Chicago, IL) gave my family many opportunities to deal with racial adversities.

My parents, DJ Turner and Fleecy Mae Broadway–Turner were from the South (Brinkley and Moro, Arkansas). They came to Chicago in the early 1950's for a better life. They sought decent wages for their labor unlike the South, where they had to work long hours in the fields for 'little to nothing'.

North Migration. When southerners first started migrating north, they were told that jobs were plentiful. But hear this, racism came along with it and showed discrimination regularly. They were allowed to ride the buses, but still had to go to the back of the bus for their seats. It was the same with the restaurants. African Americans were not served at the White restaurants; certain neighborhoods didn't allow African Americans to live in them nor could they be caught in a White neighborhood.

Home. I was born in 1954, one year before the biggest Civil Rights Bus Boycott in United States' history. Being born in that era, I had no idea what I would be facing in this society. I remember being a kid about six years old who lived at 3333 West Fulton Street on the Westside of Chicago in a second floor apartment.

We were happy kids at that time; it was four brothers: my older brother Conel, Dwayne (Peewee), Michael (Bay Bay) and myself. We didn't have a lot. I remember before we could afford a color TV in our household, we made our own color TV by putting plastic color paper on the front of the TV.

We put green at the bottom, red in the middle, blue at the top and with all that, we had a color TV, which at that time it was pretty cool. My brothers and I used to play baseball a lot in front of the house using the front porch steps for the strike zone.

This game was called 'strike em out'. We would use a hard rubber ball and bat. The ball was thrown as hard as one could 'strike em out'. This was so much fun. We would play marbles, dig a hole, draw a big circle around the hole and shoot marbles against each other.

I would always have a pocket full of marbles when I went in the house. We were in our own little world not knowing what it was like to be a person of color out in that mixed up world of the Civil Right era.

By this time I am about eight years old; I was in love with collecting baseball cards. I loved the bubble gum that came inside. Man, I was a huge collector. In order to support my addiction to baseball cards, I had to hustle pop bottles to get refunds from the empty bottles.

Our next-door neighbor was an old White lady that never left the neighborhood. Her name was Mrs. Albright; I would do chores for her. I did things like, go to the store, help with her groceries and of course, take her empty bottles to support my habit. She would always give me a quarter; I would spend it all on the baseball cards.

I really cared for Mrs. Albright. I never looked at Mrs. Albright as a White person; I just looked at her as being an old lady. I thought all people were like her, friendly, polite and harmless regardless of the color of their skin.

She was the first White person I really knew, not to mention my schoolteachers. When Mrs. Albright passed away, I was deeply saddened. I felt I lost a dear friend. Shortly after that, Mom and Dad decided it was time to get a bigger place to live.

White Flight. We were now a family of eight, actually nine because our Uncle Buck lived with us and moved along with us. Two of my younger brothers, Peewee, Bay-Bay, and I were really hurt by the move. We didn't want to leave all our friends.

We cried and carried on so badly that Mom and Dad had to bring us back to the old neighborhood to spend a couple of days with our friends to calm us down. This was 1965 and I was eleven years old. The house Mom and Dad bought was a nice two family flat at 4628 West Adams Street in an all White area with the exception of two other Black families.

We were the third Black family to move there. So now, the old world I was accustomed to is nonexistent; I was in a whole new world. This meant trying to make new friends. At first everything seemed like it was going to be all right, some of the White kids even gave us a helping hand moving in.

Then suddenly, I noticed a strange change in some of their behaviors, not wanting to play with us and moving out of the neighborhood. Then one day, I realized it was something much bigger than I thought, it was racism, my first experience with it. Someone or a group of people had painted in big green letters on a real big tree in the front of our house the word NIGGERS. My first thought was "why" what did we do?

My parents informed us not to worry about it. Not knowing they had probably heard this or seen this type of stuff before in the South. During 1965, it was truly an experience. President John F. Kennedy was killed; that hurt as well. Still, I really wasn't angry toward White people. In 1968, a lot of things happened: Martin Luther King was assassinated by a White man. I was a top newspaper boy who won a trip to New York. My boss, Steve, was White who was very friendly and helpful.

Recognized Racism. Mom got me a job working at the Pick Congress Hotel as a busboy at the age of fourteen. While working there, I learned a lot about other races and all of them weren't as bad as it appeared.

Things changed a little bit by my first year in high school. We sometimes were chased away by White students because we were not welcome there. As time went on and I became older, I could recognize racism. For, it exposed itself to me many times in our society.

Those events caused me to rebel against racism. In the late Seventies and early Eighties, I saw a change in how I looked at racism. I did not believe that all Whites hated Black people nor were they all racist. As a matter of fact, a couple of my close friends were White.

In 1980, I got married to my wonderful wife Gloria. Additionally in 1984, we both obeyed the gospel and were added to the Church of Christ. This really helped me see through racism. I realized those who chose to be racist were really a form of ignorance and that they don't know God. If they did, they would know that God is love and not of hate.

Don't Fear Racism. How can one say that they love God but hate their brother? To this day, I can say that I don't fear racism. I don't look or judge a person by the color of their skin but what I look for in a person is their character and their heart. We have children who married someone of another race. They have children as well and we love them all just the same. Our children are Kanika, Jermaine and Felicia. Kanika has two wonderful daughters, Kaela and Kristian. Our son Jermaine has five wonderful children, Breanna, Jalen, Ashante, Passion and Miangel. Our youngest daughter Felicia has a wonderful son; his name is Oliver Jerome. Jermaine is married to Shacondra and Felicia is married to Louis Newman. We are one happy family. We just hope one day the whole world will see through the window of racism as we have and learn to love one another regardless of their skin color.. *Love, Peace and Happiness*

32. VISIT WITH MARY STATON IN BURNSVILLE, NC
As Told by Mary Staton

Mary Staton is a Black woman from Burnsville, North Carolina who lives with her family not far from the slave graveyard. Eugene telephoned and asked if he could talk with her about North Carolina's Broadways.

Ms. Mary Staton mentioned two grave yards which were all grown up with weeds and vines. One graveyard was near the church and another near the go-cart track.

She directed us to a Ms. Delores Hammond, who is a Broadway and one of the granddaughters of an elder Broadway. "Go see her. She might be able to tell you something." Mary gave detailed directions to Delores' house. She stated she did not know much and she was 73 years old, but too young to remember the 1800s. The older family members had died and her house had burned which caused her to lose all her biblical records.

Mary told us of a White man who started plowing up the graveyard. "I don't think he knew any better," said Mary; but they made him stop disturbing the graveyard. They told him he had to erect a monument with the grave names he plowed up on this big tombstone. So a 10-foot tombstone was erected in honor of the Black peoples' graves that were disturbed.

The cemetery is located near Fairfield Church on the right. There was a write-up in the newspaper about the graves being disturbed.

The interview ended with everyone praising the Lord for such a beautiful day, the interview that took place, and the possibility of finding another branch of our family tree. "That is the best I can do." said Ms. Staton. Eugene took a picture with Ms. Staton and said, "Thank you and good bye."

33. MARSHALL BROADWAY'S DAUGHTER — LESSIE BROADWAY BEASLEY WILSON
As told by Earnest Beasley on January 19, 2011

Adolphus and Lessie Beasley became a couple a long time ago thus giving birth to many children. Elijah Beasley was their youngest child. He was nine years old when his father, Adolphus died on March 25, 1927 in Lee County according to Ancestry.com – Arkansas Death Index, 1914-1950. Elijah grew up and fathered Earnest Beasley who was his oldest child.

"People get the other Earnest Beasley and I mixed up." Two brothers named their kids, Earnest Beasley. One Earnest (Earny B) lives in Moro, Arkansas and the other lives in Little Rock, Arkansas. (Rev. Earnest Beasley at Holy Cross Baptist Church) When Elijah was born in 1924, his mother, Lessie Broadway Beasley, was thirty-eight years old according to Elijah's birth record. Elijah died in 1990.

After my Grandfather, Adolphus died, Grandma Lessie married Sandy Wilson of Moro, Arkansas, who is originally from Mississippi. Sandy helped to raise my Dad, Elijah.

My father, Elijah, who later moved from Arkansas to Pontiac, Michigan, then to Muskegon, Michigan, used to visit with Bobby Lee Broadway Stedman. He would take her fish, sometimes. Another Elijah Beasley of Moro and Little Rock, Arkansas at one time, and now Memphis, Tennessee; He is the son of Clifton and Esther Beasley. Elijah also told me Adolphus was from North Carolina, Tennessee, and then Arkansas. Additionally, he said Adolphus had a brother in Mississippi County in Osceola, Arkansas who used to visit him.

Most recently, family members are buried at the St. Paul Baptist Church Cemetery in Moro, Arkansas. Before that, most of them were buried in Springfield Baptist Church Cemetery.

Incidentally, Adolphus was married before Lessie. According to a Tennessee State Marriage License, Adolphus Beasley was married to Sallie Caldwell on July 31, 1882 in Giles County, Tennessee. It is estimated Adolphus was about thirty-four years old.

According to the Ancestry.com - U.S. General Land Office Records, 1796-1907, Adolphus Beasley was issued 160 acres of land on April 30, 1890 by the State of Arkansas. This record depicts the first time Adolphus purchased land. No record at this time shows he owned land in his original home state of Tennessee.

Then on August 1, 1900, 120 acres of land (S ½ NE ¼ & NE ¼ Sec 5 T 2 N 1E) was purchased for $500 by Adolphus Beasley and Bettie Watson in Moro, Arkansas. One acre was reserved for burial grounds. This information was found on a deed in the Marianna Recorder of Deeds Office, Book 31, and Page 97.

Later an Ancestry.com - Tennessee State Marriage License, 1780-2002 was found for A B Beasley and Bettie Watson. The license is dated July 27, 1904 in Wilson County, Tennessee. Adolphus was then about forty-four years old and was again issued a marriage license.

It was rumored Adolphus had about fifteen children in Tennessee when he came to Arkansas. Sam Broadway told us some of those stories. Sam Broadway was born in 1901 in Moro Arkansas, Springfield settlement and he loved family. He was a walking history book. Oliver, father of Sam Broadway, was a brother of Lessie Beasley; so Lessie Broadway Beasley was an aunt of Sam Broadway.

When Cousin Sam would visit churches like Springfield, St. Paul, or New Hope, he would see and talk with a group of men who were mostly family members; he would always tell stories of how we were kin. He would tease about how good-looking he was and so on. The guys got a kick out of that; he continued all the way up until he couldn't even back up his car when he drove to the churches. We would back his car out of the parking spot and he would get in and go on back home to Garret Grove Community. Cousin Sam was something else; he was a joy to be around.

Adolphus brought two or three children with him from Tennessee. When he married Lessie Broadway, it is believed the four children listed on the 1910 United States Federal Census belonged to his previous wife, Bettie. The children were Corra, Bessie, Mauid, and Maretine Beasley. On this Census, Lessie is about twenty-two and Adolphus is listed as forty to forty-eight, but is believed to be approximately fifty-four.

Lessie was born Julia L. Broadway to her parents, Marshall and Silvia Broadway in Hampton, Lee, Arkansas on October 1887 according to the 1900 U.S. Federal Census. During the 1900 Census, Lessie was twelve years old and living at home. Additionally, Lessie's parents were originally from North Carolina.

During the 1920 Census, Lessie (Lizzie Beazley) was reported as married to Adolphus (Adolphin D Beazley). Lessie was listed as thirty-two years old and Adolphus was listed as sixty-four. Also, seven children were in the household with them.

While being interviewed by Marie Broadway Toms, Earnest Beasley referred her to Ethel Lee Wilson Murray of Oakland, California for additional information. Ethel is the granddaughter of Sandy Wilson who was a husband of Lessie Broadway Beasley Wilson.

34. ETHEL CALLED LESSIE BEASLEY WILSON, GRANDMA
As told by Ethel Lee Wilson Murray of Oakland, CA on January 19, 2011

According to Marie Broadway Toms, Ethel Lee Wilson Murray is an eighty-four year old professional lady with a historical gold mine who lives in Oakland, California. She was born in Blytheville, Arkansas, moved to Hughes, Arkansas, and then moved to Oakland, California in 1964 for high-wage work. "When I got a job, within one day, I was making more than I was making in Arkansas all week. So, I stayed."

Ethel is the daughter of Lula Wilson. Lula's parents are Sandy and Leela (Bessie/Leola Harris Foster) Wilson. Leela was Sandy's first wife. Leela had a brother, "T", who would visit. Additionally, Ethel Lee Wilson is the granddaughter of Sandy Wilson, who was later married to Lessie Broadway Beasley Wilson.

Ethel Lee remembers Lessie's children who would visit. They were Marshall, John (oldest one), Adolph, Opel, Silvia, Willie Mae, Clifton, Elijah, J.D. and Melvin. Ethel Lee also remembers Sandy's children: Florence, Carrie, and Lula.

Lessie Broadway Beasley Wilson is remembered. Ethel was asked if Lessie was buried in St. Paul's cemetery. Ethel said, "No, she was buried in Springfield's cemetery." It was asked, "Are you sure?" and she said "Yes, I know she was." Then she was asked, did she have a tombstone?

"They didn't do tombstones very often back in those days; so I don't know. They just had little things sticking up with the name on the grave. There were grave markers to indicate a grave was there. Eugene Broadway asked, "Was the daughter's name Beth who she lived with in Cotton Plant?" "No," she hesitated and then said, "Her name was Silvia. When you get to be eighty-four years old, you forget."

When Sandy and Leslie were married, did they both have kids from previous marriage? Ethel answered, "Yes. They both had kids and they brought about three to four kids each to the marriage."

"The four kids who were with my grandmother were Silvia, Willie, Elijah and a baby boy, but I can't think of his name right now. And my grandfather had three and their names were Florence, Carrie and Lula."

Then another question and answer session started. Ethel did a very good job answering the questions:

Do you remember the name of Sandy's previous wife?
"Sandy's previous wife's name was Leela. My mother's name was Lula."

Do you know Sandy's birthday?
"My grandfather was in his eighties when he died. He was born in the late 1800's. He died in the 60s." "I got a cousin, Evelena, Sandy Wilson granddaughter, who stayed with them. She might remember more about it than I do. If you could just hold on I'll get her number for you. I'm in a wheelchair but I'll find it."

Did Leslie get sick and have to move to Cotton Plant?

"Yes, she moved with her daughter Silvia. She was a diabetic and they had to amputate her leg. Later, her daughter came to get her and took her back where she lived in Cotton Plant, Arkansas."

Do you remember any Broadway's down in Arkansas?

"I have a cousin who is married to one of the Broadway's in Little Rock, Arkansas. Her name is Lena and she's married to QT Broadway down in Little Rock."

"I used to go to school with some of the Broadways; but that's been so many years ago. We went to school at Motten School until 9th grade. "

Ethel Lee took our numbers and wrote the information down. She noted Eugene lives in Atlanta and Marie lives in St. Louis.

She took Eugene's address to send a picture of Leslie and she said she thought Linda's daughter may have a picture of Sandy.

She was taking notes like a champ. "You sound like such a professional person; I wondered if you worked with computers?" She said, "No dear. But you'll hear from me, Baby. Thank you so much. Good talking to you, love you too."

35. MY GRANDPARENTS: LESSIE BROADWAY BEASLEY WILSON AND SANDY WILSON
As told by Evelena Wilson Jones of Birmingham, Alabama on January 19, 2011

I am Evelena Wilson Jones who was born November 1, 1941 in Moro, Arkansas in the Springfield Community. One had to cross Springfield Lake to get to our house. My Grandfather Sandy did own some land in that area. I am the daughter of Florence Wilson. Florence is the daughter of Sandy and Leela Wilson. Lessie Broadway Beasley became my Grandma.

When Mr. Beasley died, Lessie Broadway Beasley married my Granddaddy, Sandy Wilson. Consequently, once Leela died, Sandy married Lessie. Some of Sandy's kids were still at home and some of Lessie's kids were still at home. They combined families with their children who became sisters and brothers.

Lessie's first husband, Adolphus Beasley, died in 1927 and they had Gretrude (11), John (9), Clifton (7), Adolphice D. (4), Marschell (3), Silvester (1), Melvern (6) according to the 1920 U.S. Federal Census; but according to the 1910 Census, Adolphus and Lessie had the following children: Corra (16), Bessie (14), Mauid (9), and Maretine (2). It is likely the kids in the 1910 Census belong to the wife of Adolphus' previous marriage.

Additionally, before the 1930 U.S. Census, Adolphus and Lessie had given birth to more children: Opel, Silvia, Willie Mae, J.D., Melvin (1920) and Eliah (1924). But when Sandy and Lessie got together, they had no other children. Sandy brought Carrie and Florence, who was Sandy's youngest, to the household. Sandy's daughter, Florence Wilson, stayed with them for a while after Florence's baby girl, Evelena Wilson was born. Lessie helped raise Evelena. As of 2011, Evelena is the only living grandchild who lived in the same household with Sandy and Lessie.

Lessie brought Silvia, Willie Mae, and Elijah, who was her youngest child to the household. When looking through the 1930 Census reports, it was noticed Sandy Wilson filled out a 1930 Census report for the Wilson's address and Lessie filled out a 1930 Census report for the Beasley's address.

Remembering Grandma Lessie as a tall and brown-skinned woman with shoulder length hair is rather accurate because her black-and-white picture shows that to be true. Lessie frequently wore her Sunday hat with a feather on the side. Grandma weighed about 200 pounds and wore long dresses as was the trend back in the day.

Grandma Lessie was sick for a while after cutting her leg on a barbed-wire fence. She was going to the fields while dew was on the ground and the weather caused her injury to get worse. Plus she did not get the proper treatment. It set up an infection. It got worse and worse. They treated her with no success. The man who was treating her was a family member. They called him "Little Doctor" but his name was Tom Martin. He would fix up home remedies to put on her leg. Lessie's leg eventually had to be amputated. They then found she had "sugar"; she was a diabetic. Marshall Beasley, Lessie's son, used to come over every day to give her the diabetic shots.

Grandma Lessie had frequent visits from her children, especially the boys. I don't know any of her brothers or sisters. The only people who came to visit her that I can remember were her kids.

My mom, Florence used to cook and was the homemaker for the family. Since Grandma Lessie couldn't work in the fields any longer, they traded jobs. Florence went to the fields to work and Lessie stayed home with me and became the homemaker.

Snakes were plentiful in Moro, Arkansas. One day when Grandma and I were outside headed toward the garden. I used to push her around in her wheel chair. I had pushed her to the garden where she would gather vegetables for dinner. I think Grandma saw a snake. Grandma jumped a mile high and ran like she had two legs. I have played this over and over in my mind, thinking it was impossible what I saw. But the only thing I could come up with was it happened. She was in another place in the yard after I saw it. What do you think?

Grandma Lessie later moved to Cotton Plant, Arkansas with her daughter, Silvia Beasley Milton. She needed more care. Silvia was named after her grandmother, Silvia Clark Broadway.

When a picture of Marshall and Silvia Broadway was shared with the Broadway family in the 1980s, it came from and was maintained under the loving care of Silvia Beasley Milton.

Lessie died in 1952 and Sandy died in the early 1960's. Lessie was buried in the Springfield Baptist Church cemetery in Moro, Arkansas.

Evelena was told by the interviewers Marie Toms and Eugene Broadway that she seemed to really know her family history. She responded with, "I get all my information from Ethel Lee Wilson Murray. We talk every night into the early mornings until one or two o'clock."

36. GRANDPA OLIVER BROADWAY
As Told by Franklin Delano Miller on January 24, 2011

Oliver Broadway was his name. He was called Grandpa. I didn't know his full name for a long time. He was short like Uncle Sam Broadway but a little stockier. According to the draft registration card of 1942, Oliver was medium height, stout build, brown eyes, and black hair.

From what I can remember, Grandpa didn't work a lot. I don't know if Grandpa was too sick to work or maybe he was just pretending. I don't ever remember him working. I don't ever remember him missing a meal, either. When you are sick, I didn't think you should feel like eating three times a day. But he sure could get to the table fast. He was a big eater. Also, Grandpa loved peaches.

Grandma Dotsey (Mary Broadway) was Oliver's wife at the time. Additionally, Grandma Dotsey was my mother's mom. My mother's name was Fleecy Miller. When Grandpa and Grandma married, it was about their third marriages. I didn't realize Grandma Dotsey was more or less like a professional cook. She used to work for this White guy named Delehay. He had a house where she would go to cook; but Grandma's house would never be too far from his house. The house was located on a rock road immediately pass Chalk Lake Bridge like going to Moro, but one would make that immediate right. The big farm started right there. Delehay's house was about midway between Highway 238 and Highway 79.

I thought Delehay owned all that land and the house was like a plantation. They really weren't plantations; because there weren't many plantations in Arkansas. However, there were a lot of plantations in Mississippi. A lot of Black people owned their own land in Arkansas.

Joe Broadway, John Ed Farmer, another White guy and some others, I don't remember their names worked for Delehay, too. Wherever, Delehay moved, he would help find a place for them to live. Grandma would always get a good house about a block from his house. At first, I didn't understand why Grandma Dotsey always had a nice car and food year round. He bought food for her to cook for him and she was free to take enough for herself. Other folks in the community became very short on food during the winter and Grandma had food year round.

Grandma had a nice house. It would be clean and a big old bed. You would have to jump up to get in bed. Grandpa used to get after me about getting on my knees to say my prayers. I was lazy. I would get down on one knee or no knees.

My belly was full; I just wanted to jump in bed. Grandpa was watching. That's why I say he wasn't that sick. He was watching because I was trying to get away with stuff.

He would say "get on bended knees." I didn't want to get on bended knees. I would be trying to look over there to see if he was asleep. He would be sitting in that chair. I was going to say my prayers but I was going to stand up and say them. Time, I would get ready to get in bed; he would say, "Get back down and get on bended knees."

Was Grandpa Oliver a minister?
"Yes, he supposed to have been a minister. Yes, they called him Rev. Broadway."
So, did you ever hear him preach?
"Nope! Never heard him preach or pray either."
I stayed with Grandma during the summers for a week or so and Mom, Fleecy Miller, and Dad, Oscar "Mann" Miller, would come pick me up.
When the government took that land from Delehay, he moved to West Helena. When Delehay moved from Moro, he took Grandma Dotsey, Joe Broadway, and John Ed Farmer with him to West Helena to help him farm. None of them owned any of that land. I found out later on Delehay was leasing land from the government and we thought Delehay owned all that land. Delehay was basically managing the farm.

Was Grandpa an old man at that time?
"Well, to me they were all old." As a kid, you think everybody is old. Though they weren't too old; Grandma Dotsey would go up town and she would take him (Grandpa) with her. They would go out and party on Saturday night. I think Grandpa had died before Grandma Dotsey moved to West Helena because I don't remember him being down there in West Helena.

I used to go down to Helena and stay with Grandma Dotsey. She stayed near the Mississippi River. When the water would go down, you could see the black top after the water receded. It was a steep hill that would go down to the Mississippi River and Oliver, Joe's son, and I would go down and watch the steam boats. They had some good land and cotton grew really well. Grandma Dotsey would pick cotton sometimes, but most of the time, she would be up there cooking. That is how she made her money year around.

One day Oliver Broadway, Grandpa Oliver's grandson, and I were rolling down the hill and doing really crazy stuff. We would get on top of the hill and roll all the way down to the edge of the Mississippi River. Oliver and I were about the same age. Oliver was older than his sister, JoeElla Broadway. I could swim but I don't know if Oliver could. But those currents were so high, if we fell in, we would have not been able to get out of there.

That was crazy stuff. I wouldn't do that for nothing in the world, now. We put our hands to the side and rolled all the way to the bottom. We were about eleven or twelve years old. I remember Grandma Dotsey was looking for us one time; she was just hollering and screaming for us. We were out someplace doing that crazy stuff. It was really crazy stuff.

Mama would let me and Mardell go down and stay for a week or so with Grandma. I was one of Grandma's picks. Mardell and I both were her picks. We felt Grandma Dotsey liked us because we were light-skinned.

I think Grandma had married Mr. Walter Kibble when she moved to Helena. I remember I was down there in Helena for about a week. At that time, we used to stack hay. Another young boy and I were running around the haystack playing. You know, everybody called me "Brother". He had a nick name, too. So one day, he said, "Man, I get tired of calling you Brother, you ain't my brother." He said, "What's your name?" I said, my name is Franklin D. Miller and the "D" is for Delanor. He said, "Man, don't try to be funny because somebody done told you my name is Franklin D. Miller and you are trying to be funny.'" Naw man, that's my name." He said, "That is my name, too." We had the same name. It was spelled the same and we were born on the same day. We were both born December 15, 1941 with the same name. My Aunt Minnie Broadway, Sam Broadway's wife, named me.

Grandma Dotsey moved back to Garrett Grove into the Little's family old house. The house was back where the side road, next to the Little's new house, led to the big red house back in the woods.

Uncle Sam Broadway, Aunt Cynthia Broadway Burnett and Uncle Green Broadway would visit Grandpa Oliver. I don't remember Oliver owning land. Uncle Joe and John Ed didn't own any land, either. Uncle Sam and Aunt Cynthia/Uncle Eddie owned land. Uncle Eddie used to have a brand new car.

He would have Odell and his brothers push the trailer out to the road; hook up and pull the cotton trailer behind the car then pull it to the gin. His family would pick two bales of cotton per day. Uncle Eddie would come by the house on Highway 238 and be pulling the trailer about ten to fifteen miles per hour.

Sometimes, he would stop and have me drive him to Moro to the gin. I remember Uncle Eddie would turn as red as a coal of fire sometimes. He looked like a White man anyway.

When I was around Uncle Sam and Joe, I was really young and too young to know their business. When I would see something I didn't suppose to see or hear, they would say something like, "Oh no, you didn't see that."

The way I remember Grandpa, he, more or less, just slept away into his death. They had a funeral but I don't remember any details.

Uncle Sam used to have an old Cub tractor. He would plow one row at a time. I would always say that I could plow more field with a mule than Uncle Sam did with his little tractor. Uncle Sam didn't do much work that I can remember either. For a long time, I thought Uncle Sam was my biological uncle. But his father, Oliver was my step-grandfather.

37. GRANDMA DOTSEY
By Marie Broadway Toms

Grandma Dotsey (Mary Broadway) was a step grandma because she was married to Oliver Broadway at one time and helped raise step-sons and a step-daughter. While growing up in the neighborhood and in church, I remember a little about her.

She was still alive when I graduated from high school in 1970. She was a good dresser, wore pretty high-heel shoes, and she shouted a lot in church. So during our family research, I was curious to learn more about her.

By 1910, Mary Byrd was twenty years old and married to a George Byrd who was twenty-eight with a four year-old child named Fleecy Byrd who was born 1906 in Arkansas and an adopted daughter by the name of Minnie Davis who was eight years old. Mary and George lived in Proctor, Crittenden, Arkansas.

Then, Hampton, Lee County, Arkansas is where Mary at twenty-eight is married and renting a place with her husband, Lee R. Abernathy, twenty-nine. Lee is originally from Alabama. Mary may have lived in Alabama for a short time because the 1920 Census said Mary was also from Alabama. Mary's daughter Fleecy Bird, fourteen, is living with them. Fleecy is the step-daughter of Abernathy.

Other events happened in Mary's life and by the 1930 Census, Mary at thirty-nine is found living with her husband, Oliver Broadway fifty-five in Dixon, Monroe County, Arkansas. Living with them was Mary's sister-in-law, Amy Abernathy, eighteen. Oliver Broadway is my great-grandfather and after Grandma Dora died, Mary Abernathy married Oliver Broadway and she became our step-great grandma. Dotsey was a nickname, so the kids called her Grandma Dotsey.

Mary married Walter Kibble who once lived at Route 1, Box 73, Moro, Arkansas in Lee County according to his U.S. World War II Draft Registration Card, April 27, 1942. At that time, Walter was fifty-seven years old and the record stated that he was born March 14, 1885. Walter was light brown complexion, bald, brown eyes, 66 inches tall and weighed approximately 164 pounds. The name of the person who would always know his address was Julius Thomas, Route 1, Moro, Arkansas.

Mary's 1959 Arkansas SS Application identifies her as being Mary Ivory Kibble who was born August 4, 1890 in Bolivar, Mississippi. Her father was Jackson Ivory and her mother was Bettie Jane Robinson. Mary's Social Security Death Index record identifies her as Mary Kibble of Brinkley, Monroe County, Arkansas. She died December 1982.

Lastly, according to her obituary, Mary Kibble's life ended on Wednesday, December 8, 1982 at 1:40 p.m. in Cla-Clif Nursing Home, Brinkley, Arkansas.

She left three step-sons: Sam Broadway of Moro; Green Broadway of Chicago; and Joe Broadway of Brinkley; Two step-daughters: Cynthia Burnett Roberts of Brinkley; and Mrs. Irene Dotson of Detroit, Michigan and a host of other relatives and friends. Her daughter, Fleecie Miller, preceded her in death in 1979.

38. PROUD TO BE A MEMBER OF THE BROADWAY FAMILY
By April Chatwood

My name is April Chatwood. I'm twenty-five years old and the youngest child of Eugene Broadway. A childhood memory, I will never forget is the year I met four of my sisters on my Dad's side, J'hane, Michelle and twins Crystal and Cocoa. I was so excited because for one, I used to see Crystal and Cocoa out all the time but I never knew they were my sisters. So, that day came and we all met.

Of course, I was shy and they were very outspoken except for Michelle. She was pretty, shy and quiet like I was. We met at one of the Broadway family reunions. Since, everything went well with the meet and greet; the idea was brought up that we should spend the summer with our Dad. That made me even more excited. So, here comes the summer. I believe I was about twelve years old and they were fourteen. I think it was only the twins and me who went to spend the summer with our dad. Considering I'd always wanted a twin sister; I thought it would be so cool to spend the summer with my twin sisters. But, oh did that backfire!!

It started off with Crystal and me being the closest because Cocoa was the mean one. Sorry Cocoa, but you were. "LOL" Then they switched on me; Cocoa and I were the closest. Then, the big day came and they both turned against me. "LOL" and there was a big fight in the room we shared. I mean, there were pillows thrown and the whole nine yards. All of this came about because they thought I was getting treated better because I was the youngest. Boy, they did not like that.

Our Dad was a Vietnam Veteran; he did things in an orderly manner, meaning we said our grace together and we ate together. The part I hated the most was no one could be excused from the table until EVERYBODY was finished eating. The reason I hated it, because I ate very, very slow (and I still do "LOL"). They would take it out on me because they would have to sit there and wait!!! A house full of estrogen equaled a house full of bad attitudes. We would fight over whose panties were whose, down to who had the biggest boobs. Keep in mind, we were young and everybody was in an A-cup, if not a training bra.

So being in the house for a while, the idea came up to go to six flags and everybody was excited. So, we woke up that morning to get ready for the big day. And low and behold another fight came because they were mad I had drooled on their pillow. I couldn't win for losing. So we called a truce on that and it was time to get dressed.

We walked in our room and my Dad's wife had our clothes laid out on the bed. The bad part was; she had us all dressing just alike as if we were triplets. I didn't like that at all and neither did they. After going to six flags, we all were starting to bond. I guess the reason for that trip was not only for us to bond and get to know one another but to realize that we were all some strong willed women in the making.

The strong had to fight the strong to get stronger. It was a vacation/trip I will never forget because to this day we are all VERY strong women and that shows how strong and anointed the Broadway blood is. I pray that it continues as new legacies are born. I am proud to be a member of the Broadway Family!!!

39. REMEMBERING AS A TEENAGER
By Danny Broadway

I remember on my sixteen birthday, I asked my father to take me to get my driver's license. He did! I, of course, was excited, young and dumb. He asked me if I had everything I needed. I said yes. We waited in a long line to discover at the end of the line, I forgot my social security card. I felt like such a loser. He was disappointed that I was so forgetful. He said what he had to say and life went on. I'm glad that he took the time to take me. He always had a way of showing up when you wanted him to.

40. THE DAY THAT CHANGED MY LIFE
By Geraldine Broadway

I was twelve years old residing at #9 Richmond in Granite Mountain (the Projects) in 1972. This particular place was in Little Rock, Arkansas on the south end of town. This day I would not wish on anyone. It started out as another regular fun school day. I remember telling the kids at school that I would not be at school the next day, just in jest.

When I got home from school the only people there was my Mom, Danny, Skip, Linda and myself. My mom was on one couch; Danny was asleep. Skip was playing with his electric football set and Linda was in the other room. Well late that evening, I was sitting on the couch doing my homework, right next to the front door.

There was a knock at the door, kind of soft. My sister Linda answered the door and there was a man asking to see our oldest brother Danny. Linda woke Danny up to see the person at the door. After Danny approached the door, he looked out the window and said "It's no one here."

Then something in his mind told him to open the door and look out. As Danny opened the door to look around the corner, I heard a pop (sounded like a fire cracker). Then I heard multiple fire cracker pops as I sat on the couch. I then saw Danny back up; push Mom off the couch and lock the door.

At this time, I saw glass flying everywhere barely missing mama's head. I dropped my homework and started to run into the bedroom along with my Mom. The shooting went on forever; it seems like all was dark. All of our lights were out and the only sound I could hear was Skip making sounds while playing on his football game.

My Mom yelled and asked Skip to check on Danny. Next thing I saw was Skip walking in the room wiping thick blood on his white t-shirt. Skip made a statement saying "Danny has been shot in the head."

Then all you could hear was my Mom yelling, "Call 911!" Linda and I were screaming uncontrollably. After the ambulance made it there, (which they took their time when called to Granite Mountain) Danny was in worse shape. They put him on the stretcher as we followed close behind. While we followed the stretcher, Danny's head fell to one side as though he had died right then.

We ran back in the room until our father (Daniel L. Broadway) and the pastor from our church (Marine Web Williams) showed up. We ended the night in prayer with the pastor and waited on the status on Danny.

The doctor stated that he would be in a vegetated status if my parents allowed him to live. My mother and father decided that would not be the best way for him to live; therefore he departed from our life as we knew and loved him.

My childhood pretty much ceased at this point, because the ten men who shot up our apartment that night was supposed to have been his associates. It really affected the way I would trust people for a long time. It turned out that this horror was based on a lie that was provided by his best friend to the assassins. Danny was innocent in it all, just guilty by association.

41. THE DAY THE EARTH STOOD STILL
By Linda D. Broadway Plummer

My name is Linda D. Broadway. I was born on Dec. 14, 1958 to Lee Esther and Daniel Broadway. I was the sixth child and also the second girl. As far back as I remember, I've always had spiritual encounters. I could see spirits just like I see the living. They are with me everywhere I go. Still even today, I can feel their presence.

I had a very sad day come in my life at the age of thirteen. On January 10, 1972, I was sitting on the couch doing my homework and there was a knock at the door. I got up and asked "Who is it?"

And they replied, "Is Danny here?" I opened the door and it was dark and I said "Wait a moment." I proceeded to go to Danny's room and woke him up. He asked me who was it? I said I don't know. He said "tell them I'll be there in a moment." I went back to the door and fear came over my body; I stood behind the door until he came.

After Danny opened the door, they commenced to shooting at my brother. A spirit had me held and covered with wings and I couldn't move. I could feel the breeze of the bullets. They were so close I thought I was shot. Once Danny fell and hit the floor; I fell and laid right beside him. Then Mama screamed, "Call 911!" When the ambulance arrived, the paramedics came to me first because I was covered in blood. They stripped me of my clothing to make sure I wasn't shot. And as they took Danny out the door on the gurney, he turned over and looked at me with his bloody eyes. This is why I have lived so many years blaming myself for his death.

I got up shaking from head to toe trying to do as I was told. I tried dialing 911. I was too nervous to even hold the phone. I kept hanging up. They would call me right back and pleaded with me not to hang up again and to please stay on the line till the police and ambulance arrived.

From that day forth, I didn't really talk no more, my voice had been taken. And I fully blamed myself for my brother's murder. I held that guilt for twenty years and then one day, I called my brother Gene and told him I was ready.

He came and got me with his three little girls and we went to the cemetery. I had written Danny a poem entitled "Twenty Years Has Passed Me By." Gene videotaped me and took pictures that day; I also shall never forget. I was exactly thirty-three years of age. I was grown with a daughter (Nia) and a son (Nicholas).

I am now fifty-two years old with a husband (Bobby Plummer) and three grandchildren (Jason, Jania and Joylyn). I have much more to tell but I'll just wait for Gene's next book. Since the time that I lost my voice in 1972, I found myself through writing poetry. I continue to write today.

42. THE DRUG KILLER
By Linda Broadway

I was blind, but now I can see
That this particular drug was killing me
I was no longer motivated for future references
Or dedicated to family preferences
I shut myself off into my own shell
Not knowing that it would lead me straight to hell
At first, it made me feel grand as a king
Because it brought me prosperous things
Like money, power and diamond rings
The use of the drug formed me a habit
Which gave me the strength of a rabbit

Always hopping from door to door
Trying to find somewhere to get more
I spent my money; I pawned my rings
Not caring anymore for anything
Then it took me into a state of depression
Making me look at my true confession
Which made me realize that this was not me
I am loving, kind and caring as can be
I want my life back in control
The first place I'll start is renewing my soul
I'm praying for the ones that I've lost
Due to this bad drug cost
I'm taking myself a new route
Where drugs are not "In" but "Out"
This drug is considered as a pleasure high
But it really amounts to ad "Do or Die"
Deal with reality and do not cry
Because things you've done that brought forth the shame
Does not have to continue to be the same

43. THE NIGHT MY BROTHER DIED
By Nathaniel (Skip) Broadway

From what I can recall from off the top of my head, I was in the room next to the front porch when Danny died. If you were facing the house from the street, the room was on the left hand side and the window was covered by a bush. I was playing with my electric football set and when I heard the noise at the time, I was thinking it was fireworks going off. But I learned afterwards, it was gunshots.

After I heard the commotion going on in the living room, I went in there to find my brother lying on the floor in a pool of blood. Someone was holding him, maybe my mother. They asked me to hold him and when I did, he wiped the blood off his face with a rug.

All I remember after that was when my Daddy made it to the house afterwards getting the phone call at his job, the hospital. It became the saddest day of my life.

44. MY BROTHER DANNY BROADWAY
By Eugene Broadway

I was twenty years old and had been in the Marine Corps for two years when we lost him. I'm trying to say in so many words that it is very hard to go back that far and explain how it was from a child's point of view.

170

Danny took his position as being the oldest child in the house as a very important position. As long as I can remember, I was always taller and larger than Danny. I must say to this day, I have never just beat Danny down.

It was something about me being younger than him that he could not ever let me win a fight. If I thought I won, he would make me fight him again. We took a lot of pride in being the older two in the family. We felt responsible for the rest of the family.

Danny had a learning problem and was assigned to Special Education classes where all the rough and tough kids were; he held his own.

In sixth grade, we had a great teacher, Marvin Woods. Mr. Woods took Danny from Special Education classes and put him in his classroom with me. Danny was so proud of being in class with me. He turned into an 'A' and 'B' student.

A lot of people don't know to this day that Danny and his crew were big protectors of me at Central High. He would show up unannounced to make sure everything was okay with me.

I remember once when my brother went to a football game looking for me and got jumped on (beat-up) by five guys. Danny came home with bumps and bruises and told me about the fight. I was somewhat afraid to go and find the guys but I suggested it. He told me he would take care of it.

Within the next two weeks, he hunted them down one by one and beat them up. As I think about it, Danny saved me from lots of trouble; he took the blame. I took up one of his tactics talking fast and insulting to a person to avoid a lot of fights. He taught me to always hit first. My brother did think he was tough and he was. He didn't let too many people in his comfort zone. Inside, he was good as gold. We worried about Danny a lot. We didn't know what he was capable of doing.

Although I was not there; I do know on November 1, 1971, Danny's life changed drastically. His only child Deshondra was born. However, I did talk to him a few times before his death (1/10/1972). He was truly a changed person for the good. He started working a full time job (bicycle factory) and got engaged to marry because he wanted the best in life for his daughter. My brother meant the world to me; he was my best friend.

To this day, our family does not quite know what or why Danny was killed. In 2010 my cousin Jerome Turner and I made a pact to fill the void our older brothers left in our lives. Also in 1976, I named my only son, not Eugene Broadway Jr. but Danny Eugene Broadway in honor of my brother. I love you, Danny, and I miss you very much.

45. THE PAST, PRESENT AND HOPE THE FUTURE
By Mary Booker

I am so thankful for my God, my family and friends that have been in my life and for the seventy plus years to date I have lived. There were ups and downs, sorrow and happiness, many roads of uncertainties, and commitments.

The path I took was chosen and I learned on the way. My bed was lumpy but I laid there and got up. I married, had two sons, went back to school and received my BA/MA degrees. I taught in Chicago; when I divorced, moved to Atlanta, taught and retired here.

I grew up in a small town, Robbins, Illinois – no sidewalks, plenty of mud, snow and floods. I walked to elementary school. We only had one but we were taught. Being the only girl with three brothers did leave me spoiled but not rotten. My parents were loving but strict.

When I went anywhere, my father always said, "Take a dime for the phone, never order any food you cannot pay for and keep gas in the car." All these sayings stayed with me; to this day I still remember and honor what he instilled in me. Growing up was a good time, because my childhood was fun. There were chores to do but they weren't difficult. Others found their chores were too hard for them, but looking back, the chores were preparing us for "what was coming." Most of the time, we played and no one bothered us.

I learned to roller skate in Mr. Witcher's hard floor rink. This was one of our Saturday/Sunday outings. There wasn't much to do in Robbins, when I look back, but it was a lot then. We walked everywhere and almost all the people knew each other.

I met many people along my way, but few good friends. Some friends too numerous to name, but true friends who have been there when I needed them are few: Anner Williams, Velma Elly, Jennifer Ransom, Rosemary Funches, Gracie Allen Brown, Ernestine Roe, Mildred Cheeks Holiday and my Cousin Bill Broadway, Andrea my god-daughter and most recently, my cousin Eugene Broadway.

I have been blessed to travel and the memories can never be replaced. Anner, Penny, Agnes and I traveled by car from Chicago to Vancouver one year; it was a trip to remember. Anner was our guide. Penny and I traveled to Alaska which was another dream of mine.

A classmate of mine, Charles Henry and his wife lives in Anchorage and they took us on a tour. One thing comes to me was when we went to the "ole animal zoo." I mentioned to Charles if a grizzly bear would chase me that I would climb the closest tree. While at the zoo, he pointed out two black grizzly bears resting in a tree; there went that theory.

When I think of the good times, bad ones appear also. So, many good times outweigh the bad. Every year I go home (Robbins), see and greet ole friends and reminisce about the good ole days and laugh until I cry. When I talk about the bad times, I remember my parents who have now gone, my two oldest brothers, also gone.

Did I get a spanking to remember? My father told me to stay close to the house and I did not and when he came looking for me I was elsewhere. Never did that again. I also told my third grade teacher when she asked me to do something that "I was cute and knew it, had big legs and could show them and I wasn't going to do anything."

When I started walking down that dirt road towards my house, I looked up and saw my father and my mother. I knew that my teacher had called.

There weren't many telephones during that time but my father had an ice business and needed the phone. My parents said "Come here, Miss Cutie". When I went to school the next day with bruises from the switch I had to get, my teacher, Ms. Searcy said, "Mary will you do…" Before she could get the words out I told her, "Anything you want me to do I will do it." I only needed those two spankings and the last one taught me well.

46. THE SPIRIT
By Crystal Broadway

We went to visit our father (Eugene Broadway) one year and this is what he said to me. Do you remember when you all came to my house in Georgia for the first time and you and Michelle said you saw that spirit? We looked at each other and then looked at him and said "Heck Yea!" in so many words. Ooh wee, what a day!!!!

My sister Michelle was fifteen and my twin sister Cocoa and I were fourteen when we went to visit our Daddy in Georgia during the summer for the first time. Our Daddy lived in a big beautiful house. We had never seen anything like it in our lives.

It was a big two story house with a big yard. He lived in a very exquisite neighborhood. We used to go to the pool every day and go swimming. It was great until one day.

We were at the house having a fabulous day. (Oh, and just in case you didn't know it, my sisters and I used to sleep in the same bed).

We had a good day but that night when we went to bed, we were lying there and I got into it with both of my sisters. They left me in the room by myself. So, as I was lying there looking at the ceiling, I turned and looked to the side of the bed and there was a spirit there…Yes, you guys, a spirit.

I almost peed on myself but then I stopped and thought, hey girl get a hold on yourself. My momma always said, if it's a bad spirit all you had to do was pray and it would go away.

So you know what I did...... No, I did not get on my knees. I laid there, closed my eyes and started to pray. After I was done, I opened my eyes and looked again. And what do you know? It was still there; so I closed my eyes and went to sleep.

The next morning when I woke up the spirit was gone. So, I immediately got up and apologized to my sisters. I told them what happened. They were like dang! That's crazy; but we went on with our day.

Later that day, our daddy said he had to run into town and we were not to go out of the house for any reason at all. We were like, okay daddy, but being kids you know how it is.

So, we were at the house chilling and my twin sister Cocoa and I got into it with our sister Michelle. So, Michelle went upstairs and she was like, forget ya'll. About thirty minutes later she came running down the stairs yelling. She said to me, did the man you saw have on a purple shirt?

I was like, yes he did. I said how do you know? She said I just saw him. We started to scream and the lights went off. I don't know how that happened. All I know is we were outside when our daddy came home. We got in trouble and we still talk about it to this day. Crazy huh!!!

47. THE TRAUMA SUBSIDES
By Jackie Morrison

It's funny how some life tragedies stick with you for a lifetime. As time goes by, they transform into funny stories and the trauma subsides:

I vividly remember the beginning of the school year when my sisters and I were so excited about starting school after a long hard and laborious summer. We had saved our earnings from our summer labor in the fields and all purchased a huge array of fashionable clothes for the upcoming year (beginning fifth grade for me).

After the second day of school, we arrived home on the school bus and were preparing to hop off the bus and make a mad dash into our relatively new brick house - only to find that our brick house was no longer there but was replaced with fire and ashes.

Although, most of my sisters stood in disbelief and confusion as to how our family valuables and belongings would be restored, my oldest sister literally fainted. We later learned that she fainted due to the loss of a new wardrobe and not the loss of our homestead. We now reminisce and laugh about her reaction to our unfortunate loss.

48. DATING STRATEGY
By Jackie Morrison

Growing up in Arkansas, my Mom and Dad were quick to enforce old traditions, especially when it came to dating. From my oldest sister to my youngest, upon approaching the appropriate dating age, dating was only allowed as long as a younger sister could tag along....LOL. This tradition continued for as long as I could remember.

49. A TREE'S VALUE
As Told By Parlee Broadway on July 23, 2010

An old pine tree located on the right front of my house was planted by my husband's grandmother, Martha Miller. Grandma Martha transplanted the tree from the woods on the old Miller place. The house that sat next to the tree burned long ago.

Around 1954, Lenner and Parlee Broadway built their first home next to that tree. Every year the tree was adorned with Christmas lights. The house set at an intersection so that all could see the blinking lights during the Christmas season. It was a tradition in our family to decorate the living tree.

The tree escaped its death on a few occasions. The tree was attacked by insects and nearly died. I remember Lenner treated the tree with some type of medicine. It was administered to the roots of the tree. The tree suffered a heat stroke and almost burned to death. It was watered back to health. We never needed to chop down a tree for Christmas, but we did. We would always place one inside, too. Lenner and I loved Christmas, just as well, as the children.

Lenner took a class on planting and taking care of trees. He planted pecan trees for nuts and also for shade. Former neighborhood folks would stop by from year to year and gather under that big pecan tree on the left side of the house.

It has been an inviting site on a summer hot day to stop and grab a seat on the picnic bench under that tree. Every other year, it produces a crop of pecans that could be marketed. Sometimes, they are good; sometimes they are not so good.

Cedar trees were planted for shade, decoration and as a windbreak. The family car would be parked near a tree in the hot summer afternoons to keep the car's interior from fading and becoming too hot. It was also a thing to do. You would see many properties on the Arkansas roads surrounded by cedar trees. Additionally, the purpose of the windbreak was to slow the wind down and protect the house.

I also planted cherry and plum trees for the fruit. They were delicate trees. They would produce occasionally. After Lenner died and when the trees got sick, I became the doctor. Not only did Lenner plant trees but he used to log. Logging is the process in which certain trees are cut down for timber. Lenner, of course, was logging during the late 50s and 60s as a way to make money during the non-harvesting season. The logging was done on family members' land that had not been cleared.

The work was difficult, dangerous and low-paying but it gave us some income. It took a lot of strength to log. I remember seeing the trucks with loads of huge logs being taken to the mills in Wheatley, Arkansas.

I, also, remember Lenner talking about the dangers. He used to work a lot in the woods barefoot with the chance of stepping on anything that may have been hidden under the leaves in the woods. He said he was a little more careless during those times.

I can also imagine the toll that the lifting, swinging the axe and the vibration of the chainsaw had on his body. I thought that was masculinity at its best. As Lenner grew older, he suffered from arthritis in the shoulders and more.

The trees that were logged were the ones that were in demand by the mill. According to the agriculture guys, trees sold for wood. Tons, cords, cubits and thousand-board-feet are common measurements used to buy and sell trees. I did not understand that. Lenner could barely read but he was great at figuring that stuff.

Trees really could be worth some money. Several factors affect the value of trees. These factors include current markets, the kind of trees, their quality and size. High quality trees are straight tall trees with few branches on the lower portion of the tree.

Defects and bends in the truck can reduce the value of the tree. Generally, one would have to log an assortment of thirty trees (pulpwood, hardwood, red oak, white oak) from an acre of land to earn about $2,300.

All trees are either hardwood or softwood. Hardwood species lose their leaves and their wood is hard. Softwood species produce cones and their wood is softer. Softwoods are also referred to as resinous trees because of their thick sap (resin) that keeps them green all year long.

Every part of the tree is useful: the leaves, roots, wood, and bark! Trees provide food, clothing, and shelter. They are also sources of energy, medication, detergents, cosmetics, and countless other products.

50. VALUE OF WORKING HARD
By Parlee Peppers Broadway

When I was at home, we never had a job like you guys have now. But most of the time, we worked on the farm; it was eleven kids in the family and people knew we were good workers. So much so, they would come by our house and say to us that they wanted to hire us for a day because they wanted to get a good bale of cotton or finish a certain crop. They knew we were a large group and hard workers and we could get it done. When all of us were at home, we could pick two bales of cotton a day. The Peppers family worked for some of the White folks who needed us to get things done quickly. We also worked for Ocie Broadway, a lot. He used to hire us to pick cotton and to chop cotton, too. He would hire the whole family, all but Mama and Daddy, Minnie and Madison Peppers.

Anyone who hired us knew when the heat was hot; they didn't have to stand over us and watch. We would do a good-days-worth of work for good-pay. After working, if we needed furniture, Mom would figure out how much we needed to work to get it. Sometimes, we had to combine the money to get it.

Yes, we worked for Ocie Broadway a lot of times. He would tell us, "If you come and work for me during the summertime, I will take you all to the revival and the baptism at Mac Nella Lake near Aubrey." It was a big affair; seemed like we were going to some kind of town or something; it would be so many people there.

We had good revivals in the summertime. We belonged to Mt. Moriah Baptist Church. We knew we had to ride on the back of the truck; it was so many of us, we didn't mine. We would have a free ride; it was a joy to us. We didn't have a car at that time.

Finally, Mama got us to raise this little crop. Mom rented some land from Mr. Cooder Smith, a White guy. We did the work of chopping the cotton and picking the cotton but he furnished the other part: cotton seeds and the tools to farm.

The agreement was that Mr. Smith made half-and-half. We cleared some money from it; my brothers wanted a car so bad. Mom said to us, your brothers want a car real bad. You need to lump your money together to get the car.

The car cost $1,000. We did it; but we did not like it so well because it was shorting us from getting our clothing that we really wanted. However, the money left was divided among the girls who wanted clothing.

When they first got the money together to get a car, they did not know how to pick a car. So they asked Duke Broadway, a person who knew about cars, to go with them over to Memphis to help pick a good car. He went to Memphis with them and helped them pick a 1939 black Chevrolet.

It was really pretty. Most of the time in those days, the car colors were black or white, even the clothing we wore were basic colors. The dealership didn't have all the colors we have now-a-days.

It was the family's first car but the brothers called it their car. The boys wanted the car to go out at their convenience. None of my brothers knew how to drive but all of them learned how to drive with that car.

The brothers got along well with the car but we never got a chance to ride in it; at least not that much because the boys always had some place to go. Furthermore, it wasn't room for us to ride. Yes, we sacrificed for the brothers through Mom.

Truly, if it wasn't for Mom, we probably wouldn't have done it. We had a large family, five girls and six brothers. They took care of it and kept it a long time.

Dad didn't worry about a car; he still had his mule and wagon. When we went to church, our church was close by, so we walked.

Of course, when Dad went to church, he would hook up the mule and wagon and drive, but all the time he didn't go. So you see, we set our goals, worked hard, and got some of the things we wanted back in the day.

51. THE MAN, LENNER BROADWAY
As told by Frank Miller

George Washington Carver High School was my school. I left Arkansas for Chicago, Illinois in 1961. I went to AM&N State for a while. I have known Parlee Broadway for a long time. I remember her when Lenner used to visit her before they got married. I would tag along with Lenner when he would go to date her. The Peppers lived in the Oak Forest Community off of Highway 79.

Marie asked, "What was dating like in those days?" I said, "I was too little to know." I just tagged along with Lenner a lot. I tagged along because Lenner wanted me to play center field for him and I was his little cousin. My father, Mane Miller, and Lenner's mother, Minnie Miller Broadway were brother and sister. I used to be at church and I would look out the window and see him and ask if I could ride along.

Lenner taught me how to play baseball. He and I used to go to the movies during the week and that was unheard of. We used to go up to Brinkley, Arkansas and eat ice cream. Shuhhh, we used to hang a lot. Marie asked, "Was he driving?" I answered, "Yes." Lenner had that old white Ford truck that he bought from Billy Gordon, a White guy that he used to work for and with.

I said "work with" because Billy treated Lenner like a friend. The two of them had a long and good relationship. When Lenner was working for him, Lenner could do just about whatever he wanted. Mind you, Lenner was a good worker. He was a hard worker, too. Then Lenner started renting and farming other people's land. He continued to do that along with owning a little land.

Lenner farmed Rev. Little's land. He used to cut logs. I used to be with him. Lenner had a chain saw and everybody else used manual chain saws. Lenner Broadway loved technology and gadgets. He loved quality things.

52. GRANDBABY
As Told by Ms. Kirstein Cheron Mosley Broadway

On February 19th, 1978 at the Baptist Hospital in Little Rock, Arkansas, Ms. Kirstein Cheron Mosley Broadway was born to the proud parents of the late Mr. Calvin Broadway and Ms. Rosemary Mosley. Kirstein, whose name means "The Anointed One", was named by her Aunt Carol Johnson (mother's sister). Although a Little Rock native, Kirstein grew up in a small town not too far away called Monroe, Arkansas where she was raised by her grandparents (her mother's parents)

The Late Rev. Wornester Mosley & Mrs. Margaret Mosley. Often times she was also raised by her grandmother The Late Mrs. Eula Wiggins Broadway who lived in the neighboring town of Moro, Arkansas. Growing up, Kirstein preferred to be called by her middle name "Cheron" as most family members know her by best. Her grandparents gave her strong upbringings in the church (Macedonia M.B. Church) as she confessed to Christ at the age of thirteen.

Kirstein was known as the overall "grandbaby" and recalls having the strongest and deepest love for them and at times admits she may have even been spoiled. As a young teen, Kirstein remembers very well the passing of her grandmother Eula. It was during the celebration of Grandma Eula when Kirstein was first united with her lost connection of the Broadway Family.

She remembers being embraced with open arms with relatives that she had only heard about and never met. It was truly a bittersweet memory as she may have lost one, but gained many more. Kirstein has other Broadway siblings: Corey, Jameel, Kamal (brothers) and one sister Chastity.

She attended school kindergarten through twelfth grade in the Clarendon School District, and graduated from Clarendon High School in 1996. Shortly after graduating from high school, she moved to Memphis, Tennessee which is where her mother resided. In the fall of 1996, she pursued her education even farther and attended an HBCU (Historically Black College) by the name of LeMoyne-Owen College in Memphis, Tennessee.

Her first intentional studies were Biology as she wanted to be an Optometrist until she discovered her true passion of Business MIS (Management Information Systems). While in college, she was heavily active as a Student Ambassador, Pre-Alumni Council, Student Government, Krimson Kourts, Inc., and a plethora of other student organizations. Despite being known as the quiet and shy one, she quickly grew out of that phase and became a very social and networked on many levels. She quickly found her other hidden passion of planning and coordinating events.

Living in Memphis, Tennessee she was always exposed to our African American history/culture as she is a member of NAACP and always supported functions of the Civil Rights Museum. In researching and finding out more about not only about our cultures, she dug deep and start researching more about her family history and cultures.

She has always been one that was a seeker of knowledge and advocate of truth; therefore she never closed her eyes on information. Even though she was raised up and taught the early teachings of being a Christian as her religious faith, she was also aware and accepted the fact that her family history also was of Islamic teachings.

She simply adored her uncle, The Late Eugene Ali (Broadway) Al-Ugdah, as he was also like a father to her. He always gave her great words of wisdom and told her that she was always loved. Kirstein was a member of New Hope Baptist Church in Memphis, Tennessee as she will follow her Christian faiths and beliefs; however she would often time visit the mosque of Masjid Al-Mu'minun where one of her best college girlfriends' father was the Imam (preacher) there.

There isn't anything that Kirstein doesn't touch and not give it her all with either being heavily active or dedicated to it. In November 2003, Kirstein joined the Fraternal Order of Eastern Star, (Noah Boyd Memorial Chapter #106)Prince Hall Affiliation in which she later elevated into other houses of the beautiful order such as the Heroines of Jericho (Eureka Court #19), Heroines of Templars Crusade (Wolverine Guild #3), & Daughters of Isis (Moolah Court #22). Once again, she keeps walking in the footsteps of her family legacy as many of her past ancestors on her fathers and mothers side were members.

Kirstein had the habit of sometimes humming to herself the tune of "This Little Light of Mine...I'm Going to Let It Shine" as a way of displaying happiness. She will admit all days were not always happy, especially in the year of 2008. Kirstein recalls receiving a phone call on February 20th, 2008 from her sister Chastity informing her of the passing of her father Calvin Broadway.

Being the big sister, she had to stay strong and keep her fellow siblings and cousins uplifted. It was months later that year that the family got hit hard again with the passing of her uncle Eugene Ali. Eugene Ali's wife Jacquelyn (Green) Broadway preceded him in death, however they had three children: Jacquetta, Amber, & Quadir. It was on this day that all siblings and cousins stated that they must continue to keep the Broadway legacy ongoing and make our family trailblazers proud.

They recalled going back to the old little house of Grandma Eula's in Moro, Arkansas which still stood in tact with the exception of various parts that had weathered away through the years.

September 15, 2009, Kirstein moved from Memphis, Tennessee to Atlanta, Georgia for the purpose of seeking and advancing her career. She was always informed that she had relatives in the area but had never gotten a chance to know who they were. In November 2010, Kirstein traveled to Little Rock, Arkansas to visit family for the Thanksgiving holiday. While visiting, she ran into her cousin by the name of Earnest Beasley. He informed her of the names and how to contact relatives in Georgia.

In the age of technology that we live in, Kirstein quickly found a cousin also by the name of Eugene Broadway. Eugene and his wife Shianne met Kirstein and embraced her with open arms. Kirstein was so elated in meeting them. They were very knowledgeable of the family history that had been traced back to the original plantation in North Carolina of the family's descendants, Marshall and Silvia Broadway.

As she was enlightened on her family history, it gave her more insight on things and the drive to continue assisting her cousin Eugene with findings that at the time were missing pieces to the puzzle. Eugene gave her several projects that have been accomplished including the story you have just read "Grandbaby."

53. MY DADDY KNOWS EVERYBODY
By Michelle Broadway

Throughout my childhood, I have very few memories that I share with just me and a parent. Being a child that came from having so many siblings, most of my memories are shared.

Well I have one particular memory that every time I recall in my mind, I have to chuckle. This memory I share with my father, Eugene Broadway.

Now in order for you to find this story as funny as I do, you have to know my father and his personality. He is a very charismatic man who has the ability to be social to a point that a person feels as if they've known him for years.

Well, one day my father took me out to a basketball game. As I watched my father, it seemed he spoke to every single person and referred to them by name. Even though looking back, a lot of them, he did call by nickname. For example, he called them: (Coach, Man and Superstar), but in my mind, he must have known everybody in the world.

So, I asked my father "Daddy, do you know every person in the world?" He looked at me, smiled and said "Yes, Baby I do." Well, to a child that meant literally everybody. So, everyone who we encountered I asked, "Daddy do you know her? Daddy do you know him?" Until my Daddy replied, "Baby, I don't know everybody." I still laugh about that moment to this day. And even though my Daddy didn't know everybody, it sure seemed like it to me.

54. WHIPPING AS A DISCIPLINARY ACTION
By Eugene Broadway

Before integration, spankings were acceptable to Blacks and Whites as a form of discipline. We seem to think even after we are grown that it helped us to a certain extent. We basically did away with whippings. I feel that it took a certain element of fear away from a child and basically that is what causes some of them to be out of control.

When public schools were first integrated, one of the biggest problems that the

White masses had was how do you justify a Black teacher whipping a White child? It might just have caused total chaos. Laws were instituted and analyzed to say spanking a child causes a child to grow up and be an abuser. So spankings were immediately taken out of schools. This was done before a massive riot could ever happen.

When African Americans were slaves, whippings controlled them very, very well. For the master's purpose, it was working. It was a deterrent method of punishment for most. It was working in the individual Blacks' and Whites' households; but it wasn't going to work throughout integration.

Whites even spanked their kids; that was a form of parenting. When the child got out of hand at school and at home, he was spanked. But what we had was Blacks spanking Blacks and Whites spanking Whites.

Whippings/Spanking were used in the 1960s. A seventh grader was spanked on her hand after she missed a question that was asked by the science teacher. She did not get another spanking in school. She became the valedictorian of her senior class.

An elementary child in the 1980s at a Black intercity school was whipped for fighting a child in school who picked on his god-sister. His father came to school and used the principal's office to whip him. He did not do that again. It served as a deterrent.

Whippings happened in the 1960's during integration. Throughout the 60s whipping were dished out at the Black schools. When I went to high school in the late 60s, paddling in the school were not allowed.

Some students thought it was the best thing that could have happened. But after becoming adult, they were not so sure. The psychology of spankings back-fired, we now have some bad ass kids.

55. YOU JUST NEVER KNOW - A TRIBUTE TO EUGENE
By Mary Booker

When I first met Eugene, I was surprised by his greeting. It was as though you had known me a long time and I was not a stranger. His smile, you're welcome, and your "Hi, I'm Eugene the cousin you talked to on the phone," made me feel so warm. There is a demeanor about Eugene that makes one want to be a part. You do not want to be left out and left behind because you will feel as if you will miss something that he wants to partake of.

From the time that we met, he has been an inspiration to me. Our trip to North Carolina showed me his true character and what he was about, "family heritage." No pretence of falsehood, only the truth. Eugene made me want to explore more and see what he envisioned. I was in the moment with him.

He expressed what he was looking for and this made me get more hyper. Eugene has shown me so much and for this I am beholden to him. When Eugene took me to Arkansas (this was my first trip there), I was amazed at what he knew.

When he showed me our great grandparents' grave site, I was too taken back. This brought tears to my eyes because this was something, a cousin he had just met, he wanted me to see. This was the birthplace of my mother, of which I did not know.

I cannot begin to tell what Eugene means to me. Words just seem too impossible and yet I know that they are there. He is a cousin one meets only in a life time because he truly cares about family members. He showed that he cared about me. He wanted to see what I only imagined was there but never knew was there.

He made it possible for me to have kindred feelings for what was a part of me all the time, my family. He has given me family that I never knew I had. And out of all the things, he was in my "back door" all the time. I am so glad he entered my life last year and now it will be impossible for him to erase me because he will always be a part of me, my cousin Eugene.

I love you Cousin Eugene and should you need me, I am here because you are truly my friend in all ways possible. May God Bless you!

56. JUST AS SHE REMEMBERED — LEE ESTHER BROADWAY
By Marie Broadway Toms

In 2011, eighty year old Lee Esther Smith Broadway was as witty as ever. She said she was doing laundry and asked if it was o.k. for her to talk while doing laundry. She said, "Yes, I'm not going back to the old way of washing. I can do this at the same time." While being interviewed, her voice was full of enthusiasm and laughter.

Lee Esther was born in Aubrey, Arkansas and raised in a community called Mount Pilgrim. Aubrey is a small city in Lee County with a population of approximately 200.

Later, Lee Esther's Dad bought some land and the family moved to Moro. Lee Esther was born in September which allowed her to start first grade on time. She went to a community elementary school through eighth grade. High school for Lee Esther and her sister were at Robert R. Moton High School in Marianna.

There weren't any buses to ride to school. So, their father rented a room in a personal household within walking distance of the school. They prepared and carried their lunches and paid for their books. Their dad had taught them how to save.

Lee Esther did not remember if there was tuition that her Dad paid. Her sister attended high school until she got married. Lee Esther finished twelfth grade.

Daniel Broadway and his mother's family lived in Helena. Daniel and Lee Esther married and had three kids right away. Daniel only worked during farming season when they were first married. Later, Daniel went to Helena and started working at the mill.

Buying groceries during the 50s was done by Daniel walking down to Moro to the store. Also, Lee Esther's brother owned a truck. He would take them to Marianna to shop from time to time. Groceries were paid for with cash, not credit, and to ease the budget, they would usually raise a little vegetable garden.

Just thinking about the other things Lee Esther remembers: (1) they used to walk to the first Baptist church in Moro. (2) She remembers a cotton gin in Aubrey. Also, a Black man owned a gin in Marianna. (3)They actually lived in Moro community.

However, it was down a little trail from Moro, not on a rock road or highway. (4) She remembers voting for the first time; she voted in Little Rock, Arkansas after moving in 1954. She did not remember any problems with voting in Arkansas.

Daniel and his mother, Nazaree, used to stay in Helena. When Daniel's mother passed, he came down to the funeral and stayed with Mama Lee Hansberry. When Daniel's mother died from cancer, he left in 1952 for Chicago to find work. Lee Esther was staying across the lake. She had two boys and one girl, Naz, who was born December 25. Daniel got a job in Chicago at a factory. I went to stay with my parents.

After Daniel came back and worked on the farm a little bit, the final straw was when Daniel got mad at a man for not getting a truck for him as promised for the work he did. Working hard, driving a truck, and taking things to Wheatley were some of the things Daniel did to earn money.

I remember he worked so hard. Daniel and his family moved to Little Rock. There, they had four more kids. Lee Esther did not go out a lot because she concentrated on raising the children. Daniel and Lee Esther divorced and went their own way for about five years. When they got back together, they bought a home using his Veteran Administration Loan.

One of Daniel's favorite things when he needed help was to call one of his sons, Eugene and let him serve as his lawyer. Daniel used to call him his little lawyer. Lee Esther is proud of her oldest living son for researching until he found his oldest sister from Daniel's first marriage.

At eighty years old, Lee Esther still keeps in touch with her friends and family by sending cards and making phone calls at Christmas and on birthdays. She even knows how to operate the advanced features on her phone: call waiting and three-way.

57. MASTER BARBER
By Cocoa Broadway

My name is Cocoa Broadway, daughter of Eugene Broadway. I'm writing this short story about my life of twenty-seven years.

My birthday is July 3, 1984. When I was born, the Lord blessed me with a twin sister by the name of Crystal who is beautiful, and so am I. We do everything together. We are the closest twins you could ever meet in life.

When Crystal and I turned twenty-three years old, we decided to move to Stockton, California. We wanted to pursue a career in the Hair Profession and follow in our father's footsteps. We drove to Stockton, California in my car, on the way to pursue our dream of owning a beauty shop and starting our own business. For some reason, it just didn't happen like that.

During our drive there, it was raining so hard we could barely see how to drive. The rain started to become hail. I knew it was unsafe to drive and we were going to have a wreck. I wanted to stop but one of my closest friends figured we could make it to our destination so we just kept driving. The hail became snow. It was so horrible. We finally made it to our destination ready for a brand new start. The whole time we were there, it was horrible.

Things did not turn out the way we hoped. We prayed about it and decided to go back home to Little Rock, Arkansas. We got in the car and headed home. We hit the highway late that night. The unexpected happened. We had a flat tire and ended up not knowing where we were.

So, we got out of the car to change the tire. Almost being successful, Crystal went to throw the flat tire in the trunk and would you believe it, the car fell off the car jack and we were stranded. Not knowing what to do and crying on the side of the road (lol), I just started screaming.

Someone finally pulled over and helped us. It was really weird how he got it done but it got us on the road. We stopped to get a room for the night and the trip turned out perfect. We stopped in Las Vegas and had so much fun. It was a wonderful trip on the way home.

So basically I'm saying, it was meant for me to come back to Little Rock, Arkansas to become a great barber. I went to school and became a Master Barber just like my father, Eugene Broadway. I realized that I wasn't supposed to be in California, at least not at that time.

58. GARRETT GROVE'S CHURCH AND SCHOOL CONNECTION
By Marie Broadway Toms

Since I grew up in the Garrett Grove Community in Moro, Lee County, Arkansas, I will talk about that community. The community was inhabited before 1891 but according to the Garrett Grove Church history, the church was established in 1891.

It was mentioned that there was a great exodus from Georgia, South Carolina, and Mississippi. The record states that there were non-denominational Christian folks there who met from house to house on Sundays to hold services. There was no mention of a school at that time.

After thirty-six members of the church decided that it was time to establish a permanent structure so that all could worship at the same time, they gained permission from the church council to establish a Baptist church in August 1892. The male members met north of a sycamore tree in the cemetery, sought and found a beautiful grove to build a bush arbor to hold services. The next day was a Saturday, the thirty-six members and pastors of New Salem, Mt. Cannon, and Long Cain churches gathered to build the bush arbor.

According to Millie Wilson, a Lifewriter's website, a brush arbor was made, by cutting down tall trees, which were small in circumference. The tall posts were set in the ground and long poles were fastened to the tops of the posts. Cross poles were placed close together; then the freshly cut brush with thick foliage was piled on top of the cross poles, to give the congregation protection from the sun. Pews were crudely made, benches with no backs. Also, in front of the pulpit was a long mourner's bench, on one end of it sat a bucket of water with a dipper. During the sermon some people, women in particular, would shout and faint. Based on what was told, it sounds like Garrett Grove's bush arbor was very similar.

Of course, Garret Grove was a rural area of Lee County, Arkansas in the 1920s. The Church was the hub of social life. Revivals were held every summer by traveling ministers or evangelists in a brush arbor. Almost every church in the area held a revival. There was Bible school for children in the morning, singing for adults in the afternoon and every night the visiting minister preached to a packed house. He spent the week with one of the families of the Church, but was invited to different homes for noon and night meals. Almost everyone in the community attended these services no matter what their denomination.

The church was declared an independent body on the second Sunday, 1894; their delegates received the right hand of fellowship in the C.W.R. Association. They named it Garrett Grove with Brother Jessie Garrett being the oldest citizen. The same day, they ordained Bro. Peter Brim, Bro. H. Rogers, and Bro. John Hicks as deacons. The first meeting day, they elected Rev. Doo Stephens, Pastor.

Bro. Garrett bought a small building and sold it to the county for a school house for $25.00, so they held services there. In 1897, they built the old Church with the help of Mr. J. L. Smith. From 1892 to 1912, the pastors who served were fourteen in number. Rev. Doo Stephens was the first pastor of Garrett Grove Missionary Baptist Church. Twelve more pastors served through 1916. Additionally, there were twenty-three more pastors who served through 2010. Noted among the many, many deacons who served at Garrett Grove were relatives of one of the founders and my grandfather and father: Jim Garrett, A.F. Garrett, Jesse Garrett, Sylvester Garrett, Sam Broadway, and Lenner Broadway.

On January 19, 1910, the church purchased land from Mr. R. B. Smith and his pastor. They built the Church on said land.

Rev. Tony was called to pastor in 1960. The School house and four acres of land was purchased by Garrett Grove under his administration. The original Church was repaired August of 1972 and then destroyed by a tornado storm on November 23, 1973. Services were held in the school building. The school house was repaired in 1974 and later became the permanent place of worship.

Under the administration of Rev. Williams, bathrooms were repaired and the wall was put up between the kitchen and the sanctuary. Under the administration of Rev. Joe Lewis Patterson, the Church members purchased pews and replaced the bathroom doors. Under the administration of Rev. Clark Sims, a handicapped ramp was installed. Also, under the administration of Rev. Clark Sims, a new church building was near completion when tragedy struck the Garrett Grove community again in 2009.

The church building was burned to the ground along with the old school house church building by arsonist(s), but no arrests were made. Yet, again in 2011, Garrett Grove Baptist Church members are bouncing back and the rebuilding has begun under the leadership of Pastor H. Burton.

59. AMERICAN SOLDIER
By Ma'isah McMillan

Stepping onto the battlefield,
I hold my head up high.
I know I'm doing what's right,
even if I die.

I've got a family back home,
A lovely wife and kids.
They're always on my mind,
I send them good bids.

I think of what's ahead of me,
of all the cries of war.
And when I finally pass away,
I hope my soul will soar.

I fight my best for freedom,
hoping I will soon make it home.

60. FAMILY RESEARCH WITH COUSIN MAEZEL
By Eugene Broadway

Since September, 2009 I have been on a joyous ride of learning and researching my family history. This book titled "The Journey" is mostly about my paternal grandfather's side of the family, the Broadways. My father's maternal side is the Hansberry family. In doing my research I obtained much information and many pictures of the Hansberry family from my cousin Maezel Johnson. As I've felt before, this has been a spiritual journey for me.

Well, cousin Maezel being eighty-two years young filled in a lot of gaps for me. We spent many hours just talking about family members of the past. I would talk to her and just mentally put myself in that time period.

Being born in 1951, I shared a part of the past when things were not at the level of progress for our people as it is today. Some of the gaps that she filled in for me, no other person alive could have done that. Wow!!!! Cousin Maezell, that means you were a miracle for me.

You did miraculous things such as helping to find the death certificate for my grandmother, explaining to me how Sussie changed her name at eighteen years old, sharing more with me about my father's younger years and letting me see my grandmother at a late age in her life. I can go on and on. Thanks cousin Maezell for all your help.

I got so involved in this journey that I went so far as to research In-laws families and Slave Master's family. I am pleased to say that I have all of this research saved in a public family tree. The name of the tree is "Broadway." It is located on Ancestry.com and will be a lifelong project for me. Please feel free to visit this site and view the "Broadway" family tree.

61. A REWARDING EMAIL
By Carolyn Broadway Thompson

Marie Toms and Eugene Broadway were so excited to hear from someone representing their great uncle's family on February 9, 2012. Especially since, they had not found that Nathaniel Broadway had children.

Their goal has always been to bring the family even closer together, so the email touched their hearts because it was exactly the kind of results they were seeking. Acknowledging the hard work of many family members and seeing the Broadway family reaping the benefits is so rewarding.

THE FOLLOWING IS WHAT WAS WRITTEN ON BEHALF OF VIRGLE:

I would like to add our family to the new Broadway book that will be coming out soon. My dad is not listed in the first book and neither am I nor the rest of his children. My grandfather, Nathaniel Broadway, is listed on page 55 of the first book. So Oliver Broadway would be my great grandfather. Would you please send the form in order for me to list my siblings?

My father was George Broadway, now deceased. My mother, Ophelia Doss, had eight children and was never married. My father also had children with three other women, two of then he married. My sister got to talk to our grandfather on the phone in Chicago and tried to see him when he was in the hospital before he died but was not allowed in to see him. However, when my sister did get him on the phone that one time, he admitted that he knew my grandmother Odessa.

We are all in contact with each other, meaning my brothers and sisters. So can you get the form to me so that I can make sure the rest of my siblings get one and can also be added?

The book was a great find to me. I got it from a new-found relative that I met by chance a month ago. We, the rest of the Broadway family, would love to be in the next book and to one day meet our family we don't know.

God Bless you for the work that you have done. The book is such a fine work. I never knew the place of our origin until I got this book "Broadway Generations - North Carolina." My name is Virgle James Broadway; my sister, Carolyn, is emailing this for me. I am George Broadway's 7th child among my siblings.

SECTION 9

FEATURED PEOPLE AND EVENTS

FEATURED PEOPLE AND EVENTS

THE SENIOR GENERATION

Last Living Grandchildren of Marshall Broadway

Interviewer *Eugene Broadway* said to William Van on January 20, 2011, "I know why your blood is so strong. You are one of six of the last living grandchildren of Marshall Broadway. Marshall was born in 1854."

The elite living family group consists of Julius Broadway's children who are grandchildren of Marshall and Silvia.

Julius Broadway was born August 6, 1894 in Lee County, Arkansas and died August 1966 in Moro, Lee County, Arkansas. His children who are still living are:
1. Emanuel Broadway of St. Louis who was born January 15, 1938 in Moro, Bradley, Arkansas
2. Georgia Mae Welch, who is Julius' stepchild of Moro, Arkansas

Additionally, among the elite living is Senior's children who are also grandchildren of Marshall and Silvia:

3. Julius Broadway of California who was born July 13, 1926

4. William Van Broadway of Flint, Michigan who was born August 18, 1934

5. Joan Grace Broadway Lewis of Flint Michigan who was born December 16, 1936

Furthermore, among the elite living is Morris' child who is also a grandchild of Marshall and Silvia:

6. Lavenia Broadway Allen of Chicago, Illinois was born February 25, 1933

Reminiscing
By William Van Broadway

Not laying any blame, but back in the day when adults started talking, they would send the children out of the room. They didn't talk about the past; sometimes, the past was horrible; they may have done something wrong and didn't want anybody to know; they could have changed their name; or it just may have been adult conversation.

I remember Morris Broadway; I met him in Chicago, Illinois. I thought when I saw him that he looked like my dad, Senior; Morris was dark-skinned and Senior was light-skinned. Morris also had a scar on his upper lip. When we were visiting, we would meet at Ocevia's house. In Arkansas before Senior left for Chicago and then later to Michigan, Senior and Lula stayed with Marshall Broadway, Senior's father.

A Historical Visit with Joan Broadway

As told by Joan Broadway on January 19, 2010

I am the daughter of Senior Broadway whose parents were Marshall and Silvia Broadway. My parents, Senior Broadway and Lula Williams were born in Moro, Arkansas; but I was born in Flint, Michigan. I married a man who was from North Carolina. His father and grandfather were from Atlanta, Georgia.

Senior, my father was born in 1896 and his father was from North Carolina. Daddy was a light-skinned Black man and Mama was kind of White or light-skinned, an Indian. Even though Silvia, a Cherokee, came from North Carolina with Marshall, there were also a lot of Indians in Arkansas, especially on the Arkansas River area. Silvia Clark's parents were Anna Wright and Buck Clark.

My father, Senior, was not a common name. He was found with his family in the 1900 U.S. Federal Census. His name was spelled "Penior". He was listed as a Black boy born October 1892 (7 years old) to Robert (a name sometimes used by Marshall) and Silvia Broadaway.

Living in the household were one older brother, William Cannie, August 1885 (14) and one older sister, Julia Lessie Broadaway, October 1887 (12). Also at home were younger siblings: Julius Broadaway, August 1894 (5), James Morris Broadaway, October 1896 (3), and Mary E. Broadaway, March 1899 (1). Grandfather Marshall stayed with Senior, Lula, and Ophelia according to the 1920s United States Federal Census.

Dad or mom used to say that they had a brother who went away and they never found him again. It may have been a case of Klu Klux Klan violence.

Senior worked so much in the foundry. People always thought that he died of a heart attack, but he died of black lung disease.

I was just reading the forward of the Broadway Generations book today. I was reading about our grandmother Silvia. I thought about it. My daughter-in-law's name was Silvia Broadway and that is why Senior was so crazy about her. She had the same name as Senior's mom, Silvia Clark Broadway.

Did you get to see that picture of Lessie Broadway Beasley that I sent today? That was a God Send. My father never did talk about his sister. He would talk about his brother and his nephew. There were some Beasley's that used to work with my husband; I wonder if those Beasley's were related to me and I did not know it. I did go back to Marianna, Arkansas to see where my Mom and Dad were married at the courthouse. The courthouse was located on a hill on unpaved roads.

Children of John and Morris used to visit Flint, Michigan to see Senior's kid. I looked in the book to see who QT's parents were. This book Broadway Generations is a wonderful fantastic resource. I never did know who QT's parents were. I found it by looking in the book that QT's father was Samuel Broadway.

His daughter lived on the next street from us and we didn't know she was QT's daughter. QT Hunt Broadway died about ten years ago. QT was Sam's firstborn by Ms. Hunt. Sam later married Nazaree Hansberry; he had two kids by her, Daniel and Geraldine. Sam married again. He married Minnie Miller and his firstborn with her was Lenner Broadway. It is a small world.

Joan was asked about her experience when she met QT Broadway. It was wonderful. We met over to his daughter's house. He said he was in the painting business. He was so nice. We would go over there to his daughter's house and she would fix big meals for us. He had a granddaughter who lived in Flint, Michigan. The granddaughter's name was Cheron; she had three or four kids.

A lot of the Broadway's were known to be business minded. I remember someone saying that Abner Broadway was in the trucking business. In Flint, Michigan, Odell was married to John Broadway and most of their kids are in Arizona. Odell taught school since she was fifteen years old. She had to verify that she taught school in order to retire. She worked for some foundation at the University of Michigan and they named a scholarship in her honor. Odell was so proud to be a Broadway.

Joan asked, "How did you find Lessie Beasley's picture." Eugene answered; there was a lady, Delores Thompson, in her early 70s at the Broadway family reunion this summer who is the daughter of Julius Broadway. This Julius Broadway's father's name is William Cannie Broadway. This daughter had never met her Broadway family. Julius Broadway had two sons Calvin and Eugene Broadway.

Calvin who died a couple years earlier had some children and a daughter name Cheron. Cheron had moved to Atlanta and was looking for family to communicate with. A cousin in Little Rock Arkansas connected her to Cousin Eugene Broadway.

Eugene Broadway and Shianne, his wife, set up a meeting with Cheron. Once that dinner meeting happened. Cheron connected us to her cousin, Earnest Beasley. We found there were two Earnest Beasleys in the immediate family and we had been communicating with the wrong one. The rest is history.

Joan, who is a daughter of Senior Broadway, wanted to know if there were pictures of Marshall and Silvia Broadway other kids since she had heard that there were about sixteen of them. Eugene answered, we have pictures of John, Senior, Morris, Lessie, Julius, but we do not have a picture of Marshall and Sylvia's oldest son, Oliver. Additionally, we would love to find a picture of William Cannie Broadway.

We used to go up to Troy every year to a church convention. Joan, William, and Rose would attend the convention. We used to go to the country in Belleville, Michigan. About thirty to thirty-five years later, we moved to Belleville.

I am dancing on my toes for the picture of Aunt Lessie. Bye, before you guys will have me dancing on the ceiling. When is the next reunion?

SECTION 10

BROADWAY FAMILY TREE

The "Broadway Family Tree" is a work in progress. It is composed largely of direct descendants of former slave, James Broadway. All of the Black Broadway descendants have been changed to be spelled "Broadway" even though our ancestors did not change the spelling of their name until they moved to Arkansas. I intentionally included and spelled the White slave descendants as "Broadaway".

Many of the White people are left in the tree in order to gather hints to expand and cause more in-depth research. We are continually looking for the connection between the Mulatto brothers James, Robert, and Harry (Hany, Cannis) Broadway and the White man's side with John and Harriet Broadaway.

Additionally, a few of the researchers in the tree provided information on both sides of their family to take advantage of that added benefit of hints and source files.

The following is a Broadway family tree using Eugene Broadway's lineage: James, Marshall, Oliver, Sam & Daniel Broadway. You can form your own tree with Ancestry.com by linking to the "Broadway" tree.

1. **Rev. John Broadaway, Slave Master (1811-1870)**
   Harriett Staton Broadaway
   Burnsville, NC
   William Cannie Staton

2. **James Broadway (1820-1884)**
   Margaret Broadway (1840)
   Burnsville to Lanesboro, Anson, NC
   Marshall Broadway (1854-1926)

3. **Marshall Broadway (1854-1926)**
   Silvia Clark Broadway (1857-1916)
   Lanesboro, Anson, NC to Lee Co., AR

   Oliver Broadway (1874-1950)
   Mary F. Broadway (1875)

John W. Broadway (1876-1936)
Annie Ella Broadway (1879)
William Cannie Broadway (1885-1928)
Lessie "Julia" Broadway Beasley (1888-1952)
Julius Broadway (1891-1966)
Morris Broadway (1892-1955)
Senior Broadway (1896-1956)
Mary E. Broadway (1899)

4. **Oliver (James) Broadway 1874-1950**
North Carolina to Arkansas
Mary Ella Gilbert
Dora Reese (1884 – 1921)
Children:
Samuel Broadway (1901- 1992)
Nathaniel (Nate) Broadway (1905-1982)
Green (Joe) Broadway (1908-1998)
Marshall Broadway (1912-1926)
Cynthia Broadway Burnett (1915-2005)
Joe Broadway (1919-2005)
Mary Byrd (1889-1982)
    Fleecie Byrd Miller (1906-1979)

5. **Samuel Broadway (1901-1992)**
Moro, Lee, AR
Mattie Hunt
    Q.T. Hunt (Broadway) (1918-1991)
Nazaree Hansberry (1902 – 1949)
    Daniel Lee Broadway (1920-1999)
    Geraldine Broadway Parker (1922-2010)
Minnie Miller (1907-1980)
    Lenner Broadway (1927-1991)
    Bobbie Lee Broadway Stedman (1930-1990)
    Fleecy Mae Broadway Turner (1932-2001)
    Sam Ella Broadway McKenzie (1935-)
    Vonitha Broadway Ward (1939 -)
    Fannie Broadway Neely (1946 -)

6. **Daniel Lee Broadway (1920-1999)**
Moro to Little Rock, AR
Lelia Thompson

Dana Broadway
Pearl Jean Smith (1926-2001)
Carol Broadway Smith Martin
Lee Esther Smith Broadway
Daniel Lee Broadway (1950-1972)
Eugene Broadway
Nazaree Broadway
Bobby Broadway
Nathaniel Broadway
Linda D. Broadway
Geraldine Broadway

SECTION 11

FAMILY PHOTO ALBUM

FAMILY PHOTO ALBUM

MARSHALL & SILVIA CLARK BROADWAY

MARSHALL

SILVIA

MARSHALL & SILVIA BROADWAY'S FAMILY

NOT PICTURED

OLIVER
MARY F.
ANNIE L.
WILLIAM CANNIE
MARY E.

JOHN

MORRIS

LESSIE

SENIOR

JULIIS

OLIVER BROADWAY'S FAMILY

OLIVER
&
WIFE, DORA
BROADWAY

NOT
PICTURED

SAMUEL

SONS, MARSHALL
&
THEOPHIS
BROADWAY

NOT
PICTURED

GREEN

JOHN W. BROADWAY'S FAMILY

DIMPLES

JOHN W. BROADWAY AND EDITH

LOLITTA FOXWORTH

HONER (H.D.) & ROSIE BROADWAY; CORA & IVY MCCOY
DIMPLES, CHARLIE, DIANE, & LOLITTA MCCOY

ROSEMARY

NATHANIEL

MARIE BROADWAY   NICK MATTHEWS   ODELL   JOHN C.

ETHEL

JOHN C. & ODELL GARRETT BROADWAY

JOHN W. BROADWAY'S FAMILY

WILLIAM CANNIE BROADWAY'S FAMILY

WILLIAM CANNIE
BROADWAY'S
FAMILY

WILLIAM CANNIE BROADWAY'S FAMILY

WILLIAM CANNIE BROADWAY'S FAMILY

LESSIE BROADWAY BEASLEY'S FAMILY

LESSIE BROADWAY
BEASLEY WILSON

CLIFTON BEASLEY

REV. ERNEST BEASLEY

ESTER BEASLEY

JAMES BEASLEY

ERMA BEASLEY

GEORGIA MAE BEASLEY

ELISHA BEASLEY

JULIUS BROADWAY'S FAMILY

MORRIS BROADWAY'S FAMILY

SENIOR BROADWAY'S FAMILY

SAMUEL BROADWAY'S FAMILY

SAMUEL BROADWAY

DANIEL

GERALDINE

NAZAREE HANSBERRY
BROADWAY

SAM BROADWAY

MINNIE MILLER BROADWAY

LENNER   BOBBIE LEE   FLEECY

SAMELLA   VONITHA   FANNIE

NATHANIEL BROADWAY AND GREENE BROADWAY

NATHANIEL BROADWAY

NATHANIEL CYNTHIA EDDIE JESSIE WEST FAMILY

GREENE BROADWAY

ODELL BROADWAY

GREENE BROADWAY

GREENE & SAMUEL BROADWAY

JOE, SAM, & GREENE BROADWAY

CYNTHIA BROADWAY BURNETT'S FAMILY

EDDIE BURNETT

JESSIE WILLIE MAE JAMMIE BETTYE EDNA

CYNTHIA BROADWAY

MARY ANN

ANNIE MAE BURNETT 1929-1930

NOT PICTURED

ROSIE MAE

DORETHA

MARION

MARICE

ODELL

SAMUEL

JESSIE MAE

WILLIE MAE

JAMES

EDNA

BETTYE

JAMMIE

ARDELL

JOHN

CYNTHIA BROADWAY BURNETT'S FAMILY

CYNTHIA

JOE BROADWAY'S FAMILY

JOE BROADWAY'S FAMILY

DANIEL BROADWAY'S FAMILY

DANIEL/LEE ESTHER BROADWAY'S FAMILY

LEE ESTHER SMITH BROADWAY

LEE ESTHER

LEE ESTHER

LEE ESTHER

LEE ESTHER

EUGENE

DANNY

BOBBY

SKIP

LEE ESTHER & GIRLS

GERALDINE

NATHANIEL "SKIP"

LINDA

DAVID SMITH FAMILY

SAMPLING OF DANIEL BROADWAY'S ACHIEVEMENTS

DANIEL   EUGENE   EUGENE

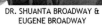

DR. SHUANTA BROADWAY &
EUGENE BROADWAY   LEE ESTHER SMITH
BROADWAY   CRYSTAL AND COCOA
BROADWAY

EUGENE BROADWAY   BOBBY BROADWAY   DANNY, NOAH, EUGENE BROADWAY

EUGENE BROADWAY'S FAMILY

EUGENE BROADWAY'S FAMILY

EUGENE BROADWAY'S GRANDCHILDREN

HANSBERRY FAMILY ELDERS

HANSBERRY ELDERS

The Late

WILLIAM HANSBERRY

JOHN HANSBERRY

LEE ETTA HANSBERRY

EVA WOODARD

MARY HANSBERRY

ADA HANSBERRY

FRED WOODARD

EVA WOODARD

PEARCE HANSBERRY

HANSBERRY FAMILY ELDERS

LEE ETTA HANSBERRY
NAZAREE HANSBERRY

SAMUEL
BROADWAY

NAZAREE
HANSBERRY

GERALDINE

DANIEL & LEE ESTHER BROADWAY

DANIEL

LEE ESTHER

GERALDINE BROADWAY PARKER'S FAMILY

JOHN & LEE ETTA HANSBERRY
GREAT - GRANDPARENTS

LEE ETTA HANSBERRY
DAUGHTER & MOTHER

SAMUEL & GERALDINE BROADWAY
FATHER & DAUGHTER

BROADWAY-PARKER FAMILY

JAMES &
PAULINE

JONATHAN

HAZEL

MABEL

FELIX JR

PARKER GUYS 1N 1965

CURTIS PARKER FAMILY

LENNER BROADWAY'S FAMILY

GRAND/GREAT-GRANDKIDS: SHARNETTA & MIRANDA BROADWAY, MEGAN WORSHAM, SHEKINAH BROADWAY, KILIAN TOMS, BR.RAL TOMS, COUSIN JEROME TURNER, KAMEIL LEVIN, SAM BROADWAY, TASMONETTE KATES WALKER & MELISSA KATES BROWN

234

BOBBIE LEE BROADWAY STEDMAN'S FAMILY

FLEECY BROADWAY TURNER'S FAMILY

SAMELLA BROADWAY MCKENZIE'S FAMILY

FANNIE BROADWAY NEELY'S FAMILY

MARY F. BROADWAY'S FAMILY

ANDREW BROADWAY, 2ND FROM LEFT,
FAMILY & FRIENDS

FRONZIA BAILEY &
ROBERT BROADWAY
& FAMILY

ROBERT BROADWAY
&
MARY BENNETT

RONALD BROADWAY

ROBERT BROADWAY &
FRONZIA BAILEY

NADINE BROADWAY

ROBERT BROADWAY JR.

ROBERT PONCHO
BROADWAY III

ROBERT BROADWAY III

KWANE BROADWAY
& FAMILY

ARLANDER BROADWAY'S FAMILY

ELBERT

ATLEAN & THOMAS

CUBA

Q.T.

DORTHULA

MINOR JONES

NOTES

NOTES

1. Ancestry.com. (2009). 1870 United States Federal Census [database online]. Provo, UT, USA.

2. Ancestry.com. (1942). Draft Registration of James (Oliver) Broadway. World War II Draft Registration Card 1942 . Provo, UT, USA: Ancestry. com.

3. Broadway Deeds 1885-1920. (2010). Arkansas, Lee County Registrar of Deeds . Marianna, AR, USA: Lee County Registrar of Deeds.

4. Broadway, C. (1908). Land Complaint: Norment Heirs to John Broadway. Lee County Chancery Court . Marianna, AR, USA: Lee County Chancery Court.

5. Broadway, J. (1914, March 18). Complaint and Depositions. Lee County Chancery Records . Marianna, AR, USA: Lee County Chancery Court.

6. Brook, R. E. (1828). History of Rocky River Baptist Church.

7. Claims Resolution Act of 2010. (2011, February 15). Retrieved November 12, 2011, from USDA: Office of the Assistant Secretary for Civil Rights: www.ascr.usda.gov/cr_act2010_.html

8. Deeds, A. C. (1875). Registrar of Deeds: Charles Beverly to Marshall Broadway. Anson County Registrar of Deeds . NC, USA: Anson County, NC.

9. Early, G. (n.d.). Black Migration. Retrieved from PBS: Jazz - A Film by Ken Burns: http://www.pbs.org/jazz/places/faces_migration.htm

10. Eye Wittness to History. (2005). Retrieved from Life on a Southern Plantation, 1854: www.eyewitnesstohistory.com

11. Lancaster, G. (2010, April 9). Cotton Pickers Strike of 1891. Retrieved May 31, 2011, from The Encyclopedia of Arkansas History & Culture: http://encyclopediaofarkansas.net

12. Lapucia, B. (2011). Migration North to the Promised Land. Retrieved 11

13, 2011, from Yale-New Haven Teachers Institute: http://yale.edu/ynhti/curriculum/units/1978/2/78.02.05.x.html

13. Lee County, A. (1885). State of Arkansas to Marshall Broadaway. Registrar of Deeds: Commissioner of State Lands . AR, USA: Lee County Courts.

14. Peurifoy, D. R. (2009, April 24). Retrieved November 2011, from Find a Grave: www.findagrave.com

15. Racial Tensions in Omaha - African American Migration. (1921). Retrieved from Nebraskastudies.org 1900-1924: http://www.nebraskastudies.org

16. Staton, R. J. (1960). Staton History: Every Staton We Could Find in the World. Granite Bay, CA: Brooks Litho.

17. Stockley, G. (2001). Blood in Their Eyes: The Elaine Race Massacres of 1919. Fayetteville: University of Arkansas Press.

18. Taylor, Q. (n.d.). William T. Sherman issued Field Order No. 15. Retrieved February 2011, from Black Past: www.blackpast.org

19. Teske, M. African American Children Chopping Cotton Near Marked Tree, AR in 1930s. Encyclopedia of Arkansas History and Culture. Arkansas History Commission, Marked Tree (Poinsett County).

20. The African American Experience. (2010, January). Retrieved June 19, 2011, from Historic Latta Plantation, North Carolina: ProQuest Web

21. Times, A. (1881, May 19). Retrieved from Anson County, Polkton, NC Genealogy Services.

22. Vernon, D. I. (n.d.). Chopping Cotton. Retrieved October 23, 2011, from www.kerns.com

BIBLIOGRAPHY

1. Act No. 151, "An Act to Remove the Free Negroes and Mulattoes from this State." February 12, 1859. Acts of the General Assembly of the State of Arkansas. Little Rock: General Assembly of the State of Arkansas, 1859, pp. 175–178.

2. Acts of Congress Relative to Refugees, Freedmen, and Confiscated and Abandoned Lands. Washington, D.C.: Government Printing Office, 1865.

3. Alexander, John Brevard, The History of Mecklenburg County: from 1740 to 1900, http://books.google.com/books, Charlotte, NC, August 1902

4. Alwood, Evan. Diary. Mary Lee Chapter, No. 87. Arkansas History Commission,

5. Ancestry.com - Tennessee State Marriage License, 1780-2002 was found for A B Beasley and Bettie Watson

6. Ancestry.com. 1750 - 1930 United States Federal Census [database on-line]. Provo, UT, USA: Ancestry.com Operations Inc, 2002.

7. Ancestry.com. Arkansas, County Marriages Index, 1837-1957 [database on-line]. Provo, UT, USA: Ancestry.com Operations, Inc., 2011.

8. Ancestry.com. Cook County, Illinois, Deaths Index, 1878-1922 [database on-line]. Provo, UT, USA: Ancestry.com Operations, Inc., 2011.

9. Ancestry.com. World War I Draft Registration Cards, 1917-1918 [database on-line]. Provo, UT, USA: Ancestry.com Operations Inc, 2005.

10. Anson County, North Carolina Genealogy Services and Anson Times issue of May 19, 1881, Polkton, North Carolina

11. Apple, Nancy, and Suzy Keasler, eds. History of Lee County, Arkansas. Dallas: Curtis Media Group, 1987.

12. Application of Hallwood Petroleum, LLC, established Exploratory Drilling Unit, Sections 7&8 – T3N – R1E Lee Co.

13. Arkansas Death Index, 1914-1950. Publication: Name: database online, MyFamily. com, Inc., original data: Division of Vital Records, Arkansas Dept of Health; Location: Provo, UT; Date: 2005;

14. Arkansas Oil and Gas Commission, Mr. Lawrence E. Bengal, Director, El Dorado, AR

15. Arkansas the Natural State. African-American Heritage. Heritage and Civil Rights Pathways in Arkansas. http://www.arkansas.com

16. Avirett, James B. (James Battle), 1837?-1912

The Old Plantation: How We Lived in Great House and Cabin Before the War

Baum, D. "Burdens of Landholding in a Freed Slave Settlement: The Case of Brazos County's "Hall's Town"." Southwestern Historical Quarterly 113.2 (2009): 185. Research Library, ProQuest. Web. 19 Oct. 2011.

17. Beine, Joe. Online Death Indexes & Records – USA – Search Rootsweb. 2004-2011.

18. Bentley, George R. A History of the Freedmen's Bureau. New York: Octagon Books, 1970.

19. Beverly, Charles and Beverly, Charlotte. Sold land (133 acres) to Marshall & Silvia Broadway. March 8, 1875, $566, Anson County, N.C., Book 19, page 358 & 359

20. Black Masters. A Family of Color in the Old South, Michael P. Johnson and James L. Roak New York: Norton, 1984), p.64.

21. Brinkley, Arkansas. http://www.brinkleyar.com (accessed September 18, 2011).

22. Broadway, Cannie. Chancery Records, Marianna, Arkansas, 1908

23. Broadway, J.M. Lee Chancery Court, March 18, 1914, the plaintiff's Atty. W. L. Ward, Esq. and the defendant summoned and heard the complaint and depositions

24. Broadway, M.B. & Sylvia J. Sold land to W.C. Staton. March 1888, North Carolina, Anson County. Clerk of Superior Court, March 21, 1885, Register of Deeds.

25. Broadway, M.B. Purchased land (80 acres) from the State of Arkansas. November 23, 1893 (April 4, 1887, March 3, 1891, May 16, 1888, February 1892.

26. Broadway, Marshall & Silvia. Purchased land (133 acres) from Charles & Charlotte Beverly. March 8, 1875, $566, Anson County, N.C., Book 19, page 358 & 359

27. Brooks, Rev. Edgar. History of Rocky River Baptist Church, pages 108-109

28. Brundage, W. Fitzhugh. Lynching in the New South, University of Illinois Press

29. C. Vann Woodward, The Strange Career of Jim Crow (New York: Oxford University Press, 2002): 82.

30. Chancery Records, John Broadway vs. 2375 – Decree. Ella Norment et al. (Cannie Broadway assigned said contract) Dec 14, 1908, Marianna Courts, Lee County, Arkansas

31. Claims Resolution Act of 2010, On December 8, 2010, President Obama signed law.

32. Cobb, William H. Commonwealth College. In The Encyclopedia of Arkansas History & Culture. Retrieved October 21, 2004, from, www.encyclopediaofarkansas.net/.

33. Confederacy included South Carolina, Mississippi, Florida, Alabama, Georgia Louisiana, Texas, Virginia, Arkansas, North Carolina, and Tennessee.

34. Cox Forman, Linda (728). Capt. Frederick Staton, www.lindapages.com , (accessed 6/22/2010)

35. Dennis, Jane. Brinkley (Monroe County). Staff of Encyclopedia of Arkansas History and Culture, http://encyclopediaofarkansas.net (accessed January 24, 2010), Little Rock, Arkansas.

36. Diary of Susan Cook," Mar. 10, 1865, in Phillips County Historical Quarterly, V (1957), 38.

37. Documenting the American South – The Church in the Southern Black Community. New York; Chicago: F. Tennyson Neely Co., 2004 by the University Library, The University of North Carolina at Chapel Hill.Dougan, Michael B. Life in Confederate Arkansas, ARKANSAS HISTORICAL QUARTERLY, Volume 31 (Spring 1972).

38. Emily Yellin. "Lynching Victim Is Cleared of Rape, 100 Years Later."New York Times 27 Feb. 2000, Late Edition (East Coast): ProQuest National Newspapers Core, ProQuest. Web. 19 Oct. 2011.

39. Encyclopedia of Arkansas History & Culture, African-American sharecroppers' Cotton Pickers Strike of 1891 in Lee County

40. Encyclopedia of Arkansas History & Culture, Cotton Pickers Strike of 1891 that was retrieved on May 31, 2011

41. Everything.com: The Life of a Slave - Slavery in America | American History - Everything.com http://www.everything.com/life-slave/#ixzz0yWZnp0d8

42. Fauntroy, Michael K., Republicans and the Black Vote (Boulder, CO: Lynne Rienner Publishers, 2007): 41.

43. Finley, Randy. From Slavery to Uncertain Freedom: The Freedman's Bureau in Arkansas 1865-1869, 2008.

44. Forman, Linda Cox. Granite Bay, CA. Bible Records, Land and Court Records, Wills, and Staton History by Rev. John Staton.

45. Ginzburg, Ralph. 100 Years of Lynching, , Black Classic Press; Lynching in the New South, W. Fitzhugh Brundage, University of Illinois Press, http://www.ccharity.com/lynching

46. Gregory M. Lamb. "Deadly shots heard around suburbia; an ordinary Black man becomes a hero in volatile 1920s America: [ALL Editions]." The Christian Science Monitor 21 Sep. 2004, ProQuest National Newspapers Core, ProQuest. Web. 19 Oct. 2011.

47. Grif Stockley and Jeannie M Whayne. "Federal troops and the Elaine massacres: A colloquy."The Arkansas Historical Quarterly 61.3 (2002): 272-283. Research Library, ProQuest. Web. 19 Oct. 2011.

48. Grooms, Robert M. DIXIE'S Censored Subject Black Slave Owners, www.seanbryson.com

49. Hanks, George H. Photograph by Kimball, NYC. Wilson Chinn, a branded slave from Louisiana--Also exhibiting instruments of torture used to punish slaves. Library of

Congress Prints and Photographs Division, Washington, D.C. 20540 USA. 1863.

50. Harry A. Ploski and Warren Marr's. The Negro Almanac (New York: Bellwether Co., 1976).

51. Higgins, B. "The Big Hat Law: Arkansas and Its State Police, 1935-2000." The Arkansas Historical Quarterly 68.3 (2009): 345-347. Research Library, ProQuest. Web. 19 Oct. 2011.

52. Higgins, Billy D. "The Origins and Fate of the Marion County Free Black Community." Arkansas Historical Quarterly 54 (Winter 1995): 427–443.

53. Higgins, Billy D. Act 151 of 1859 (Act to Remove the Free Negroes and Mulattos from the State, Arkansas's Free Negro Expulsion Act of 1859. University of Arkansas at Fort Smith

54. Historic Latta Plantation, North Carolina. Early American Life: Christmas 2010 1 Jan. 2010: Research Library, ProQuest. Web. 19 Jun. 2011.

55. History of Mecklenburg County: from 1740 to 1900

56. Hogue, Wayman. Back Yonder: An Ozark Chronicle, 1880's

57. Hundley, E.E., Robinson, W., and Robinson, H.M. Negroes for Sale, Public Auction at Spring Hill, Hempstead County, January 6, 1842.

58. Illinois, Cook County Deaths 1878–1922." Index. FamilySearch, Salt Lake City, Utah, 2010. Illinois Department of Public Health. "Birth and Death Records, 1916–present." Division of Vital Records, Springfield, Illinois.

59. John W. Brown Diary, Sept. 11, 1862, in University of Arkansas Library, microfilm. (Hereafter cited as Brown Diary).

60. Jones, Joyce. Going to Town [1963-1969], From Sharecropper to Manhood [1963-1970], School Days [1963-1970], School Desegregation [1970-1975], The chosen One [1971-1972], Dr. King. Ontario Black History Society (responsible for initiating the formal celebration of February Black History Month at all levels of government in Canada), 1978. Canada.

61. Journal of Southern History > Vol. 2, No. 3, Aug., 1936 > A Dangerous Pamphlet...

62. Journal of the Senate of Arkansas. Little Rock: Price and Barton, 1870.

63. Kaye, A. "Neighborhoods and Nat Turner: The Making of a Slave Rebel and the Unmaking of a Slave Rebellion. " Journal of the Early Republic 27.4 (2007): 705-720. Research Library, ProQuest. Web. 19 Oct. 2011.

64. Kaye, Anthony E. Joining Places – Slave neighborhoods in the Old South, 2007, John Hope Franklin fund of The University of North Carolina Press

65. Land Deed, Grantor Beverly, Grantee M.B. and Silvia Broadway

66. Lee Chancery Court. Depositions of J.M. Broadway, Sam Carter, and Cannie Broadway, March 9, 1914. Office of T.L. Ward, Marianna, Arkansas, Plaintiff J.M. Broadway and

Defendant Leella Broadway (Lella or Luella). Married Dec 11, 1912, Leella committed adultery with John Broadway and Albert Breazwell. Divorced March 18, 1914 (page 37)

67. Lee County Sesquicentennial Committee. History of Lee County, Arkansas Curtis Media Corporation -1987, Dallas, Texas.

68. Lee County, Arkansas History and Genealogy, Hearthstone Legacy Publications book on CD, "Biographical and Historical Memoirs of Lee County, Goodspeed Publishing Company, 1890.

69. Lerone Bennett Jr. "Excerpt from the new Before the Mayflower: The African-American Century. "Ebony 1 Jul 2003: Research Library, ProQuest. Web. 19 Oct. 2011.

70. Library of Congress, Prints & Photographs Online Catalog.

71. Life on a Southern Plantation, 1854, Eyewittness to History, www.eyewitnesstohistory. com (2005)

72. Lilly, J. Paul. Agricultural History of North Carolina, North Carolina Agricultural History, Associate Professor Emeritus, Department of Soil Science , North Carolina State University

73. Marianna & Lee County, Arkansas. http://www.mariannaarkansas.org/ (accessed January 24, 2010).

74. Marianna, AR (Lee County visit court house, public library, city park) during 2010 and 2011

75. Marianna, Lee County, Arkansas Land Records. Broadways. 1885 and 1900s

76. Matthew Shaer. "In America's Deep South, a front seat for Freedom Riders." The Christian Science Monitor 13 Jul 2011, ProQuest National Newspapers Core, ProQuest. Web. 19 Oct. 2011.

77. Microsoft Word Reference Books, Redmond, WA

78. Miller, Frank and Dora Miller Word. Phone Interviews.

79. Miller, Franklin Delano (2011, January 24). Grew Up with the Broadways (M. Toms, Interviewer.

80. Millie Wilson, a Lifewriter's Website

81. Morgan, Sam. An Oral History of the Judd Hill Plantation. Arkansas State University and Mike Gibson, Trustee Judd Hill Foundation. http://juddhillplantation.org/history.html

82. Moro, AR (Lee County visit cemeteries) (March 20 & December 16 2011): Mt. Moriah Baptist Church Cemetery, New Hope Baptist Church Cemetery, Garrett Grove Baptist Church Cemetery, Springfield Baptist Church

83. Nebraska Studies.org "Racial Tensions in Omaha",

84. Negro in Politics, 12 December 1887, Washington Post: 5.

85. Ninth Census of the United States. Washington, D.C.: Government Printing Office, 1872.

86. Office of History and Preservation, Office of the Clerk, Black Americans in Congress, 1870–2007. Washington, D.C.: U.S. Government Printing Office, 2008. http://baic.house.gov/historical-essays/essay.html?intSectionID=23 (October 30, 2011).

87. Patty, W. (2011). A Little Rock Boyhood: Growing Up in the Great Depression The Arkansas Historical Quarterly, 70(2), 210-212. Retrieved October 17, 2011 from Research Library. (Document ID: 2476416401).

88. Perkins & Trotter, PLLC, A Professional Limited Liability Company, Attorneys and Counselors, Little Rock, AR 72225-1618

89. Peurifoy, Dr. Robert. Capt Frederick Staton, record added April 24, 2009, Fredrick Staton Cemetery, Burnsville, Anson County, North Carolina. www.findagrave.com (accessed September 18, 2011).

90. Plessy v Ferguson Supreme Court decision of 1896

91. Powell, Delores Broadway. (2010, April 1). Resident of Burnsville, NC. (E. Broadway, Interviewer)

92. Quintard Taylor of www.blackpast.org on January 16, 1865, Union General William T. Sherman issued Special Field Order No. 15

93. Rayburn, Otto Ernest. Moonshine in Arkansas, The Arkansas Historical Quarterly, Vol. 16, No. 2 (Summer, 1957), pp. 169-173

94. Report of the Commissioner of the United States Bureau of Refugees, Freedmen, and Abandoned Lands. Washington, D.C.: Government Printing Office, 1865.

95. Resolutions Passed by the Convention of the People of Arkansas on the 20th day of March, 1861

96. Rev. Edgar book, "History of Rocky River Baptist Church"

97. Robert Cochran. "Blood in Their Eyes: The Elaine Race Massacres of 1919. The Arkansas Historical Quarterly 61.2 (2002): 204-207. Research Library, ProQuest. Web. 19 Oct. 2011.

98. Ross, Margaret. "Mulattoes, Free Negroes Ordered To Leave Arkansas on Eve of War." Chronicles of Arkansas. Arkansas Gazette. February 15, 1959, p. 3E.

99. Simkin, John (BA, MA, MPhil), Spartacus Educational, retrieved on August 29, 2011 http://www.spartacus.schoolnet.co.uk/USAdonaldD.htm

100. Slave Trader - History's Most Ignoble Trade? 2003-2008 Son of the South. http://www.sonofthesouth.net/slavery/slave-trader.htm (accessed 8/28/2011)

101. Smith, C. Calvin, ed. "The Elaine, Arkansas, Race Riots, 1919." Special Issue. Arkansas

Review: A Journal of Delta Studies 32 (August 2001).

102. Smith, C. Calvin. (2003). Victory at Home: Manpower and Race in the American South during World War II. The Arkansas Historical Quarterly, 62(3), 340-342. Retrieved October 17, 2011 from Research Library. (Document ID: 470056111).

103. Smith, Ted J. (1999). Mastering farm and family: David Walker as slaveholder. The Arkansas Historical Quarterly, 58(1), 61-79. Retrieved October 17, 2011 from Research Library. (Document ID: 41367858).

104. Staton, M. (2010, April 1). Resident of Burnsville, NC. (E. Broadway, Interviewer)

105. Staton, Rev. John Samuel edited. Staton History: Every Staton We Could Find in the World, Printed Privately for Staton Families, Brooks Litho of Charlotte, North Carolina, 1960.

106. Stockley, Grif & Jeannie M Whayne. (2002). Federal troops and the Elaine massacres: A colloquy. The Arkansas Historical Quarterly, 61(3), 272-283. Retrieved October 17, 2011 from Research Library. (Document ID: 203950561).

107. Stockley, Grif. Blood in Their Eyes: The Elaine Race Massacres of 1919. Fayetteville: University of Arkansas Press, 2001.

108. Stoddard, Brooke C. and Daniel P. Murphy, Ph.D. The Life of a Slave. Netplaces.com, a part of The New York Times Company.

109. Tallahassee, FL, The Florida Department of Business and Professional Regulation, Lee County Man Arrested for Running Illegal Moonshine Still, March 11, 2011 Division of Alcoholic Beverages and Tobacco (ABT),

110. Thomas Cemetery, Burnsville, Anson County, North Carolina

111. Thurmon, John. Commissioner of State Lands, Little Rock, Arkansas, www.cosl.org/

112. Time Line: Lerone Bennett's Before the Mayflower (Chicago: Johnson Publishing Co., 1982),

113. Toms, Marie. Broadway Generations, Butterfly Press, 2011

114. Traveler's Guide to Arkansas 1541-1699, Timeline of Arkansas History. (Accessed January 24, 2010)

115. Tri-County Genealogy. Marvell, AR: Tri-County Genealogical Society (1986–).

116. U.S. World War II Draft Registration Cards, 1942 Record. Publication: Name: database online, MyFamily.com, Inc., original data: United States Selective Service System, World War II: Fourth Registration, National Archives and Records Administration; Location: Provo, UT; Date: 2006; Repository: Name: Ancestry.com

117. U.S. World War II Draft Registration Cards, April 27, 1942

118. United States Congress. Report of the Joint Committee on Reconstruction. 39th Cong., 1st sess., 1865. Reprint, Westport, Conn.: Negro Universities Press, 1989.

119. USDA: A history of American Agriculture 1776-1990

120. Vance Family Papers. Arkansas History Commission, Little Rock.

121. Vanderberry, Herb. NCDA&CS Agricultural Statistics Division, Raleigh NC

122. Vernon, Dr. Ivan R. Chopping Cotton, 10/23/11, http://www.kerens.com/phpnuke/modules.php?name=News&file=article&sid=287

123. W. Augustus Low and Virgil A. Clift's Encyclopedia of Black America (New York: Da Capo Press, 1984),

124. Wadesboro, N. C. (Anson County visit courthouse, library,) during summer of 2010

125. Whayne, J. "Black Farmers in the Red Autumn: A Review Essay. The Arkansas Historical Quarterly 68.3 (2009): 327-336. Research Library, ProQuest. Web. 19 Oct. 2011.

126. Whayne, Jeannie M. "Low villains and wickedness in high places: Race and class in the Elaine riots."The Arkansas Historical Quarterly 58.3 (1999): 285-313. Research Library, ProQuest. Web. 19 Oct. 2011.

127. Whitaker, Robert. On the Laps of Gods: The Red Summer of 1919 and the Struggle for Justice that Remade a Nation. New York: Crown, 2008.

128.   Wikipedia DVD Selection is sponsored by SOS Children, www.wikipedia.org. Ku Klux Klan

129.   Williams, W. "Left Hits Founders as Racists." Human Events 18 Jul 2011: Research Library, ProQuest. Web. 19 Oct. 2011.

130. Wilson Jones, Evelena (2011, January 19). Grandmother Lessie Beasley. (M. Toms & Eugene Broadway, Interviewer)

131. Wilson Murray, Ethel Lee (2011, January 19). Grandmother Lessie Beasley. (M. Toms & Eugene Broadway, Interviewer)

132. Wintory, Blake and Hampton, Ashan R. "Mosaic Templars of America", Mosaic Templars Cultural Center. Department of Arkansas Heritage. http://www.mosaictemplarscenter.org/ (accessed January 25, 2010).

133. Wintory, Blake. Lee County, Staff of Encyclopedia of Arkansas History and Culture, http://encyclopediaofarkansas.net (accessed January 24, 2010), Little Rock, Arkansas.

STORY INDEX

STORY INDEX

Beasley, Earnest	M. Broadway's Daughter – L.Broadway Beasley Wilson,157
Booker, Mary	Choice, 128
Booker, Mary	Don't Turn Around, 137
Booker, Mary	The Past, Present And Hope The Future, 172
Booker, Mary	You Just Never Know - A Tribute To Eugene, 182
Broadway Martin, Carol Jean	Letter of Love to My Brother Eugene, 115
Broadway Plummer, Linda D.	The Day the Earth Stood Still, 168
Broadway Smith, De'Shondra	About My Two Fathers, 119
Broadway Thompson, Carolyn	A Rewarding Email, 188
Broadway Toms, Marie	Garrett Grove's Church and School Connection, 185
Broadway Toms, Marie	Just As She Remembered – Lee Esther Broadway, 183
Broadway Toms, Marie	Forty Acres and a Mule, 78
Broadway Toms, Marie	Closer to Heaven or Hell – Chopping Cotton in Arkansas, 152
Broadway Toms, Marie	Fascination with Obituaries, 148
Broadway Toms, Marie	Grandma Dotsey, 165
Broadway Williams, Wanda	Grandpa....Tell Me about the Good Ole Days, 140
Broadway, Bobby	Missed Opportunities, 147
Broadway, Cocoa	Master Barber, 184
Broadway, Crystal	The Spirit, 173
Broadway, Danny	Conversations at the Barbershop, 133
Broadway, Danny	Remembering As a Teenager, 167
Broadway, Ed	Out Of Touch in Touch, 124
Broadway, Eugene	My Brother Danny Broadway, 170
Broadway, Eugene	Loss of Civility, 118
Broadway, Eugene	Whipping As a Disciplinary Action, 181
Broadway, Eugene	Family Research with Cousin Maezel, 188
Broadway, Eugene	Spiritual Journey, 130
Broadway, Geraldine	The Day That Changed My Life, 167
Broadway, Joan	A Historical Visit with Joan Broadway, 195
Broadway, Linda	The Drug Killer, 169
Broadway, Linda D.	Give Me a Nickel, 117

Broadway, Marie   Higher Education Aid Denied In 1970, 141
Broadway, Michelle   My Daddy Knows Everybody, 181
Broadway, Nathaniel   Childhood Story, 127
Broadway, Nathaniel (Skip) The Night My Brother Died, 170
Broadway, Parlee   A Tree's Value, 175
Broadway, Parlee   Driver's License Experiences, 139
Broadway, Shianne   A Letter to Eugene, 15
Broadway, Shianne   The Journey – The Trees, 132
Broadway, Shuanta   New Broadway Generation, 145
Broadway, Virgle James   A Rewarding Email, 189
Broadway, William Van   Reminiscing, 194
Broadway-Early, Jhane'   A Match Made In Heaven, 144
Broadway-Early, Jhane'   The Power Of DNA, 142
Broadway-Early, Jhane'   Uncle June, 143
Chatwood, April   Proud To Be a Member of The Broadway Family, 166
Hansberry Reunion Fam.,90 Genealogy
Hansberry Reunion Fam.,90 A Family's Demand to the U.S. Government
Kates, Oneadia   Cousins, 133
McMillan, Ma'isah   American Soldier, 187
Miller, Frank   The Man, Lenner Broadway, 178
Miller, Franklin Delano   Grandpa Oliver Broadway, 162
Milliken, Deborah Hall   Faithful Is Our God, 122
Morrison, Jackie   Dating Strategy, 175
Morrison, Jackie   The Trauma Subsides, 174
Mosley Broadway, Kirstein C. Grandbaby, 178
Murray, Ethel Lee   Ethel Called Lessie Beasley Wilson, Grandma, 159
Peppers Broadway, Parlee   Value of Working Hard, 176
Pride, Naz   Life with My Six Siblings, 113
Staton, Mary   Visit with Mary Staton in Burnsville, NC, 156
Toms Jr., Leonard "Hanif" Decisions, a Reflection of Time, 134
Turner, Dennis Jerome   The Color of Our Skin, 153
Turner, Jerome   Found Grandpa Marshall's Grave in Chicago, 148
Tweedie, Olaf Lacy   An Extraordinary Woman, 120
Tweedie, Olaf Lacy   Me and My Mother, 120
Tweedie, Olaf Lacy   More than an Uncle, 144
Tweedie, Olaf   The African-American Race, 151
Wilson Jones, Evelena   My Grandparents Lessie Broadway Beasley Wilson and Sandy
Wilson, 159

ABOUT AUTHOR

Eugene Broadway, a retired Postal Worker and Barber is the second child born to Daniel and Lee Esther Broadway. Mr. Broadway was born in Moro, Arkansas and moved to Little Rock, Arkansas at the age of five.

He holds a Bachelor of Arts Degree in Business Administration from *Philander Smith College* in Little Rock, Arkansas. He also holds a Barber Instructor and Cosmetology License.

After working with his cousins on the 2010 Broadway Family Reunion Committee, Broadway was encouraged by cousin Marie Broadway Toms to pursue one of his aspirations in life which was to write a book.

Mr. Broadway and his wife Shianne now live a retired life in Powder Springs, Georgia.

OTHER RESOURCES:

Eugene Broadway's Website
http://www.eugenebroadway.com

TO ORDER MORE BOOKS:
The Journey

Butterfly Press
http://www.butterflypress.net/store/

or

Eugene Broadway
P.O. Box 2012, Powder Springs, Ga. 30127

DEDICATION TO SMALL BLACK FARMERS, LEE COUNTY, ARKANSAS

GARRETT GROVE
MORO, ARKANSAS

LENNER
BROADWAY

LENNER

LENNER BRAODWAY
A FARMER

SOY BEAN
COMBINDER

TRUCK UNDER SHED

COTTON CHOPPERS

COTTON
FIELD

10 FT.
COTTON SACK

COTTON GIN

CPSIA information can be obtained at www.ICGtesting.com
Printed in the USA
LVOW112256150312

273340LV00001B/1/P